DATE			

COMPARATIVE AND INTERNATIONAL EDUCATION SERIES

Volume 5

Community Financing of Education

Issues and Policy Implications
in Less Developed Countries

COMPARATIVE AND INTERNATIONAL EDUCATION

Series Editor: PHILLIP G. ALTBACH, State University of New York at Buffalo, New York

Editorial Advisory Board:

SUMA CHITNIS, Tata Institute of Social Sciences, Bombay, India

S. GOPINATHAN, Institute of Education, Singapore

GAIL P. KELLY, State University of New York at Buffalo, USA

KAZAYUKI KITAMURA, Research Institute for Higher Education, Hiroshima, Japan

THOMAS LA BELLE, University of Pittsburgh, USA

GUY NEAVE, Institute of Education, University of London, UK

NOTICE TO READERS

Dear Reader

An invitation to Publish in and Recommend the Placing of a Standing Order to Volumes Published in this Valuable Series.

If your library is not already a standing/continuation order customer to this series, may we recommend that you place a standing/continuation order to receive immediately upon publication all new volumes. Should you find that these volumes no longer serve your needs, your order can be cancelled at any time without notice.

The Editors and the Publisher will be glad to receive suggestions or outlines of suitable titles, reviews or symposia for editorial consideration: if found acceptable, rapid publication is guaranteed.

ROBERT MAXWELL
Publisher at Pergamon Press

Community Financing of Education

Issues and Policy Implications in Less Developed Countries

Edited by

MARK BRAY
Department of Education
University of Hong Kong

with

KEVIN LILLIS
Institute of Education
University of London

PERGAMON PRESS

OXFORD · NEW YORK · BEIJING · FRANKFURT
SÃO PAULO · SYDNEY · TOKYO · TORONTO

U.K.	Pergamon Press, Headington Hill Hall, Oxford OX3 0BW, England
U.S.A.	Pergamon Press, Maxwell House, Fairview Park, Elmsford, New York 10523, U.S.A.
PEOPLE'S REPUBLIC OF CHINA	Pergamon Press, Room 4037, Qianmen Hotel, Beijing, People's Republic of China
FEDERAL REPUBLIC OF GERMANY	Pergamon Press, Hammerweg 6, D-6242 Kronberg, Federal Republic of Germany
BRAZIL	Pergamon Editora, Rua Eça de Queiros, 346, CEP 04011, Paraiso, São Paulo, Brazil
AUSTRALIA	Pergamon Press Australia, P.O. Box 544, Potts Point, N.S.W. 2011, Australia
JAPAN	Pergamon Press, 8th Floor, Matsuoka Central Building, 1-7-1 Nishishinjuku, Shinjuku-ku, Tokyo 160, Japan
CANADA	Pergamon Press Canada, Suite No. 271 253 College Street, Toronto, Ontario, Canada M5T 1R5

Copyright © 1988 Pergamon Books Ltd.

First edition 1988

Library of Congress Cataloging in Publication Data

Community financing of education.
(Comparative and international education series; v. 5)
1. Education—Developing countries—Finance—Case studies. I. Bray, Mark, 1952– . II. Lillis, Kevin. III. Series.
LB2826.6.D44C66   1987   379.1'2'091724   87-20963

British Library Cataloguing in Publication Data

Community financing of education: issues and policy implications in less developed countries. —— (Comparative and international education series; V.5).
1. Education —— Developing countries —— Finance
I. Bray, Mark   II. Lillis, Kevin M.
III. Series
371.2'06'091724   LC2826.6.D44
ISBN 0-08-035858-6

Pergamon Books wish to acknowledge with gratitude the sub-stantial financial contribution made by the Commonwealth Secretariat towards the publication costs of this book and for their willing co-operation at every stage since its conception.

Printed in Great Britain by A. Wheaton & Co. Ltd., Exeter

Introduction to the Series

The Comparative and International Education Series is dedicated to inquiry and analysis on educational issues in an interdisciplinary cross-national framework. As education affects larger populations and educational issues are increasingly complex and, at the same time, international in scope, this series presents research and analysis aimed at understanding contemporary educational issues. The series brings the best scholarship to topics which have direct relevance to educators, policy-makers and scholars, in a format that stresses the international links among educational issues. Comparative education not only focuses on the development of educational systems and policies around the world, but also stresses the relevance of an international understanding of the particular problems and dilemmas that face educational systems in individual countries.

Interdisciplinarity is a hallmark of comparative education and this series will feature studies based on a variety of disciplinary, methodological and ideological underpinnings. Our concern is for relevance and the best in scholarship.

The series will combine monographic studies that will help policy-makers and others obtain a needed depth for enlightened analysis with wider-ranging volumes that may be useful to educators and students in a variety of contexts. Books in the series will reflect on policy and practice in a range of educational settings from pre-primary to post-secondary. In addition, we are concerned with non-formal education and with the societal impact of educational policies and practices. In short, the scope of the Comparative and International Education Series is interdisciplinary and contemporary.

I wish to acknowledge the assistance of a distinguished editorial advisory board including:

Professor Suma Chitnis, Tata University of Social Sciences, Bombay, India.
Professor Kazayuki Kitamura, Research Institute on Higher Education, Hiroshima University, Japan.
Professor Gail P. Kelly, State University of New York at Buffalo, USA.
Dean Thomas LaBelle, University of Pittsburgh, USA.

Dr S. Gopinathan, Institute of Education, Singapore.
Professor Guy Neave, Institute of Education, London.

PHILIP G. ALTBACH

Foreword

DURING the global economic depression of the 1980s, many governments became increasingly conscious of the cost of education and of the need to secure alternative sources of revenue. The ninth Conference of Commonwealth Education Ministers held in Cyprus in July 1984 recommended that 'a study should be conducted on a cross-country basis of the experience within the Commonwealth of raising additional and alternative funds for education' (Commonwealth Secretariat, 1985, p.33). Economic stringency was particularly severe in the Third World member states, and most governments felt that financial problems contributed to major shortcomings in the quality and quantity of education.

In response to the Cyprus recommendation, in 1985 the Commonwealth Secretariat organised a workshop on community financing of schools. It was held in Botswana, was given some financial support by the Economic Development Institute of the World Bank, and was chiefly attended by delegates from the Commonwealth countries of central and southern Africa. Among the main outcomes of the meeting was a resource book which seeks to provide policy-makers and practitioners with a practical guide to issues and strategies (Bray, 1986). The book, entitled *New Resources for Education: Community Management and Financing of Schools in Less Developed Countries*, may be obtained from the Publications Unit of the Commonwealth Secretariat.

A decision at the workshop that the issues deserved further study has led to the production of the present book. The chapters on Nigeria and Kenya were presented at the 1985 meeting and are reproduced here in revised form. The chapters on Zambia and Botswana were written specially for the book, but also owe direct inspiration to the meeting. They have been combined with additional case studies, a comprehensive analysis in Part I, and a discussion of policy implications. The result does much to fill a gap in the literature. Many writers have made passing reference to community financing, but few have discussed it in depth.

It will be observed that the book covers many non-Commonwealth countries as well as Commonwealth ones. We are happy to see this feature, for although the Secretariat of course exists to serve member states, we

vii

consider it important both to learn from the experience of others and to disseminate our own experiences beyond the Commonwealth.

PETER R. C. WILLIAMS
Director, Education Programme
The Commonwealth Secretariat

Contents

Part II Case Studies

Part III Policy Implications

List of Tables

Acronyms

APE	Association de Parents d'Elèves
BBK	Brooke Bond Kenya
CCP	Chinese Communist Party
CES	Church Education Secretary
CJSS	Community Junior Secondary School
CPE	Certificate of Primary Education
EACE	East African Certificate of Education
GDP	Gross Domestic Product
JPRS	Joint Publications Research Service
KANU	Kenya African National Union
LMS	London Missionary Society
MP	Member of Parliament
NCNA	New China News Agency
P&C	Parents' and Citizens' [Association]
PRC	People's Republic of China
PSIP	Primary School Improvement Programme
PTA	Parent–Teacher Association
SCMP	Survey of China Mainland Press
SDA	Seventh-day Adventist
SETA	School Equipment Trust Account
TAPA	Tanzania Parents' Association
UN	United Nations
Unesco	United Nations Educational, Scientific and Cultural Organisation
Unicef	United Nations International Children's Fund
USAID	United States Agency for International Development
UPE	Universal Primary Education

Currencies

Country	Name of Currency	Symbol of Currency	Approximate Value (US $)
Botswana	Pula	P	0.48
Burma	Kyat	K	0.14
China	Yuan	Y	0.27
Guyana	Dollar	G$	0.10
India	Rupee	Rs	0.08
Kenya	Shilling	KSh	0.06
Malawi	Kwacha	K	0.50
Nigeria	Naira	N	0.80
Papua New Guinea	Kina	K	1.02
Swaziland	Emalangeni	E	0.39
Tanzania	Shilling	TSh	0.02
Zambia	Kwacha	K	0.18
Zimbabwe	Dollar	Z$	0.59

Note: The exchange rates shown were the official ones in mid-1987. They do not necessarily reflect the values of the currencies at the times referred to in the text of this book.

Acknowledgements

The editors wish to acknowledge the help of the Commonwealth Secretariat in producing this book. The Secretariat organised the 1985 workshop in Botswana which provided much of the initial impetus for the book, and has assisted with materials and financial support. Within the Secretariat, particular thanks are due to Peter Williams and Service Farrant. The assistance of the Economic Development Institute of the World Bank should also be recognised, for it helped sponsor the Botswana workshop. The editors would also like to thank various readers of the manuscript, particularly Clive Whitehead, Rosemary Preston and Simon Pratt. Finally, the contributions of Chicago University Press and Unesco should be acknowledged. The Press publishes the *Comparative Education Review*, Volume 30 Number 1 of which contained an earlier version of Robinson's chapter on China. Unesco publishes *Prospects*, Volume 59 Number 3 of which contained an earlier version of Paul, Hamilton and Williams' chapter on Guyana.

Introduction

In recent years issues relating to community support for education have come increasingly to the fore in many countries, especially in the Third World. Only a minority of non-industrialised countries have yet achieved universal primary education, and in most Third World nations universal secondary education remains a distant goal. In many instances the quality of education is lamentable, even when enrolment rates are low and expenditure is high. During the last decade most countries have also found themselves increasingly hard-pressed on the economic front. And while goals are proving elusive and resources are becoming scarcer, most governments also experience expanding demands arising from rapid population growth and escalation of popular expectations about education as an avenue to individual prosperity. The result is a logistic and economic crisis.

One way to alleviate the crisis, many governments feel, is to spread the burden of educational financing. Accordingly, recent years have seen a resurgence of interest in self-help and community support schemes. As well as contributing resources, it is sometimes argued, such schemes can also improve the impact of education. It is suggested that people who directly pay at least small amounts for education and other services come to value those services more highly than when they are handed out anonymously and apparently without cost. Self-help projects can also promote desirable forms of social cohesion.

In some respects the widespread resurgence of these arguments represents a return to an earlier model of educational financing. During the early nineteenth century, the education systems in most countries relied on religious bodies—especially Christian, Islamic and Buddhist ones. Only as the nineteenth century progressed did governments decide that they also had major responsibilities in education, and in many cases it has only been in the twentieth century that governments have had enough resources to contemplate fully meeting these responsibilities. Accordingly, in a wide range of countries religious bodies were first given official assistance and then almost completely taken over. Yet during the 1970s and 1980s the pendulum began to swing again, this time for the negative reason that government funds were too scarce.

1

It should not be assumed that private schools are always better than government ones, however, or that self-help schemes are always positive in their outcomes. In several countries, community efforts have been strongly criticised for creating low-quality institutions and for exacerbating regional and social imbalances. Equally, some governments have major misgivings about the extent to which religious or other groups can use the education system to foster values that may not be widely acceptable in the nation as a whole, and self-help projects can be socially divisive as well as socially constructive.

In the light of these important considerations, it is perhaps surprising that the topic has been neglected by scholars and policy-makers. This book seeks to fill a gap by examining the nature of the issues and by illuminating them with case studies. The latter cannot of course be fully representative of the Third World, which in any case is a loose category that seems to defy tighter classification. Nevertheless, the studies do provide an instructive sample with a wide range of settings and cultures, and they discuss the mechanics of community financing as well as the broad issues.

1. The Conceptual Framework

Because the subject of this book is amorphous and complex, an initial explanation of its conceptual framework is required. First, it is mainly concerned with formal, Western-type schools at the primary and secondary levels. In many countries considerable community contributions are made to pre-primary and post-secondary institutions, to nonformal education, and to alternative formal systems such as Koranic schools and Roman Catholic seminaries. However, discussion of community support in these areas would have greatly increased the length of the book, and the focus has been restricted in order to allow treatment in depth.

Secondly, although the title refers to finance, the book is also concerned with non-financial contributions—of land, labour, and materials. One draft of the book referred to community *support* rather than community financing. However, although the earlier title clearly reflected the concern with non-financial as well as financial contributions, it could have been interpreted to include moral and philosophical support. The latter are not within the main focus of the book, and since contributions of land, labour and materials are often substitutes for cash in the sense that they would have to be purchased if they were not provided directly, it was decided to retain the word 'financing' in the title.

Even with the deliberate financial focus, however, difficulty sometimes arises in the classification of fees. In so far as school fees are imposed by national governments in lieu of taxes, they are not central to the scope of this book; but where fees are set locally by communities themselves they should be considered relevant. This issue will be explored further, particularly in Chapter 4.

Another problem arises over the conception of a community, and it becomes necessary to differentiate several types. As an overall concept, a community may be defined as a group of people who share social, economic and cultural interests. Its members recognise social obligations to each other, hold at least some common values, and identify themselves with each other as 'we'. This overall definition embraces, among others, the following types and examples:

(a)   A *geographic community* is probably the most common conception, and may refer to all the individuals living in a village, rural district or urban suburb. These are relatively small geographic areas, and represent the levels with which this book is most concerned. In Kenya and Nigeria, for instance, locally-formed village development associations have become a major force in education. In some situations all the people in a country or even a continent may see themselves as a community, though this conception is less pertinent to the focus of the book.

(b)   The word community can also describe *ethnic, racial and religious groups*. Thus it can refer to the Tamil, Gikuyu or American-Indian peoples, for example, to Chinese, Europeans or Asians, or to Christians, Mormons, Jews or Muslims. Within Christian communities may exist separate communities of Roman Catholics, Baptists, Methodists, Anglicans; and within Muslim communities may exist separate communities of Ismailis, Ahmadiyya, Sufis. Whether people identify themselves as members of the overall religion or of the sect usually depends on their numbers and the context. If people are a minority and are somehow considered radically different by the majority, they are likely to join together more cohesively than in other circumstances.

(c)   Some communities are sub-divided by *sex* and *age*. In all parts of the world males and females, and children, youths, middle-aged and elderly meet in separate communities for particular purposes. Women's groups can be a strong force in local development, and Igwe's chapter in this book describes formally-constituted age group communities in Eastern Nigeria.

(d)   Communities may also be based on *common occupations or experience*. Tailors, truck drivers and academics, for instance, may form themselves into communities. The Rotary and Lions Clubs are communities of businessmen which often assist local schools. Common ties arising from past connections are exemplified by communities of ex-servicemen and, in the context of education, Old Students' Associations. Commercial companies, universities and missions commonly operate educational trusts for the children of their workers.

(e)   Communities can also arise from *shared family concerns*. Among the most important for school support are Parents' Associations, based on adults' shared concerns for the welfare of their children.

(f) Communities may arise from general *shared philanthropy*. Many schools are run by bodies which were created to fund and run schools but which have no other community functions. For example, the Tanzania Parents' Association (TAPA) runs forty-nine schools. In all parts of the world one can find similar non-profit-making educational trusts.

It will be obvious from these examples that an individual may simultaneously belong to several communities, that there is considerable overlap, and that there may be communities within communities. Equally, it will be obvious that communities may widely differ in their mode of operation. Whereas in many communities both membership and activities are voluntary, in others they are compulsory. Thus an individual may decide whether or not to join the Rotary Club and whether or not to support the Club's assistance to a school, but nobody decides on her/his birthplace, and social sanctions may make it almost impossible for an individual to opt out of a village development association project unless she/he is prepared to leave the area altogether.

Communities also vary in their educational objectives. Whereas religious communities, for example, may decide to run their own schools because they want their children to learn in a different atmosphere from that prevailing in the government schools, village development associations may decide to open schools only because the government has failed to do so. In the latter case, self-help schools generally shadow the government model, especially when communities hope that the government will eventually take their schools over.

Finally, the range of relationships which an individual school may have with the government can also vary. To demonstrate this, one may build up a model as in Figs. 1, 2 and 3.

Figure 1 is a simple model to demonstrate the range of options in two dimensions. On the left are schools which are entirely self-financed and receive no government support, and on the right are schools which are entirely financed by government with no community support. In between is a series of combinations. Of course, not all countries have schools occupying all points in the spectrum, and the centre of gravity may vary widely in different national systems.

However, Fig. 1 takes no account of private, profit-making schools. Accordingly, Fig. 2 adds an extra 'wing' to the model. Because in some countries even profit-making schools receive government grants, the private school wing also contains a range of situations. In contrast to the non-profit making system, it is hard to envisage a situation in which the government pays more than 50 per cent grants. Accordingly, the line separating government from non-government finance is not a true diagonal.

Figure 3 takes this model one stage further to allow for intermediate situations. Four situations are indicated, illustrated most clearly by different arrangements to secure new school buildings. If a profit-making business-

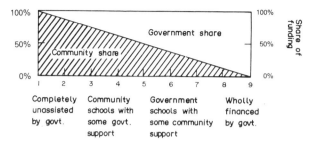

Fig 1. Community and government financing—model 1.

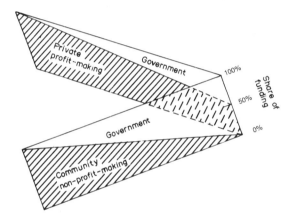

Fig 2. Community and government financing—model 2.

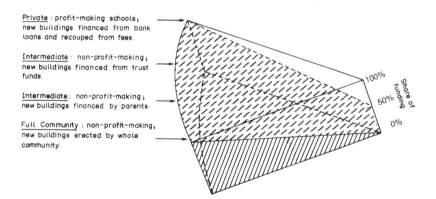

Fig 3. Community and government financing—model 3.

man wished to erect a new school building, he might take a bank loan and subsequently repay it from pupils' fees. This extreme could not be described as community financing, and is outside the boundaries of this book. The second option in the diagram is an intermediate one in which a school is non-profit-making but run from a trust. The Kamuzu Academy in Malawi, for example, is said to be funded entirely from trust funds set up by President Banda. One would not describe construction of a new building from those funds as community support. A similar argument might apply to a Roman Catholic school in Africa or elsewhere which obtains funds for a new building from headquarters in Rome or a parish overseas. The third option, however, would seem to have a stronger element of community support. In this instance, new buildings are erected by the parents of children, either directly doing the work themselves or employing a contractor to do it on their behalf. Fourthly, the most community-oriented type is a school in which the buildings are erected by the whole community, both parents and non-parents.

Just as a particular school could be located anywhere along the spectrum in Fig. 1, the same holds true of the three-dimensional model in Fig. 3. Particular countries usually have clusters of school types which can be placed in different parts of the model. In this book we are mostly concerned with the full-community end of the spectrum, but will also consider some intermediate types.

2. The Extent of Community Financing

It is also useful at the outset to indicate the scale of community financing of education in different contexts. Of course, this varies considerably between and within countries and at different points in time. Further, it is usually hard to estimate with precision (a) because little research has been conducted on the topic, (b) because figures are rarely collated by central authorities, and (c) because it is often hard to assign a monetary value to non-financial contributions.

Nevertheless, examples from widely scattered contexts indicate that contributions can be considerable. For example, Kenya has become particularly well-known for self-help. The movement there is known as 'harambee', commonly translated as 'let's pull together'. Lillis and Ayot (*infra*) indicate that in 1983 56.0 per cent of all secondary school students were in the aided sector.

Similarly, Igwe (*infra*) states that between 1976 and 1978 the Imo State Government in Nigeria spent N14,802,000 on renovation and re-equipment of secondary schools, while communities spent N12,939,000 on construction of sixty-five new ones. Over the period 1976 to 1984, he says, the number of secondary schools increased from 147 to 476, and the capital costs of all the new ones were borne by their communities. Brodersohn (1978, p.154) refers to estimates from Trinidad and Tobago, the Dominican Republic, Panama, Honduras and Cuba that between 15 and 30 per cent of both recurrent and capital costs may be financed by community inputs. In Nepal, 60 per cent of the labour for school construction is said to be provided free of charge by communities (Yannakopulos, 1980, p.125). Chapter 14 in this book portrays a similar situation in Burma, and Wu's (1984) account of Yongning Township in China's Jiangsu Province indicates that 62 per cent of primary school teachers in 1982–3 were community-employed.

In some countries, the proportion of total enrolments in self-help institutions may also be high. Thus Lillis and Ayot (*infra*) indicate that 44.7 per cent of Kenyan secondary school pupils in 1983 were in unaided institutions; and in neighbouring Tanzania, the comparable proportion in 1981 was 43.4 per cent (Carr-Hill, 1984, p.83).

3. The Dangers of Unrealistic Expectations

To balance this picture, however, one must emphasise that community support in some societies is much weaker. For example, Kaluba (*infra*) points out that Zambian communities are unable to exert the same degree of social cohesion as their counterparts in Eastern Nigeria; and Bhutan has almost no tradition of community self-help in education. In part, no doubt, the extent of community financing can be manipulated by governments; but in many cases the key factors are social or cultural, and it would be unrealistic for governments to hope to solve financial crises by trying to imitate the education systems of countries in which community forces are strong.

Phan and Cao (1973, p.109) also seem to have unreasonable expectations. They assert that increased use of community resources has the advantage that:

> The government will receive no more requests from parents asking for building more schools because they have already felt that they are responsible for their own community. In this respect, the government has gained a notable spiritual advantage. Parents and people in the community have really made their contribution to the common national plan with the spirit of a 'responsible man' because they are directly concerned with the education of their children. They will, therefore, play a more important role after having acquired a better knowledge of education and of their own community problems.

The authors advanced no data to back up their assertions, and it is difficult to believe that they could have done so. In many cases, self-help efforts are mere stop-gap measures because communities consider government provision deficient either in quantity or type, and it is naive to expect promotion of self-help to lead to a reduction in demands for government inputs.

Indeed, the experience of several countries shows the opposite to have been the case.

Similar comments apply to those who expect community financing to have a significant effect on the curriculum. For example, Nhan (1973, p.29) has stated:

> It is now time to get more involvement of parents' associations in sharing responsibilities in the education of their children as a whole. Parents' associations based on democratic principles and good-will should not only provide materials and school facilities, but also contribute to the orientation of the school curriculum towards the real needs of their daily life. In this way, school ceases to be a centre separated from the community.

And a Unesco publication (1984a, p.5) suggests that:

> Local support is regarded as a means of ensuring that the school is sensitive to the needs of the community. In its present form, the school curriculum does not focus sufficiently on local needs, and to a certain extent even alienates students from life in the community. If the school has to look to the community for support, it may generate demands from the community that schools should develop curricula which take into account its needs and problems.

In practice, although many governments welcome community financing as a way to supplement their own resources, rarely are they prepared to tolerate schools which challenge their official control and which present radically new models.

Moreover, in most countries community-run schools consciously imitate government ones. The two main reasons for this are that entry to the labour market is governed by success in government examinations, and that in many countries the government will agree to take over schools if they are already sufficiently endowed and run according to the government's own model. Further, self-help schools are usually sensitive about accusations of inferiority. Since this word generally implies that they have been compared with government schools and found wanting, many self-help institutions try to shadow government ones as closely as possible.

In addition, although some authors assert the right of communities to determine their own priorities (e.g. Unesco, 1984a, p.17), it is also clear that resources are not always invested wisely. The history of self-help operations in Third World countries is littered with examples of poorly conceived and uncompleted projects which have consumed valuable resources and had negative outcomes. In addition, several examples in this book highlight the social inequalities that may be exacerbated by self-help projects, both between and within communities.

Moreover, in his comments on the reasons why education projects tend to be more numerous than others, Anderson (1975, p.366) presents the negative reason that effective health services, for example, are judged by cures, whilst the effects of inadequate education are less easily recognised. He also suggests that health assistants are more difficult to obtain than untrained teachers and a few books, and that roads, dams and cattle dips are unpopular because they require mass labour but are unlikely to attract many government resources. These negative reasons do not fill the observer with great confidence on the appropriateness of community priorities.

Government decisions may also be short-sighted, and there is a particular danger of policy makers giving undue weight to financial and quantitative factors but neglecting broader issues and the quality of education. For example, major problems can arise when communities are permitted to establish independent institutions, especially if community institutions are resourced at lower levels than 'mainstream' schools. The serious qualitative problems that have arisen in some countries are highlighted in Chapter 6, and they stress the need in many cases for government controls of community initiatives.

Where controls are strong, however, governments encounter the different danger of stifling initiatives. Even in such regions as Eastern Nigeria, which have a reputation for dynamic self-help operations, controls have sometimes inhibited efforts and proved counter-productive (Okoye, 1986). These factors are discussed at greater length in Chapters 8 and 17.

PART I

Issues

CHAPTER 1

Community Bodies Engaged in Fund-Raising

MARK BRAY

The Introduction has already mentioned a number of community bodies that engage in fund-raising on a school's behalf. They range from general village and development organisations to more narrowly oriented Parent–Teacher Associations. This chapter provides a more detailed profile of these bodies.

1. Local Government Bodies

All societies have systems of local government, though their nature and role in school financing may differ widely. In some countries they are based on indigenous, traditional systems of government, while in others they are part of newly created structures.

The *kgotla* system in Botswana comes in the former group, of traditional bodies which have continued to operate within the context of a new nation. Most villages in Botswana have their own *kgotlas*, which are presided over by their chiefs and which operate as democratic forums. The original proposals for many of the country's community junior secondary schools were first made in *kgotla* meetings, and Swartland and Taylor (*infra*) indicate that the bodies still act as foci for fund-raising and policy matters.

Similar bodies may be found in other countries. Igwe (*infra*) describes the Village Councils of Eastern Nigeria, and Mbithi and Rasmusson (1977, p.27) indicate that comparable organisations operate in parts of Kenya. The *barrios* or *barangays* of the Philippines have evolved out of an older system in which families were grouped under the jurisdiction of a headman, and have also been used for school development. The Philippines is well known for its community-oriented Barrio High Schools (Cruz and Calado, 1975; Orata, 1977; Manalang, 1977). The Nepali and Indian counterparts of these local government bodies are the *panchayats*, which have a similar function (Padhye, 1976; Jayasuriya, 1984).

By contrast, the system of brigades, and township and district authorities introduced in China was a new type of local government which has been used to encourage considerable inputs to schools, but which did not derive its

13

origin from traditional bodies. For example, almost Y500 million is reported to have been invested in school buildings between 1979 and 1983, of which 75 per cent came from brigade and peasant households (Robinson, 1986, pp.83–4). Likewise, Wu's (1984) account of Yongning Township in Jiangsu Province indicates that in the 1982–3 school year 62 per cent of the primary school teachers were locally appointed *minban* staff. Wu adds that 53.2 per cent of the school funds in that year came from the state, 7.7 per cent from tuition fees, and 39.1 per cent from local contributions.

2. Village Development Associations

In a large number of countries, communities have created formal development associations in order to mobilise resources and bridge the gap between what they would like to be done and what the government is able to do. For example, Brokensha (1966, p.73) examines the role of the Larteh Youth Association in Ghana, which was formed 'to promote the welfare of the town and people of Larteh and to promote unity amongst various Larteh Nationals at home and abroad', and which founded the National Secondary School. Likewise, in Tanzania the Kanyigo Development Association (KADEA) has established a flourishing secondary school. The people of Kanyigo subscribed Tshs 600,000 to establish the school, and agreed to contribute Tshs 1,000,000 a year from coffee sales to help meet recurrent expenditure. KADEA is also running a co-operative shop and a bus to help fund the school (Galabawa, 1985, p.9).

Igwe (*infra*) provides similar examples of village development associations, highlighting that connected with his own village in Nigeria. Other authors comment on their role in Kenya (Anderson, 1970, 1973), Malaysia (Rashid and Harith, 1973, p.32), and Guyana (Paul *et al.*, *infra*). Usually the associations are concerned only with local development, although Anderson points out that in Kenya they have had political undertones of national importance.

3. Religious Bodies

The contributions of the Christian churches to education are well known in most of the Third World. In many cases formal schooling began with the work of Christian missions, and only later did governments supplement and take over the missionaries' work. In many countries the churches remain very active in education. Schools are sometimes supported by overseas congregations, but an even bigger contribution comes from local sources. The Seventh-day Adventists (SDAs) remain particularly prominent in many countries because they have resisted incorporation into national education systems. They operate in countries as far apart as the Solomon Islands, Malawi and Montserrat. Sometimes schools are started by broad Christian organisations rather than by specific sects. For example, the Young Women's Christian Association (YWCA) and its Young Men's counterpart have founded a number of schools in Botswana and Tanzania (Makunga, 1985; Galabawa, 1985).

Islamic bodies have also been active both in traditional Koranic schooling and in education based on the Western model. With regard to the latter, Rahardjo (1975) provides examples from Indonesia, Fisher (1975) provides further examples from Sierra Leone, the Gambia and Liberia, and Fafunwa (1974, p.69) refers to the activities in Nigeria of the Ansar-ud-Deen and Nawar-ud-Deen societies. In many parts of West Africa the work of the Ahmadiyya communities has become particularly well known. Fisher (1975, p.188) comments on the origins of the Muslim Brotherhoods in Sierra Leone:

> The *imam* of the Ahmadiyya community in Magbwaka feared lest Arabic studies might die out, for it seemed to him that the old Koran schools round the bonfire were disappearing. Impressed with how much the government was able to do, in education, for how little in direct taxation, he envisaged a corresponding Muslim enterprise if each believer would give 10 shillings for Arabic teachers and 'schools with benches'.

Subsequently, this brotherhood evolved into an explicitly orthodox, non-Ahmadiyya body. However, the Ahmadiyya movement has had a major impact. Fisher records (p.188) that in 1973 there were five Ahmadiyya secondary schools in Sierra Leone, with applications pending for two more, and twenty-one government-assisted primary schools. Ahmadiyya communities also operate many schools in Nigeria and other parts of West Africa (Bray, *et al.*, 1986, p.91).

Ismaili communities are also notable for their interest in schooling, especially in Pakistan, India, Bangladesh, Uganda and Kenya (Aga Khan Foundation, 1985, p.3; Morris, 1968, p.151; Abreu, 1982, pp.53–71). In many cases local communities are self-sufficient, but some receive international help. For example, the Aga Khan Foundation provides grants and technical advice to encourage self-help among Ismaili communities in northern Pakistan.

Many Hindu communities also embark on self-help programmes. Worshippers in the temples may be mobilised to assist neighbourhood schools or to sponsor individual students (Nayar and Virmani, 1978, p.9). Biak Cin and Scandlen (*infra*) indicate that Burmese Buddhists have also had a long tradition of support for monastery schools which in recent years has been transferred to the Western system; and the literature makes similar observations about Kampuchea (Nhan 1973, p.29), Laos (Visaysackd, 1973, p.69), Sri Lanka (Guruge, 1977, p.19), and Thailand (Watson, 1980, p.173).

4. Political Bodies

The *minban* schools in China are among the clearest examples of school sponsorship by political bodies. Especially during the 1940s and 1950s, the Chinese Communist Party played a key role in their establishment and maintenance (Robinson, *infra*). Chapter 14 in this book also emphasises the importance of contributions by political parties in Burma. Party members supply books and teaching aids, make donations towards sports, cultural and other co-curricular activities, and offer scholarships to needy children. In Indonesia, the Nahdlatul Ulama (NU) runs a number of *pesantrens*, which are schools that teach some general subjects but which place strong emphasis on religious learning. Although the NU is a religious body, it has also played a major political role (McVey, 1983, pp.202–5; Awanohara, 1984, p.69).

Likewise, during the early and middle years of the century a range of schools in east and central Africa were run by *de facto* political groups in opposition to governments (Ranger, 1965; Anderson, 1970; Heyman *et al.*, 1972). And today, the Tanzania Parents' Association (TAPA) is affiliated to the main political party, Chama Cha Mapinduzi, and runs forty-nine schools (Galabawa, 1985, p.7).

These are explicit examples of links, to which discussion in Chapter 2 adds further elements. It highlights the ways politicians and schools may use each other in Kenya, the former gaining publicity and an improved public image, and the latter gaining financial benefits and spokesmen in the wider world.

5. Age Groups and Traditional Workparties

Many societies, particularly in Africa, have traditionally been subdivided into age groups. In some cases a new role is played by these groups in modern times. Van Rensburg (1974, p.20) named his brigades in Botswana after a traditional form of organisation in Ghana, and subsequently found out that in Botswana itself:

> the tribes had until only a few years before had a system of regiments, originally for military purposes, in which all young men of the same age-group were called up to undertake public works in time of peace.

Likewise, among the Kamba in Kenya, self-help efforts have been partly based on the traditional workparty or *mwethya* (Mbithi, 1972; Hill, 1974, 1975). Hill (1975, pp.2–3) reports that:

> Since independence the Kamale *mwethya* has built a nursery, well, village road and the first stages of a primary school. In large-scale and costlier projects, it combines with other groups—as on the Maluma sub-location cattle-dip (six groups) and the *harambee* secondary school in Nzimbani (26 groups).

Similarly, Igwe's chapter (*infra*) indicates that age groups are important traditional bodies which have been directed to new uses in Eastern Nigeria. His village has fourteen age groups, which are mobilised by the Village Council and which compete to raise funds, usually by taxing their members. The age groups may also provide non-financial support, for example by preparing grounds for construction and by cooking food for launching ceremonies.

6. Racial and Ethnic Bodies

It is common for racial minorities to run their own schools, usually because they want their children to receive schooling in their own languages and to follow different syllabuses. Thus in cultural enclaves in Africa and Asia, for instance, one may find American or German schools catering for the children of missionaries or industrialists. In East Africa the Asian communities have established their own schools, and Abreu (1982, pp.140–83) has specifically documented the work of the Goan community. Similarly, Chinese minorities have run their own schools in such countries as Fiji, Malaysia and the Philippines.

Schools have also been organised by ethnic bodies, and again the Kenyan example comes readily to mind. Between 1922 and 1952, for example, the Kikuyu created nearly 400 self-help schools (Anderson, 1973, p.18), and others were established by the Luo, the Kamba and the Pokomo. Most of the institutions were small primary schools, but they included a few junior secondary schools and one senior secondary school combined with a teachers' college. With the advent of Independence in 1963 the political climate changed; but ethnic pressures have remained important in the post-Independence era, even though they may be disguised (Anderson, 1973, 1975; Bray, Dondo and Moemeka, 1976).

7. Business Organisations

The Round Table, Rotary and Lions Clubs are particularly well known for sponsoring students and giving small grants to schools. Mkandawire (1985, p.13) records that one Lions Club in Malawi gave K10,000 to a school in 1984. Kaluba (*infra*) comments on their role in Zambia, Nayar and Virmani (1978, pp.16, 67) refer to their work in India, and similar instances can be recorded from many other countries.

The Indian study also highlights the role of large business houses, such as the Birlas and the Tatas. It states (p.17) that 'it is a custom in the business community to set apart a certain proportion of their profits—called *Dharamda*—which is used for charitable purposes, some of which is channelled into assistance to educational institutions'. Similarly, Chapter 10 in this book highlights the role of the Brooke Bond tea company in Kenya;

Chapter 11 comments on inputs from the Zambia Consolidated Mines Company; and Chapter 17 notes the contributions of bauxite mining companies in Guyana. Unesco (1984b, p.9) adds the further example of timber companies in Malaysia.

8. Alumni Organisations

Old Students', or Alumni Organisations can provide valuable supplementary funds for schools. They generally seem to be stronger at the secondary than at the primary school levels, perhaps because individuals are able more easily to identify the impact of secondary schools on their subsequent careers. They are also stronger in élite and long-established schools, because these institutions have larger numbers of former students in prominent and prosperous positions. The old boys have played a strong role in the development of Kenya's élite Alliance High School, for example (Smith, 1973, p.265), and in Sierra Leone's Bo Government School (R. Katta, personal information, 1985). However, other institutions may not be able to call forth resources so effectively.

9. Parent–Teacher Associations

Parent–Teacher Associations (PTAs) exist in all parts of the world. Their title implies that membership is restricted to parents and teachers rather than embracing the community as a whole, but rarely are such distinctions rigid. Certainly guardians are generally included as well as parents, and some societies make the broader base explicit. In 1979, for example, the Sri Lankan Government instructed schools to widen the membership of their PTAs and to rename them School Development Societies (Sri Lanka, 1979); and Papua New Guinean schools have Parents' and Citizens' Associations rather than Parent–Teacher Associations.

Ashuntantang *et al.* (1977, p.110) indicate that in West Cameroon PTAs have a longer tradition in voluntary agency than in government schools, but that they have been encouraged in the latter and by the mid-1970s existed in 90 per cent of institutions. They add that each PTA effectively embraces the whole community, and that 'traditional political organisations at the village level, like the "secret societies", are often used to remind members of their obligations and, if necessary, force members to participate in meetings' (see also Bergmann and Bude, 1976, p.130).

It is unusual, however, for all schools to have equally active bodies: some may have very strong PTAs while others may have weak ones or none at all. The situation usually depends most of all on the attitudes and skills of the head teachers. Payne and Hinds (1986) note that in Barbados the first PTA was not founded until 1952, that further significant development did not occur until the 1960s, and that even now some primary schools have no PTAs. Interestingly, in 1973 the Barbados schools formed a wider body, the National Council of PTAs, to assist individual groups and to represent their views to government. 'Associations of associations' have also been encouraged elsewhere (see e.g. Sri Lanka, 1959, 1977).

10. Boards of Governors

Many schools have bodies called Boards of Governors, Boards of Management, or School Committees. Although the details may vary, most are responsible for overall development of their schools within the framework of the education system. They can make decisions on buildings and discipline, and in many systems can control aspects of the curriculum, pupil admission and teacher appointment. Membership is usually a combination of elected and *ex-officio* posts, the elected members being local individuals who are respected and known for their concern with education, and the *ex-officio* members usually including the head teacher and, at the secondary level, a government representative. Boards commonly engage in a wide range of fund-raising activities, usually in conjunction with their PTAs and other bodies.

11. Pupils

Many schools raise money through their own productive activities. They undertake contracts in carpentry and metal work, grow produce, and rear animals for sale. Some schools run stores which serve the neighbourhood, and others, in urban areas, supplement their incomes by collecting empty bottles for return to drinks manufacturers. In addition, pupils commonly organise dances, fêtes and other fund-raising events. In these cases, the pupils are themselves acting as a community.

A different type of example is provided by India's Tamil Nadu State, in which secondary school pupils have been mobilised to help nearby primary school children in a 'godfather' scheme. The help has mainly taken the form of labour and books (Nayar and Virmani, 1978, p.62). Parallel activities have been achieved through the 'school clusters' project in Sri Lanka (Samaranayake, 1985, p.58).

12. Individuals

Finally, many schools owe their origins to individuals rather than groups. These people may later encourage the formation of collective bodies, such as school councils or boards of governors, but the original initiatives are often individual rather than collective. In Dominica's Marigot High School, for example, a key role was played by the man who became its first principal. He has had considerable success both in mobilising the community and in attracting government support, but much of the original growth arose from his personal initiative (Roberts, 1985).

Individual philanthropists may also provide important injections of capital and land. The schools often recognise and encourage their contributions by naming buildings after them. One survey in Burma indicated that in 1972–3 individuals provided 84.7 per cent of the cost of new buildings and furniture in affiliated (i.e. community-owned) schools (Kyi, 1977, p.40). This compared with 13.3 per cent from PTAs and 2.0 per cent from the government. Another study (Nayar and Virmani, 1978, p.67) recorded that educational trusts established by philanthropists were widely found in India.

Individuals also help schools by contributing their services. Retired teachers and local craftsmen may teach children on a voluntary basis, for example, and local government officials may assist with technical advice on construction and accounting. They do this in a personal capacity rather than as representatives of a larger group.

Summary

This profile stresses the varied nature of community bodies involved in school financing. Some are traditional bodies like the *kgotlas*, *barangays* and *panchayats*, the roles of which have been adapted to new contexts. Like village development associations, age groups and Rotary Clubs, they have broad objectives and do not restrict their focus to education. PTAs, boards of governors and alumni associations, by contrast, are specifically formed to help their own institutions.

Sometimes PTA membership is restricted to parents and teachers, though a wider community base can also be found. In these cases, referring back to Figure 3 in the Introduction, their work would be classified as intermediate rather than full-community. Even in this type of body a wider social base can often be found, however, and some institutions make this explicit by forming Parents' and Citizens' Associations rather than Parent–Teacher Associations.

Boards of governors are also likely to incorporate members who have no children of their own in the schools, which gives them a broad community base. On the other hand, sometimes individuals contribute to schools *as* individuals, making no claim to be part of larger bodies. Like those who establish non-profit making trusts to run schools, their activities would be classified in the intermediate category.

It is also interesting to observe the geographic spread of the different types of community bodies. Although the age groups discussed by Igwe and some other bodies are found only in specific cultures, most types can be found in all parts of the world. This suggests that although promotion of community financing in specific contexts must take account of particular cultural and other circumstances, it is possible to discern a set of common features and forces.

CHAPTER 2

Initiating and Directing Projects

MARK BRAY

The origins of many self-help schools are associated with individuals. Pedro Orata's Barrio High Schools in the Philippines immediately come to mind (Orata, 1977). Less well known but equally clear examples are Fr Cheney's school at Above Rocks in Jamaica (Houghton and Tregear, 1969), Tai Solarin's Mayflower School in Nigeria (Solarin, 1970), and the Asra Hawariat School in Ethiopia (Kinahan, 1976). One of the keys to the success of most projects is the existence of at least one individual with energy, vision and talent for organisation.

In many cases, however, schools are associated less with individuals than with broad movements. This is true of most church schools, for example, and institutions sponsored by political organisations, village self-help groups and cooperatives. And even schools which owe their origins to individuals require diversification to committees and broader structures if they are to ensure long-term stability.

Accordingly, this chapter examines leadership patterns in community projects. The first half discusses the initiation, organisation and implementation of self-help schemes. It makes particular use of Kenyan data which focusses on cattle dips, aid posts, polytechnics and water projects as well as on schools. The second half of the chapter turns to the institutional frameworks of schools, and comments on the roles, composition and effectiveness of school Boards of Governors.

1. Initiation, Organisation and Implementation of Projects

Although it makes some comparative statements, this section is chiefly based on work by Mbithi and Rasmusson (1977), who collected data on 311 harambee projects in forty of Kenya's forty-one districts. Few comparable studies are available from other countries, and the work is therefore worth reporting in some depth.

As projects develop, they move into different phases and may require different types of leadership. Mbithi and Rasmusson classified the phases as *project initiation*, in which the leaders create awareness and articulate the need by arranging discussion groups and meetings; *organisation*, in which the leaders define participation criteria and fund-raising procedures; and *implementation*, in which the leaders take charge of work groups and maintain interest and commitment. It is not always easy to distinguish between the phases, but the classification is a useful one.

Mbithi and Rasmusson collected data on the sex, occupation, educational level and age of individuals in each category, and the research findings on each will be summarised in turn. The fifth section pulls some threads together, and comments on leadership factors which may contribute to the success or failure of projects.

(a) The Sex of Leaders

Table 2.1 summarises Mbithi and Rasmusson's information on the sex of leaders in harambee projects. In the Kenyan situation, it appears, men are very dominant. The proportions of women who were initiators, committee members and work group leaders were fairly constant, and the average ranged from just 5.7 per cent to 7.0 per cent. This may be disappointing to advocates of greater female participation; but a major feature of harambee is its grass roots nature, and the composition of committees is not generally amenable to manipulation from above.

TABLE 2.1. *Percentage of Female Leaders in Harambee Projects, Kenya*

Province	Initiators	Committee Members	Work Group Leaders
Central	21.8	20.3	15.2
Rift Valley	8.8	8.4	8.0
Western	7.0	7.7	1.3
Nyanza	5.3	6.4	2.3
Eastern	1.4	4.4	5.2
Coast	2.2	2.3	2.3
North Eastern	0	0	0
Average	6.0	7.0	5.7

Reproduced from Mbithi and Rasmusson (1977, p.56), with permission from the Scandinavian Institute of African Studies, Uppsala, Sweden.

Within the country, however, Central Province showed a marked difference from the rest, with 21.8 per cent female initiators as opposed to an average of 6.9 per cent, and a score of zero in North Eastern Province. This may reflect changing cultural and religious patterns, for although the traditional place of women in Central Province was not markedly different from that in most other Kenyan societies, the area has become more economically developed than most, and the Christian churches have a strong foothold there. In contrast, Eastern, Coast and North Eastern Provinces have high proportions of Muslims; but one case study from Taita, a non-Muslim Coast Province District, showed that almost all married women participate in all functions (Mbithi and Rasmusson, 1977, p.49).

The researchers also looked at the types of projects in which female leadership was strongest. They found most female initiators in water projects, nurseries and schools, to which pattern were added churches and health centres in respect of committee membership. Most women work group leaders were found in schools, water projects and churches.

However, Mibithi and Rasmusson also point out (p.49) that the small number of women occupying formal positions is not necessarily an accurate reflection of their role. Many women, the researchers suggest, 'use' men as nominal leaders and spokespeople, requesting them to represent them on formal occasions but not needing them in day-to-day activities. Moreover, one source has estimated that women provide 80 per cent of self-help labour for harambee projects (Keigelman, cited in Unicef, 1984, p.87).

(b) The Occupations of Leaders

The occupational patterns that Mbithi and Rasmusson found are shown in Table 2.2. The role of farmers is clearly apparent, again showing the importance of grass roots initiatives in harambee projects. Overall, farmers

TABLE 2.2. *Occupations of Leaders in Harambee Projects, Kenya*

	Initiators	Committee Members	Work Group Leaders	Total
Politicians	7.2	4.4	2.5	4.8
Clergymen	7.7	6.2	5.3	6.3
Businessmen	10.6	12.0	5.3	9.9
Teachers	12.5	10.8	13.0	11.8
Clerks	1.2	2.4	1.9	2.0
Artisans	4.6	1.0	3.6	2.4
Farmers	21.7	36.4	36.8	34.7
Government Officers	27.6	22.8	29.1	25.3
Office of the President				
District/Divisional	*4.6*	*1.0*	*1.3*	*2.0*
Locational/Sublocational	*14.8*	*10.7*	*17.1*	*13.4*
Ministry of Social Services				
District/Divisional	*1.5*	*0.7*	*0.2*	*0.6*
Locational/Sublocational	*0.7*	*1.4*	*0.8*	*1.1*
District/Divisional				
Ministry of Agriculture				
Agriculture	*1.0*	*1.5*	*0.4*	*1.1*
Veterinary	*0.3*	*0*	*0*	*0*
Ministry of Education	*0.4*	*0*	*0*	*0.2*
Other	*4.3*	*7.5*	*9.3*	*6.9*
Vague	0.3	3.5	1.4	2.0
Sample Size	639	949	475	2063

Note: The figures in italics show subdivisions of the Government Officers category.
Reproduced from Mbithi and Rasmusson (1977, p.57), with permission from the Scandinavian Institute of African Studies, Uppsala, Sweden.

represented 34.7 per cent of the total. They were particularly prominent in nursery school, primary school and cattle dip leadership, which suggested an occupational preference for small projects of immediate relevance.

Government officers were the second most important category, and were the first most important at the initiation stage. The majority of them were chiefs and subchiefs (in the Office of the President), who at the location/ sublocation levels comprised 14.8 per cent of initiators and 17.1 per cent of work group leaders.

To some extent, the role of chiefs in Kenya has parallels in Eastern Nigeria. Okoye (1986, p. 268) records that:

> Soon after the creation of Anambra State, legislation was introduced for Government recognition of Chiefs in specified communities, provided they had the unanimous support of their people. In order to prove that they had the welfare of their people at heart, many new Chiefs embarked upon secondary school building programmes, seeking success in the venture to ensure their continuing popularity. Taking advantage of this, the Ministry preferred to work with the community Chief if this was possible without compromising standards.

However, Mbithi and Rasmusson note (pp. 50, 62) that although they were government officials, the chiefs did not appear to have followed directives of the provincial and district administrations. Indirectly, of course, the continued involvement of chiefs indicated that their superiors were at least prepared to tolerate their activities; but they were highly autonomous, and thus could not be seen as instruments of higher control. Again, this may be a specific feature of the Kenyan situation, but it suggests limits on the extent to which self-help projects may be susceptible to central coordination and control.

At the same time, Mbithi and Rasmusson's survey showed a weak formal role for community development officers (in the Ministry of Social Services), who represented less than two per cent in any category. The researchers suggest (p.58) that this reflected their role as 'coaches', responsible for training and inspiration but not expected by their employers to take up formal leadership positions. Keller (1980, p.32) adds:

> Local representatives of the central government frequently are aware of self-help drives and may even become involved, but this is not to say that they exert any special influence in community planning. Their advice is sometimes solicited, but how a community perceives its own needs is a much more crucial determinant of what action is taken or not taken than government objectives.

He suggests that the government is particularly wary of involvement in school projects because of their high recurrent costs. Indeed, according to Hill (1974, p.15), civil servants have been prohibited from membership of school committees. In contrast, cattle dips, health centres, bridges and wells have much smaller financial implications, and the government is generally prepared to play a stronger role.

In Mbithi and Rasmusson's sample, politicians formed only 7.2 per cent of initiators and 2.5 per cent of work group leaders. However, these low figures may have disguised their real role. The researchers pointed out that although Harambee was firmly supported by President Kenyatta, the movement has also been an expression of discontent with the central government. Thus some communities have used politicians to give them access to resources, and some politicians have used communities to foster confrontation with the central authorities. Moreover, they added (p.61) that although politicians made up only 7 per cent of all initiators, they constituted 20 per cent of all high school and village polytechnic initiators. Thus, politicians had a particularly prominent role in the larger and more prestigious projects.

Keller (1980, pp.33–4) also comments on the role of politicians, indicating that at the initiation stage patterns in individual projects may vary. Referring specifically to the education sector, he states:

> Some [politicians] take on what we might call 'passive-receptive' roles. That is, they do not necessarily initiate a school movement, but they feel compelled to support one as soon as it emerges. . . . Other members of parliament, who we might classify as 'active-supportive', are firmly in control of school development in their areas and make a conscious attempt to plan the initiation and expansion of local harambee 'spearheads of the collective initiatives of the people'. . . .

He adds that usually a Member of Parliament (M.P.) can ill afford *not* to be involved at the organisational stage:

> In many cases perhaps the major reason for his having been elected in the first place was the expectation on the part of his constituency that he would be able to deliver outside development aid. Should he fail and attempt to be re-elected, he is almost certain to be rejected. The M.P. is often called upon to lead the initial fund-raising drive, and he is also expected to use his influence and vantage point to secure funds and teachers for the school once it is functioning. Privately one such individual complained about his community's over-enthusiasm and poor resource base from which to begin a school, but publicly he was most supportive.

It is also worth noting that in several countries the activities of politicians have caused problems for bureaucrats. Hill (1974) points out that politicians in Kenya have sometimes sponsored schools which have disrupted development plans and been opposed by administrators. And Nayar and Virmani (1978, p.17) make similar comments about the Indian situation, stating that 'it has really become a problem for government to discriminate between genuine and fake voluntary effort'.

Finally, as one would expect, teachers played a particular role in all leadership categories for secondary schools. However, Anderson (1975, p.381) adds that although in theory every new secondary school can draw on neighbouring primary teachers for advice, the cooperation of the latter cannot be taken for granted. They may be especially unwilling to become involved if they are not indigenous to the area.

In addition, although some schools have received great help from Ministry of Education officials, university lecturers, and established secondary school teachers, many such people have an understandable suspicion of the lack of sophistication of many older people put into positions of authority by community selection procedures, and of the manipulation of projects by people with ulterior political or entrepreneurial motives. Again, this shows tensions between local concerns and national development, and emphasises the constraints that may hinder the channelling of self-help endeavours to truly productive ends.

(c) The Educational Background of Leaders

Linked to the above points, Mbithi and Rasmusson also examined the educational profiles of leaders. Table 2.3 shows that primary education was overwhelmingly the highest educational level reached by initiators, and an average of 11.8 per cent were reported to have had no formal education at all. This emphasises the grass roots nature of harambee. Indeed, the Taita case study suggested that:

> Qualifications for leadership includes [sic] ability of the individual, his experience of the project at hand—(for example a dip project had a progressive farmer both as a chairman and treasurer because he knew how a dip should be constructed). . . . The candidate must be faithful . . . education is not important. (Mbithi and Rasmusson, 1977, p.54)

TABLE 2.3. *Educational Levels of Leaders in Harambee Projects, Kenya (%)*

Level of Formal Education	Initiators	Committee Members	Work Group Leaders	Average
None	9.0	13.9	10.9	11.8
Primary	57.5	56.9	61.3	58.2
Secondary	18.1	11.9	14.1	14.3
Higher	6.1	3.4	5.3	4.6
Vague/Unknown	9.3	13.9	8.4	11.1
Total	100.0	100.0	100.0	100.0

Reproduced from Mbithi and Rasmusson (1977, p.59), with permission from the Scandinavian Institute of African Studies, Uppsala, Sweden.

The author of the above quotation went on to say that although education was not important, leaders should 'of course . . . be literate'. However, one may assume that many of the people whom Mbithi and Rasmusson reported to have had no formal education were only barely literate, if at all.

Nevertheless, many people did have higher qualifications. Overall, 14.3 per cent of the sample were reported to have secondary school qualifications, though only 4.6 per cent had tertiary qualifications. Proportions were fairly constant between the different types of leadership.

(d) The Ages of Leaders

The results of Mbithi and Rasmusson's question about the age of leaders are shown in Table 2.4. They were unable to obtain much extensive information on this matter, and two categories show only a 33 per cent response. Nevertheless, the findings were internally consistent. The largest group was aged 40 to 49, and the 30 to 59 age group encompassed 79 to 86 per cent of the total.

TABLE 2.4. *Age of Leaders in Harambee Projects, Kenya*

	Total number	Of which age group known for	Largest group found in interval		Three major intervals	
Initiators	696	265	40–49	34%	30–59	79%
Committee Members	1,015	340	40–49	36%	30–59	80%
Work Group Leaders	504	168	40–49	42%	30–59	86%

Reproduced from Anderson (1975), with permission from Allen & Unwin Ltd.

The researchers were not surprised by this finding. They pointed out that most harambee projects arise from a sense of relative deprivation, and that the literature on marginality suggests that a high sense of deprivation may be associated with age. In addition, most African societies place strong emphasis on age as a criterion for leadership and prestige, and in any case many rural communities had suffered an exodus of young people in search of employment.

(e) Success and Failure of Projects

Mbithi and Rasmusson also examined the factors which contributed to success or failure of projects. They did this by comparing similar projects in specific districts, and then analysing the reasons for differences in outcomes. Because the factors are numerous and complex, they will also be considered in other parts of this book, particularly in the last chapter. Meanwhile, it is pertinent to summarise some of the conclusions which apply to leadership.

One factor which Mbithi and Rasmusson considered important was continuity in leadership. Table 2.5 summarises data for 39 projects in Coast Province and 19 projects in Western Province, and indicates the extent to which the same individuals were involved in the different leadership stages. The table shows that there was often quite heavy overlap—up to 61 per cent in the case of committee members and workgroup leaders in the Coast. Obviously, complete lack of overlap would create problems of coordination and implementation. However, case studies also showed (pp.100 ff.) that in projects with very high overlap the leaders tended to be inward looking and inflexible, and thus that their projects also performed poorly.

TABLE 2.5. *Leadership Continuity in Harambee Projects, Kenya (%)*

	Percentage overlap between:		
Province	Initiators/ Committee Members	Committee Members/ Work Group Leaders	Initiators/ Work Group Leaders
Western	47	46	44
Coast	38	61	43

Reproduced from Anderson (1975) with permission from Allen & Unwin Ltd.

Secondly, Mibithi and Rasmusson (pp.104 ff.) highlighted the importance of leader-appointment procedures. For example, one nursery school on the Coast was found to be successful, in part because it had high participation and because the leaders were openly elected at a Baraza (fund-raising campaign) by counting of hands. By contrast, one factor causing the failure of a nursery school in the same district appeared to have been that its leaders were self-appointed. Lack of initial consensus was not always a problem, however, for some self-appointed leaders were able to attract enough external resources to create the necessary momentum.

Projects also tended to fail when they were 'initiated from above'. In this connection, the role of government officers is critical. On the one hand, as noted above, government officers can be valuable assets, both as open leaders and as hidden catalytic agents. Not the least important, they can also provide access to funds. However, some projects examined by Mbithi and Rasmusson (pp.113 ff.) were heavily dominated by the government, and had too small an element of local support. The researchers' conclusion (p.137) was that 'government involvement should be materially supportive, consultative and coordinatory and not imposive'.

Anderson (1975, p.378) complements these conclusions, stressing the need, especially at the organising and implementing stages, for committees with a wide range of skills:

> [W]hilst respect and popularity are obviously essential if confidence is to be maintained, the capacity to sustain a continuous pattern of work

and collections, and ultimately to support the ongoing routine of [project] life, is especially important. Naturally local people stress that in choosing committee members they choose people who are known for their hard work and reliability. But administrative ability has other aspects, in particular the capacity to understand financial matters, the longer-term implications of policies, and the attitudes of government officials or inspectors. . . .

These administrative strengths do not have to be concentrated in individuals, but they must be possessed by the committee as a whole, which needs to be able to hold together a diffuse range of interests and to focus both formal and informal activity on project development.

Many schemes also suffered from multiple leadership and from competing claims on resources. Mbithi and Rasmusson found that when leaders were committed to too many projects, they were often unable to give adequate attention to each. And sometimes, villagers were expected to contribute to a wide range of schemes. Thus, one case study commented:

> The malady with our projects is that too many are started and are expected to develop side by side. Before two projects are completed there is a third and a fourth springing up. The result of this is to overburden contributors. Overburden in time spent at meetings, work, and other barazas, overburden in money. (Mbithi and Rasmusson, 1977, p.119.)

In this sublocation, seventeen projects were started in seven years. The importance ascribed to schools, at least to begin with, was indicated by the fact that eight of the projects were educational. However, Mbithi and Rasmusson observe that as the backlog of unfinished projects increased, greater emphasis was given to cattle dips, roads, bridges and other projects which paid clear and rapid dividends.

2. Institutional Management and Boards of Governors

The first part of this chapter has looked at leadership patterns within a range of self-help projects. It was chiefly based on the work of Mbithi & Rasmusson, which itself was concerned with harambee cattle dips, aid posts, polytechnics and water projects as well as with schools.

It is now desirable to return to a more specific focus on schools, and to consider aspects of institutional management. In Mbithi and Rasmusson's terms, the work of school committees mainly comes in the organisation and implementation phases of leadership, and there is thus some overlap in the focus of the two parts of the chapter. However, because this part is exclusively concerned with schools and develops some different types of discussion, it is appropriate to present it separately. It looks in

turn at the roles, membership and effectiveness of Boards of Governors.
As a final preliminary remark it should be noted that although the general
term 'Boards of Governors' is being used here, specific systems have
different names for such bodies. Other common titles in anglophone
countries are 'Boards of Management', 'Governing Councils' and 'School
Committees'. Thus although for simplicity one may often use the general
term 'Boards of Governors', nomenclature may have to change when
discussing bodies in specific systems.

(a) The Roles of Boards of Governors

Once again, the system in Kenya can be used as a starting point. In that
country, schools are governed by School Committees. Anderson (1973,
p.365) has pointed out that each one is:

> the official body for negotiations with the educational authorities, the
> local council, self-help committees, and through the local chief, the
> government administration, in all matters concerning the school. In
> conjunction with the headmaster, the committee also determines the
> type of support which the parents will give to the school, for instance by
> arranging work days to do such tasks as constructing or repairing
> buildings or digging latrines. . . . The committee may arrange money
> collections amongst parents to provide for building materials, and it has
> to account for the funds raised and used. Further, it has to keep parents
> informed about school affairs, arrange for parents' visiting days and
> parent/teacher meetings, and also keep the headmaster and teachers
> informed of the parents' views of how the school is being run. In this
> respect, it is likely to press for good examination results and to become
> critical of the teachers if these are not obtained.

This picture is applicable to a large number of Third World countries.
Chapter 13 shows that the functions of primary school Boards of Management in Papua New Guinea, for example, are similar to their counterparts in
Kenya. Large boards usually operate through sub-committees responsible
for such matters as admission of pupils, finance, and buildings.

However, some education systems differ from the Kenyan and Papua
New Guinean ones. Government schools in Sri Lanka, Zambia and the
Cayman Islands, for instance, have no boards (Sri Lanka, 1979, Zambia,
1973, Cayman Islands, 1984). Head teachers there receive instructions
directly from government officers, and though they may be guided by
Parent–Teacher Associations (PTAs), some schools do not even have these
bodies.

In other countries, an intermediate system operates. Thus whereas the
law in Papua New Guinea (1983, Section 60.1) states that every school *shall*
have a governing body, the law in Barbados (1981, Section 16.1) merely

states that schools *may* have such bodies. It also seems fairly common for greater emphasis to be placed on boards at the secondary than at the primary school levels. Thus Ghanaian law, for instance (1981, Section 20.1), requires every secondary school to have a Board of Governors and a PTA, but only requires primary schools to have Parent–Teacher Advisory Committees.

The differences between these systems usually arise from their own historical circumstances and the initiatives of key decision-makers. In Papua New Guinea the creation of primary school Boards of Management largely resulted from personal initiatives by the Director of Education at the time of unification of government and church systems in 1970. In pre-Independence Zambia, the schools for white children did have governing bodies, but the boards were abolished at the time of desegregation of the education system and were never replaced. Governments which are keen to increase levels of community support for education might find it useful to require establishment of boards in all schools. Alternatively, if the authorities are not keen to devolve too many powers to the school level, PTAs can provide a useful, if weaker, substitute.

Boards of Governors in unaided schools are generally more powerful than their counterparts in government schools. Committees in unaided harambee schools, for example, have powers to hire and fire teachers and to determine their rates of pay. Boards of Governors in Papua New Guinean schools, by contrast, are allowed to make their views known to the appointing authorities, but in practice have rather little influence over teacher appointments. The only influence they have over the teachers' conditions of service is in the nature of housing provided. There exists, therefore, a range of powers in different systems.

It is very rare, however, for boards to be given absolute control over their schools. Most governments insist on registration of all schools, and many have regulations on maximum class size, maximum fees, basic facilities, and curriculum. In addition, governments exercise indirect control through the examination system and through influence on the types of qualifications required for individuals to gain certain types of employment. Some communities do not even seek strong control. The studies by Igwe (*infra*) and Okoye (1986) indicate that in Eastern Nigeria communities are keen to construct schools but then wish to hand them over to the government.

(b) Membership of Boards of Governors

Although most Boards of Governors have both ex-officio members and elected community representatives, the nature of representation can differ considerably. In Nepal, for instance, secondary school management committees are required by law to have nine members, who must include the headmaster and a teachers' representative (Padhye, 1976, p.89). In Botswana, by contrast, the law governing Community Junior Secondary

TABLE 2.6. Occupations of Harambee School Committee Members, Kenya, 1967 and 1968

School	Size	Farmer	Trader/business	Teacher	Chief or sub-chief	Civil servant	Minister of religion	Member of parliament	Male	Female	Party official	Local councillor	Co-operative chairman	Primary school chairman	Estimated age range	Median age	Used church buildings	Explicit church representation
Central province																		
School A (M)	11	1		4	2	1‡	3†		9	2	2				80–40	53	✓	✓
B (M)	6	2†	1	1		2*‡	2		6	1		1		1	60–40	48	✓	✓
C (G)	8	2†	2	1	1	2*‡			7	1		1	1		not obtained			✓
D (M)	14	11†‡					1		14	–					80–30	61	✓	✓
Nyanza																		
E (M)	16	5	2	2	5†	1		1	13	3	1	1		1	60–30	48	✓	✓
F (B)	9	2‡	2	2†	1	2			9	–	2	1			70–40	50		✓
Eastern																		
G (M)	8	3	2‡	2†	1				8	–					60–30	39		
H (M)	9	2	1	1	2‡	2	1†	1	8	1	2				not obtained		✓	✓
I (M)	11	2	2‡	2	2†		1	2	11	–	2				not obtained		✓	✓
Western																		
J (M)	13			5	5‡	2	1†		12	1	1	1			70–20	48		✓
K (M)	12	1	1	4‡	5*†		1		12	–		1			not obtained		✓	✓
L (M)	9		1†	3	4	1‡			8	1	1				70–20	51	✓	✓

* A retired position. † Chairman. ‡ Treasurer.　　　　M=Mixed; G=Girls; B=Boys.

Source: Anderson (1975, p.375).

Schools specifically *excludes* head teachers from membership of Boards of Governors (but does require them to be secretaries to the boards, thereby also requiring them to attend meetings), and makes no mention of teachers' representatives (Botswana, 1978, Section 6.3). Instead, the law requires each Board to include:

(a) the owner, who shall be the manager of the school, or in the absence of the owner a manager nominated by a meeting of the local community including parents for a period of five years, and accepted by the local education authority and approved by the Minister,

(b) the District Commissioner or his representative,

(c) the local Member of Parliament or his nominee,

(d) one representative of the local authority nominated annually by that authority,

(e) one member nominated by the Permanent Secretary, and

(f) four to seven members nominated by a meeting of the local community including parents, accepted by the local education authority and approved by the Minister.

In all countries, Boards of Governors in church schools usually have at least some church representation. They may be chaired by the local priests, and include members of the congregations.

The nature of representation in practice may be indicated by some examples. Table 2.6 reproduces the findings of Anderson's (1975) survey of Kenyan harambee schools in 1967 and 1968, and Table 2.7 shows the occupations of chairmen and treasurers in 214 harambee secondary schools

TABLE 2.7. *Occupations of Chairmen and Treasurers of 214 Harambee Schools, Kenya, 1967*

	Chairman	Treasurer
Member of Parliament	10	–
District Commissioner/District Officer	5	1
Chief or Sub-Chief	19	13
Education/Agriculture/Health Officer	10	16
County Area Councillor	5	3
County Council Official	4	7
Teacher	40	42
Minister of Religion	27	–
Missionary Worker	4	17
Supervisory Level	6	5
Artisan	5	1
Labourer	1	–
Businessman/Trader	22	30
Farmer	36	49
Not Reported	20	30
Total	214	214

Source: Anderson (1975, p.376).

in 1967. The latter sample represented 83 per cent of the schools then existing.

Anderson (1975, p.376) comments on the need for caution in interpreting Table 2.6, for some schools had complex arrangements involving councils, boards of governors and executive committees whilst others, although officially having only one body, seemed to accept that it should have a variable composition. He also points out that the table is unable to show the important networks of informal relationships. Yet it does show the range of occupations and leadership patterns. Chiefs, teachers and farmers were particularly common, and Table 2.7 shows that many of them were either chairmen or treasurers. Table 2.6 also shows the small number of women in official positions, though, like Mbithi and Rasmusson, Anderson comments that this may not reflect their real role. It also indicates that although there is a need to attract educated people with a knowledge of the modernising aspects of society, age must still be respected. Again, these conclusions match those of Mbithi and Rasmusson.

Chapter 13 provides comparable information, from Papua New Guinea. It finds that although Boards are supposed to be representative of the communities served by the schools, some achieve this better than others. As well as commenting on the small number of females, the chapter indicates problems in securing full ethnic, residential, socio-economic and occupational representation. It may be assumed that such problems are common in most countries.

(c) The Effectiveness of Boards of Governors

Within any country one would expect variation in the effectiveness of Boards of Governors. Part 1 of this chapter commented on the need for committees to possess a good representation of skills. Work by Anderson (1975) and by Mbithi and Rasmusson (1977) has shown that this is not always achieved in the Kenyan context, and one may assume that their conclusion is also applicable to other countries.

Another major determinant of the effectiveness of a Board is the school's head teacher. This is because the heads are the main professional link to the schools, and usually oversee implementation of decisions. Active heads request meetings and put items on the agenda while passive ones neglect matters and antagonistic ones may even seek to prevent meetings. Research in Papua New Guinea has indicated that it is possible for a Board to continue to be effective in the face of a passive or antagonistic head teacher, and even for a Board to arrange for its head teacher to be transferred (see Chapter 13). However, it is hard for Boards to operate effectively without support from their head teachers, particularly where staff are employed by the government rather than by the Boards themselves.

The views of teachers themselves are also important. Kweka's study of community participation in Tanzania (cited in Galabawa, 1985, p.21) pointed out that while teachers were happy for villagers on school committees to organise fund-raising activities and construction, they usually rejected the suggestion that villagers should make decisions on other areas of school life. The teachers stated that villagers were simply not qualified to advise on the curriculum, for example. And one might assume that few villagers would feel confident in opposing teachers' interpretations of government policy. Thus the balance of power tends strongly to favour the 'professionals', and this fact can limit the effectiveness of a board's work.

At the same time, however, Anderson's Kenyan study (1975, p.387) pointed out that boards can be very powerful, even to the point of exploitation. His survey indicated that sometimes local people obtained positions as salaried advisers to schools, often drawing their wages and expenses despite the fact that they could do very little to help:

> In some cases these advisers were eventually able to take over the running of the school and direct a portion of the fees into their own pockets. Indeed, a number of businessmen specialised in taking over schools that got into difficulties. One very good example of this was the Kenya Education Guild established by an Asian businessman which at one time controlled seven separate schools. In some cases these had been taken over and in others they had actually been set up in conjunction with local people, particularly politicians. One of the Guild's specialities was to obtain teachers and one fruitful very cheap source of these was Sudanese refugees smuggled into the country.

In this instance, eventually the government controlled the activities of the more obvious exploiters, and though one might be able to think of comparable scandals from other countries, fortunately they rarely represent the norm. However, Anderson observed that 'in more subtle forms, one suspects that exploitation remains a factor in the poorer schools', and clearly the notion cannot be dismissed altogether.

Summary

The chapter has highlighted the nature of community leadership in self-help projects in a number of countries. The first part paid particular attention to the data from Kenya, which showed overlapping but different leadership groups at the initiation, organisation and implementation phases of projects. The second part concentrated on the roles, membership and effectiveness of Boards of Governors. It ended on the sober note of potential exploitation, though it would be unreasonable to allow that to dominate the picture. Clearly, school committees are a valuable, perhaps even essential, instrument for mobilising resources and managing projects.

Readers should again be cautioned that most of the data have been derived from a small sample of countries, and it is unfortunate that comparable data from different contexts are so scanty. Nevertheless, it has been possible to highlight the nature of leadership that is likely to exist in many self-help projects, and to indicate the potential of community representation at the school level.

CHAPTER 3

Generating Resources

MARK BRAY

This chapter is concerned with both financial and non-financial resources. To some extent they are substitutable, for communities have to buy land, labour and materials if they have not been donated, and projects to generate resources frequently place as much emphasis on donations in kind as on cash.

The mechanisms for generating resources are diverse, and depend on the cultural contexts and the inventiveness and enthusiasm of the organisers. It is impossible to present a full portrait, but the chapter will highlight a number of common strategies. In many institutions, school fees are the most important source of income. However, because their existence raises major philosophical and operational issues which deserve to be treated at length, they are considered separately in Chapter 4. The present chapter concentrates on resources from within the community, resources from outside the community, and resources generated by schools themselves.

1. Resources from within the Community

(a) Launching Ceremonies

Launching ceremonies are among the most prominent ways to generate funds for capital projects, and when properly managed can be very successful. Mbithi and Rasmusson (1977, pp.27–8) describe practices in Eastern Kenya:

> In a typical self-help project, participants walk to the project site from the sublocation and surrounding areas. Those representing special groups such as clans are provided with transport by their groups. The first to arrive start playing drums or singing and some dance short rhythms just as assemblies in traditional dances usually start. . . . The dignitaries such as the chief, headman, clan leaders, project committee members, visiting politicians and wealthy businessmen and citymen sit near the table of the Master of Ceremonies. The local clans normally prepare food and supply water and young men act as marshals, dance partners and general handimen.

As all expected participants arrive the tempo of work and dance increases as each group attempts to out-perform its neighbour. . . . The Master of Ceremonies will from time to time interrupt activities to make announcements. For example, he will outline the aims of the project, the probable external and government assistance. He will introduce the dignitaries and request them to contribute. All contributions are announced publicly and all sing songs of praise to the contributor. If contributions are meagre, the songs will exalt the wealth of the conspicuously rich and appeal to their love for their local area. As contributions shift to the non-dignitaries, the Master of Ceremonies will interrupt work and dance. 'Stop dancing everyone. I have a nice surprise for you. Our School Committee, a body of men dedicated to the education of our children has donated a bull for all of you to eat'— general clapping of hands, drum rhythm and songs—'and has given to this building project sixty shillings'. Or he would shout suddenly, 'Musau son of Muli has donated fifty cents'. Clapping and general attempt to see who Musau is. Musau is pleasantly embarrassed. He grins, dances or waves. Donations which continue to pour in may be money, eggs, poultry, food, cement, a lorry full of sand or even the land on which a project stands.

As Mbithi and Rasmusson point out, the social groups within which the individuals operate are of major importance. It is within these groups that discipline is maintained, and fines are imposed on those who fail to turn up. The roles are clear, and include the captain, the song leader, the drummers, the rhythm setter, and the workers who move the soil and carry the water. Frequently the local Member of Parliament is invited to make a personal donation, and to sponsor the school in the wider world (see also Hill, 1974, 1975; Keller, 1975, 1980).

Igwe's account of launching ceremonies in Nigeria is very similar. He highlights the strong incentives for individuals to enhance their prestige by donating large amounts and perhaps having buildings named after them, and indicates that the launching ceremony for the secondary school in his own village raised over N1,000,000 in one day.

Although for obvious reasons the organisers of launching ceremonies pay close attention to the potential for attracting large individual gifts, in most contexts the bulk of project income comes from small donations. Mbithi and Rasmusson specifically make this point in their Kenyan study, and it is also true in Eastern Nigeria. Nayar and Virmani's (1978) study in India's Tamil Nadu State similarly reports (p.56) that:

under the Gudiyattam Town Teachers Association Centre conference, Rs. 72,000/- were collected for 20 schools. The analysis of the donors revealed that only 5.3% of the donors contributed more than Rs. 25/-

each. 41.1% of the contributions came from people who contributed Rs. 0.50 to Rs. 0.99 each.

Indeed in some contexts, such as socialist Tanzania, ostentatious donation of large gifts may be rare because possession of so much personal wealth is inconsistent with national ideologies.

(b) Community Taxation

Communities sometimes raise additional resources by imposing taxes on members. Rahardjo, for example (1975, p.36) indicates that part of the funds for Indonesian *pesantrens* comes from religious tithes. Donation of *zakat* is one of the pillars of Islam, and other religions also emphasise the importance of charity.

Igwe (*infra*) indicates that in his village, community members are taxed by the Council of Elders. The men are generally taxed at higher rates than the women, and the age groups are a valuable instrument for collection of the taxes. Sons and daughters who are no longer resident in the village may also be taxed, with the sanction of ostracism in the event of non-payment.

Similar comments are made by Hill (1974, p.8) about Kamba communities in Kenya. *Mwethya* workgroups require individuals to contribute labour, and:

> if one failed to work, one was fined 2/–, and if one failed to pay that, one's property was attached (as clans had always done) and something such as a chicken sold to pay the fine. Likewise, if money was being collected, say 2/– a head for school building materials, property would be attached if the due was not paid. This form of attachment is called *kithendu*. . . . In *kithendu*, the committee appointed a group of usually 12 villagers (called askaris) to go to the offender's home at night—after all the last chances to pay had been exhausted—and snatch an item of the defaulter's property by force. This would be sold unless the offender reclaimed it and paid up, plus 1/– *kithendu* costs, given to the *kithendu* party. Anything could be seized, including clothes, a mattress or blanket, or even a goat. . . .

Hill adds that urban dwellers are also accounted for. They are expected to contribute money proportionally to their earnings, though they give amounts that they themselves consider appropriate, and are not assessed. Some towns have 'outside branches' of the *mwethya*, which have their own committee members and which sponsor sub-projects in liaison with the home based committee. Hill indicates that urban migrants may escape the net if they work outside the main centres, but if they send their children back to the village school they have to pay the penalty for evasion.

Alternatively, communities might decide to tax beer in their area, to impose a toll on vehicles, or to tax market stalls and traders. These measures are usually based on the assumption that people who drink beer, own vehicles and operate businesses have more money than the average person, and can therefore afford to give extra support to their schools.

The extent to which communities can operate in this way depends, of course, on the extent to which they are well organised and can impose sanctions. Kaluba's comments on Zambia (*infra*) indicate that most communities there are much less cohesive than typical Kenyan and Nigerian ones. Kaluba does refer to one school which has been assisted by donations from sons and daughters of the village now living in Lusaka and on the the Copperbelt; but contributions were voluntary, he says, and the case was unusual. Moreover, the peoples of Eastern Nigeria tend to be even better organised than those in Kenya. Thus whereas non-resident members of Nigerian communities may be assessed to determine the size of their contributions, Hill (1974, p.8) states that this does not happen in the communities on which his research focused.

(c) PTA Collections

Collections by Parent–Teacher Associations can be another major source of income. However, it is rare for them to be thoroughly researched, and few studies of PTAs in developing countries are available. PTAs commonly raise money by imposing levies on their members, and by organising fêtes, dances and other social events.

One study of PTAs conducted in Burma (Kyi, 1977) is highlighted in Chapter 14. Table 14.3 shows a strong role played by PTAs, particularly in State High Schools. Interestingly, in affiliated schools, which are institutions in which the communities pay the teachers and erect the buildings but in which the government sets the curriculum and exerts overall control, the role of individual philanthropists seemed to be even greater than that of PTAs. The same is true of the monastery schools. Regrettably, the original survey shed no further light on this phenomenon.

In a different cultural setting. Ashuntantang *et al.* (1977) surveyed seventy-nine schools in Cameroon, and again found PTAs playing a strong role. Ninety per cent of the schools had PTAs, most of which met three times a year or more and had recently organised financial and other contributions. It is significant, however, that some schools did not have PTAs, and the researchers found that the level of participation in big urban senior schools was much lower than in the smaller rural ones. This was partly because urban communities were less rigidly organised along traditional lines: 'the social control over the individual member of the community is nearly non-existent, and thus participation in meetings of school committees cannot be ensured or enforced' (pp.110–11).

Associations de Parents d'Elèves (APEs) are also prominent in Mali. They are legally protected, and usually have salaried officials. In the past, they have been coordinated in a series of four administrative tiers which matched that of the nation as a whole: (a) at the local level the *chef d'arrondissement* was responsible for directing fund-raising according to instructions from above, (b) at the next level up the *Commandant de Cercle* was in charge of wider coordination and attention to economies of scale, (c) at the next level was a regional APE, again with responsibility for coordination but with no powers to raise funds, and (d) at the top, established in 1978, was a National Federation of APEs, responsible for overall supervision. In 1979, however, the machinery was considered too cumbersome. The bottom two tiers were abolished, in part because the formation of the National Federation made them unnecessary (Berthe, 1985).

A body to coordinate the work of parents' associations has also been formed in Barbados (Payne and Hinds, 1986). This is a non-government organisation, however, and thus differs significantly from the Malian one. Also, in Barbados, as in most countries, work on parents' committees is voluntary.

Chapter 13 in this book provides further information on parents' bodies, in this case focusing on Papua New Guinea. In that country they are called Parents' and Citizens' (P&C) Associations. As in Cameroon, the majority of schools have P&C Associations, but some do not. The head teachers are usually the most important individuals, for some are enthusiastic and actively seek parental involvement but others only tolerate or even discourage it. The chapter also highlights organisational weaknesses in many of Papua New Guinea's P&C Associations, and indicates that sometimes there is conflict between the Associations and Boards of Management. Nevertheless, it shows that parental bodies can be a major force both for fund-raising and for mobilisation of labour for the schools. It is common in Papua New Guinea, as in other countries, for parents' groups to set aside specific days of the week for community work on their schools' buildings and grounds.

(d) Alumni Associations

Igwe's paper (*infra*) comments on the role of Alumni Associations. He indicates that alumni of his own old school have recently been levied N100 each for a school bus. A fixed levy is common, though some associations ask members to contribute whatever they feel able to afford, and others set the levies as a percentage of contributors' incomes.

The Alumni Association of Bo Government School in Sierra Leone is among the latter, and is a particularly well-organised body. It sets sliding scales for expected contributions according to the incomes of the members, and is administered by a full-time officer at the school. It has branch offices in different parts of Sierra Leone and in Great Britain, Canada and the United States.

Nayar and Virmani's study of India (1978, p.72) suggests that 'the older the boy, the greater his contribution'. This cannot be guaranteed, of course, for Alumni Associations have to rely on their powers of persuasion rather than ability to enforce sanctions. Nevertheless, well-organised campaigns can generate considerable resources, especially in older and more prestigious schools whose former pupils have reached positions of eminence.

(e) Grants from Co-operatives

Some community schools, particularly in Africa, receive income from local cash-crop co-operatives. Table 3.1 gives the example of a coffee co-operative in Tanzania which has supported several schools and awarded scholarships to deserving individuals.

Anderson (1973, p.58) indicates that co-operatives have played a similar role in parts of Kenya. It has occasionally been hard to decide which schools specific co-operatives should serve, and dissent has sometimes erupted over payments which have been proportionate to individuals' earnings. In the early 1970s this caused the Kenyan Ministry of Co-operatives and Social Services to advise co-operatives against linkages with self-help schemes. Anderson considers this to have been a regrettable move. He points out that co-operatives tied self-help services to the level of production, and thus reduced the extent to which capital was drained from immediate productive use, and created extra incentives for agricultural effort.

(f) Provision of Services

Contributions of labour in school management and in construction and maintenance of buildings have already been mentioned. In addition, schools

TABLE 3.1. *Bukoba Co-operative Union Education Grants, 1969–74*

	Tanzanian Shs
Upper Primary Education	293,594
Home Craft Schools	110,000
Secondary Education Fees	433,592
Omwani TAPA Secondary School	13,694
Rugambwa Secondary School	25,000
Farm Centres' School	43,728
University Education	56,499
Moshi Co-operative College	9,416
School Buildings	155,275
Education of BCU's own employees	153,255
Total	1,294,053

Source: Galabawa (1985, p.8).

may receive help from such people as contractors whose trucks are already travelling and who are willing to fetch school supplies. In some countries women in the community cook school meals on a voluntary basis (see e.g. Nayar and Virmani, 1978, pp.54 ff.), and in many situations communities provide lodging for pupils whose homes are distant from the schools (see e.g. Bray and Boze, 1982).

Occasionally, community members also help with teaching. Priests and religious leaders are often particularly keen to work in schools, frequently without payment. Robinson (*infra*) mentions help from community members in China, and local craftsmen have also taught in Community Junior Secondary Schools in Dominica, usually in exchange for small honoraria (Roberts, 1985). On the African continent, one project in Cameroon (IPAR-Buea, 1977, p.56) hoped to improve school-community relations by using the following local resource people:

Agriculture	—a good coffee, cocoa or oil palm farmer
	—a woman recognised for good food crop farming
	—an extension officer of the Department of Agriculture
	—a clerk of the Co-operative Society
Crafts	—professional and amateur craftsmen
Traditional culture	—Chief/Quarter Head
	—heads of 'cultural associations'
Traditional medicine	—'native doctors'
	—local specialists
Health/Hygiene	—midwife/itinerant health officer
Modern national institutions	—president of party cell
	—Chief
	—civil servant
	—members of local councils
Moral instruction	—clergy and other members of accredited religious organisations
Language	—skilled story teller

However, it must be recognised that use of such personnel is rarely straightforward. The fact that the outsiders are good at their work does not necessarily mean that they are good teachers; visitors may find it hard to get to know the pupils personally, and may encounter discipline problems; it is often hard for teachers to coordinate lessons, and to get outsiders to focus on topics that fit in with other teaching; the outsiders may be unwilling to set homework or to follow up lessons; and effective use of community members requires particularly competent and confident school hosts, who may be rare in many developing country settings. The evaluation of the Cameroon project (Ashuntantang *et al.*, 1977, p.112) concluded that:

> community participation in teaching is only on paper. The good intentions of the syllabus cannot be found in practice, perhaps because teachers have never been trained to animate local people for effective participation or to find out under what conditions community members are ready to assist in the education of children.

(g) The Degree of Voluntariness in Contributions

At several points in the above discussion, it has been noted that individuals may be under such strong pressure to contribute to projects that their participation is in effect compulsory. Not all societies are able to enforce strong sanctions, but those in Kenya and Eastern Nigeria seem to be particularly cohesive and powerful. The issue of sanctions is important, for many advocates of self-help base their praise on the voluntary nature of the phenomenon. Where communities launch many projects and then impose sanctions to fund them, self-help schemes can impose serious strains on individuals.

Mbithi and Rasmusson's Kenyan research on this topic is illuminating and worth reporting in some length. It throws light both on the extent of compulsion and on the factors which make people willing or unwilling to contribute. The researchers also comment on probable future trends.

First, Mbithi and Rasmusson (1977, p.148) noted the nature of responses when people were asked what distinguished a harambee project from a non-harambee project. Table 3.2 points out that more people stressed the voluntary nature of contributions than their compulsory nature. The researchers pointed out that findings would be biased because many leaders would be unwilling to reveal that compulsion played a major role. However, the findings are important. Nyanza and Rift Valley Provinces stood out as 'centres of compulsion', and the authors pointed out that it is much easier to enforce sanctions there than, for example, among the scattered nomadic peoples of North Eastern Province.

The researchers then asked *why* individuals decided to contribute to projects. Table 3.3 shows that in response to this differently phrased question, compulsion became more prominent, and the provincial breakdown seemed to follow a slightly different pattern from that recorded in Table 3.2. Respondents had a number of practical reasons for supporting projects. In the general section, the strongest reasons seemed to be that the project was needed and that the respondent was a committee member who wanted to motivate others. With regard to schools, respondents were

TABLE 3.2. *Voluntariness versus Compulsion as a Noted Characteristic of Harambee Projects, Kenya (% of Total Score)*

Response	Nyanza	Western	Rift Valley	Eastern	Coast	Central	North Eastern
Contributions are Voluntary	5	13	14	22	37	6	50
Contributions are Compulsory	8	0	14	0	0	0	0
No. of Responses	88	52	57	120	273	157	26

Source: Mbithi and Rasmusson (1977, pp.149, 152).

TABLE 3.3. *Reasons why People Contributed to Harambee Projects, Kenya*
(% of Total)

Project	Stated reason	Coast	Eastern	Rift Valley	Central	Western	Nyanza
	1. I wanted to improve my area	16	7	12	4	31	29
	2. Compulsory—could not go against collective will—forced	—	6	—	10	13	21
	3. As a Committee Member, I wanted to motivate others to contribute	15	43	35	12	5	—
	4. I knew I would benefit from the project once completed	5	5	—	—	—	—
All	5. We very much needed the project (for unspecified reasons)	31	7	22	—	13	—
	6. Current idea and practice	4	—	14	—	—	29
	7. I only help in organising dances	2	—	—	—	—	—
	8. Our MPs encouraged us	2	—	—	4	—	—
	9. People clap at rallies when one contributes	—	—	6	—	—	—
1. Cattle Dip	(a) Eradicate ticks and restore health of domestic animals	—	18	—	14	—	—
2. Education	(b) To reduce walking distance for pupils	10	—	—	—	—	—
	(c) Provide opportunities for more successful students	5	2	—	18	9	—
	(d) So the government would take over the school	1	—	—	—	—	—
	(e) As an investment in our children for normal benefits	4	—	—	15	—	—
	(f) To reduce hooliganism and delinquency	—	—	—	—	24	—
3. Health	(g) Reduce walking distance for patients to the nearest medical facility	—	—	2	—	—	8
4. Water	(h) My home is on the pipeline	½	—	—	—	—	—
	(i) Reduce time going to draw from the well	—	7	—	—	—	—
	(j) For my grade cattle	4½	—	—	—	—	—
5. Church	(k) I contributed as a Christian	—	5	9	23	5	13
	Total	100	100	100	100	100	100
	N	302	188	91	73	38	24

Source: Mbithi and Rasmusson (1977, p.153).

concerned to reduce pupils' walking distance, provide more opportunities, attract government resources, provide an investment in their children, and reduce hooliganism.

Additional light on this picture has been thrown by Bolnick's (1974) work. He found that when respondents in a case study were asked what factors made them willing to support projects, they gave a variety of replies. Table 3.4 shows that people seemed particularly willing to contribute if projects were led by local people whom they knew personally and if they themselves stood to benefit from the schemes. Willingness was also high when rallies were chaired by national leaders.

Mbithi and Rasmusson also investigated the views of the small number of people whom they found did not contribute. Their responses are reported in Table 3.5. The most common response was that they did not have anything to contribute. Other reasons given were that they did not know about the fund-raising meeting, that they had already contributed to other harambee projects, and that there were already external sources of funds from the government. It must be stressed, however, that people may have been unwilling to express their real reasons for not contributing, and that the small number of responses distorts the percentage figures and their apparent significance.

Finally, Mbithi and Rasmusson pointed out (p.154) that two factors raised the probability of coercion in the future. First, the increased proliferation of projects arising from multiple needs, as defined not only by local people but also by national leaders, would strain local individual contributors' resources and reduce spontaneity. Second, the expanded number of projects would increase the chances that individual schemes would not receive approval from specific groups, and would lead to divergence of opinion and

TABLE 3.4. *Degrees of Willingness to Contribute to Harambee Projects, Kenya*

Characteristic of Respondent in Relation to Meeting or Project Situation	% of Respondents who contributed willingly
Rally chaired by national leader, for secondary school (HS)	86
Ditto, for health centre (HC)	79
Knew local leader speaking at rally personally (HS)	95
(HC)	90
Did not know him (HS)	52
(HC)	51
Had children in primary school (HS)	97
Did not have children in primary school (HS)	42
Hospital near home before contributing (HC)	69
Hospital not near home before contributing (HC)	82

HS = Harambee [Secondary] School
HC = Health Centre
Source: Bolnick (1974), quoted in Mbithi and Rasmusson (1977, p.154).

TABLE 3.5. *Reasons why People did not Contribute to Harambee Projects,*
Kenya (% of Total)

Stated reason	Western	Rift Valley	North Eastern	Central	Eastern	Nyanza	Coast
1. Had nothing to contribute	63.0	0.0	25.0	0.0	25.0	33.0	17.0
2. I would not benefit from the project	0.0	17.0	0.0	0.0	4.0	33.0	17.0
3. I was not resident in this locality	0.0	50.0	50.0	33.0	0.0	0.0	16.0
4. I was unaware of any fund-raising meeting	37.0	17.0	25.0	0.0	0.0	0.0	33.0
5. None given	0.0	0.0	0.0	0.0	58.0	0.0	0.0
6. I had contributed towards another Harambee project	0.0	0.0	0.0	0.0	13.0	0.0	0.0
7. I wasn't interested in the project	0.0	16.0	0.0	67.0	0.0	34.0	0.0
8. We had external sources of funds from the government	0.0	0.0	0.0	0.0	0.0	0.0	17.0
Total	100.0	100.0	100.0	100.0	100.0	100.0	100.0
N	8	12	8	6	24	6	6

Source: Mbithi and Rasmusson (1977, p.154).

support. This could lead to pressure on local people to conform with the collective will.

2. Resources from Outside the Community

(a) Assistance from Governments

Grants for self-help schools, from both central and local governments, are very common. The grants enable the governments to improve the quality of education and, by encouraging the communities, to extend the availability of schooling. They may also give the governments powers of intervention. The grants may be either for capital or for recurrent expenditure.

One example of central government capital grants, from Zimbabwe, is provided in Table 3.6. In this case, communities were entitled to the amount shown for each item, and had to meet extra costs themselves. In other cases, governments may provide 'matching' grants. In Lesotho, for example, the government has met 75 per cent of building costs but has expected communities to meet the remaining 25 per cent (Motanyane, 1985, p.10). In one state

TABLE 3.6. *Building Grants in Zimbabwe, 1980*

Administration Block	Z$9,000
Library	5,350
Classroom	2,500
Geography Room	5,500
Laboratory & Store	10,150
Woodwork Room & Store	5,650
Metalwork Room & Store	6,400
Housecraft Room & Store	5,200
Agricultural Building	3,400
Toilet Block & Tool Store	2,950
Dormitory & Toilet Block for 36 Pupils	990
Kitchen, Dining Room & Store for 144 Pupils	2,090

Source: Zimbabwe (1980).

in India proportions have been one-third community to two-thirds government, but grants have also varied according to the wealth of each area (Nayar and Virmani, 1978, pp.47, 55).

The system of matching grants in India has not always worked smoothly, however. At one time communities in Gujarat collected money, but then the government found itself unable to find its share and the communities' funds lay idle (Nayar and Virmani, 1978, p.12). It is important for governments to assess the nature of demand before embarking on open-ended commitments.

It is also common for governments to provide annual recurrent grants. The Botswana Government, for example, allocates P80 per pupil to the Community Junior Secondary Schools (Swartland and Taylor, *infra*), and the Zimbabwe government makes per pupil payments ranging from Z$8.30 to Grade 1 to Z$18.35 in Grade 7 (Zimbabwe, 1980).

In some systems, the government also pays teachers' salaries. These are not grants in the sense of monetary allocations which schools can use as they see fit, but serve a similar purpose. In Malaysia, for example, per capita grants for Chinese primary shools were replaced in the 1950s by teachers' salaries (Rashid and Harith, 1973, p.32). In Lesotho and Papua New Guinea the majority of church schools have been incorporated into a national education system, and teachers in church schools are paid through the same mechanism as teachers in government schools. A similar pattern operates in Dominica, where the staff of the Marigot Foundation High School, for example, are now paid by the government (Roberts, 1985, p.12). In Botswana, the government now pays the salaries of qualified teachers (but not the unqualified ones) in the Community Junior Secondary Schools, and some harambee schools in Kenya receive government support in the same way.

The Papua New Guinean government also gives subsidies to support Church Education Secretaries (CESs). Under the formula, churches are given the equivalent of a Level 1 primary school teachers' salary for every

100 teachers in each CES's charge. Thus if the Secretary has only 99 teachers, the church receives no grant. If the Secretary has 199 teachers it receives a grant for one salary; and if he has 200 teachers it receives a grant for two salaries. The formula is crude but workable, and to date there have been no serious pressures for change.

In addition to Ministry of Education assistance, help may be provided through Community Development bodies. For instance, Anderson (1973, p.38) indicates that in the early 1970s the Kenyan Department of Community Development had about KShs 200,000 per annum for projects in each province. Help is also provided for schools in Swaziland through their Ministry of Community Development (Putsoa, 1985) and in Burma by a similar body (Biak Cin and Scandlen, *infra*).

Local governments may also be empowered to assist schools. In the Philippines, for instance, specific provisions have been laid down for Barangay Councils to assist local high schools from real estate taxes (Cruz and Calado, 1975, p.31). Provision of education grants from provincial, state and local governments is common throughout the world.

Finally, government assistance may also be non-financial. Many District Officers provide invaluable advice on building designs, procurement of supplies, fund-raising and settlement of disputes. In many cases they also help with direct management of the schools through their Boards of Governors. Orata (1977, p.404) indicates that in the Philippines government officers have played a major role in helping villagers to raise money to pay fees and support their schools:

> The extension workers of the Bureau of Plant Industry, the Bureau of Animal Industry, the Presidential Arm for Community Development, and the National Cottage Industrial Development Authority are asked for help to enable the students and their parents to acquire the new skills and attitudes that are needed. Invariably the help is given gladly and free of charge.

(b) Assistance from Overseas Churches

Many religious schools, especially Islamic and Christian ones, receive assistance from abroad. Mention has already been made of the Geneva-based Aga Khan Foundation, for example, which has a project to assist self-help communities in Pakistan, Kenya and elsewhere. Similar projects operate within Christian communities, usually via missionary organisations. The aid can be particularly important for secondary schools which require laboratories and good quality buildings.

Acquisition and use of external help is not always straightforward. Wahlstrom (1985), for example, documents tensions which have arisen between the Church of Sweden Mission and the Tamil Evangelical

Lutheran Church in India. When the Swedish aid commenced, it was mainly concerned with school building construction. Over time, the Swedes became more interested in nonformal education, which they saw as an instrument for reducing social inequalities. The Indian church leaders objected to the nonformal programmes, not least because the projects threatened the social status quo, and wished to retain the original focus on schools. The resulting conflict of interests caused considerable ill-feeling. In this case, the Indian church leaders began to see the foreign involvement as a threat rather than a help.

Fortunately the extreme tension generated in this case is relatively uncommon. However, it is worth noting that outside agencies and local communities may have radically different views on the types of projects that they would like to be developed. Communities seeking to obtain external aid sometimes have to sacrifice some of their own priorities or adapt their own philosophies to fit those of the donors.

(c) *Donations from Local Businessmen*

Examples of local businesses contributing to education can be found in all parts of the world. Often the businessmen's motives are a combination of concern for local development and a desire to maintain or improve their own public images. Schools with specific projects may gain assistance in kind as well as in cash. For instance, they may obtain paint from manufacturers or retailers, and timber from local sawmills.

One innovative concept in Zimbabwe has been the sale of 'desk shares', in which the authorities work out the unit costs of a year's education and invite firms to sponsor students. Donations from companies have often taken the form of sponsorship for children of senior employees, but businesses have also been willing to make 'untied' donations (Zimbabwe, 1985, p.5).

Sometimes, business sponsorship takes the form of entire school construction rather than assistance to existing schools. For example, by the end of 1984 the Brooke Bond tea company in Kenya had established seventeen schools, of which thirteen were in the Kericho area where its main operations were based. The company usually provides the land, constructs the buildings, and then hands them over to the government (Lillis and Ayot, *infra*).

The Rotary and Lions Clubs are also well known for small-scale sponsorship of students and projects. Because these organisations are urban-based, they tend to give more frequently to urban than to rural schools. This helps balance the system in so far as PTAs and community associations usually operate more effectively in rural areas.

(d) Aid from Foreign Governments

Aid from foreign governments may be either bilateral or multilateral. The latter operates through such international organisations as Unesco, Unicef and the United Nations Development Programme (UNDP).

Anderson (1983, p.63) provides a case study of bilateral aid, commenting on a secondary school in Kenya which acquired funds from the US Agency for International Development and the British Council. In all parts of the Third World, schools also benefit from volunteer teachers of various nationalities. Occasionally embassies also distribute library books, sports equipment or other resources.

This type of support is usually channelled through national governments, however. Individual communities may have some success if they approach embassies on their own initiative, but the majority of bilateral and multilateral projects are negotiated at official levels. In this case, individual communities benefit only if governments decide to involve them.

Even among international agency projects, however, there are occasional exceptions. One is the Seti Project in Western Nepal, which was launched in the late 1970s by Unesco, Unicef and the UNDP. It was deliberately small, focusing just on development in one Zone. The project leaders made 'contracts' with communities, whereby the former would provide 60 per cent of the cost of buildings and other facilities if the communities provided 40 per cent (Young and Aarons, 1986).

Of course, the initial selection of Seti was the outcome of negotiation between the government and the agencies, and did not result from initiatives within Seti itself. Also, one may assume that agency and community priorities did not always coincide and that the contracts required some compromises. However, reports of the Seti Project suggest that the dedication of agency staff and the small size of the project enabled it to be more flexible than most, giving time to specific community needs and not just imposing their own priorities.

Yet this success itself sounds a warning, for it implies that it is hard to organise such effective initiatives on a larger scale. Indeed one report commented that a subsequent project was commencing under much less favourable circumstances. One of the new project's greatest problems was that it had to operate through government machinery, which was cumbersome, inflexible and often corrupt (Young and Aarons, 1986).

3. School Economic Activities

As mentioned in Chapter 1, many schools also engage in their own production through farms, canteens and carpentry or metalwork contracts. In one school in Rwanda, for instance, use of organic fertilisers on a small plot enabled eight- and nine-year-old pupils to grow potatoes worth the equivalent of US$120 and use the profits—six times what the school received from the government—for equipment (Kulakow *et al.*, 1978, p.15). In the Barrio High Schools of the Philippines, production was made part of the broader curriculum and a mechanism through which pupils could pay their fees:

> If, for example, a student is given a piglet to take care of and later on to sell, the proceeds from which he pays his tuition fees and other expenses, he is guided in the work, as part of his education, on how to take care of the piglet, how to raise its food, what to do if it becomes ill, how to prevent it from becoming ill. After he sells the pig, he returns to the Piglet Project what is left after paying tuition fees and buying his own piglet to continue raising. This amount from all the aided students is used to buy piglets for other deserving students. (Orata, 1977, p.404.)

Similar projects have been launched in parts of China (Shao, 1983) and in other countries.

Usually, school production is only a supplementary activity. Mahatma Gandhi's famous experiments in India showed that if children worked for three hours a day, a class of thirty children could raise enough money to pay their teacher's salary and still have something over for contingencies. Yet today, even in India Gandhi's principles are not followed. The chief reason for this, it is said, is that communities want their schools to be places for learning rather than production (Nayar and Virmani, 1978, pp.18–21). Nevertheless, smaller scale operations are very widespread, and can provide valuable supplementary income.

Summary

This chapter has shown that schools can secure incomes from a wide range of sources. Discussion has focused on the resources from within communities, resources from outside communities, and the ways that schools can generate their own resources.

Of course, procedures that are actually used in different contexts vary widely. Many African communities, for instance, have no need to buy land because it is communally owned and can be allocated by the chiefs (Motanyane, 1985, p.5). Also, fund-raising which relies on rich individuals ostentatiously displaying their wealth may be highly effective in capitalist societies such as Nigeria but less appropriate in socialist nations such as Tanzania. Some communities are alsoin a better position than others to make contributions compulsory. Nevertheless, it is evident from the examples that a high degree of commonality exists in many parts of the world.

CHAPTER 4

School Fees—Philosophical and Operational Issues

MARK BRAY

One of the most prominent mechanisms by which communities raise money to support schools is through the imposition of fees. In many systems, however, the existence of fees is controversial. The issues are sufficiently important to merit a whole chapter, separate from Chapter 3.

Historically, many education systems have evolved from being predominantly fee-charging to being predominantly fee-free. However, the proportion of institutions which still charge fees and the levels of those fees vary widely. Nor has the trend towards abolition of fees always been uniform, for the recent financial stringency experienced by many governments has led to an upsurge in fee imposition.

Because this book is mainly about community support for education, an initial distinction should be made about the types of fees with which it is concerned. In many systems, fees are imposed by governments as a form of direct taxation. The emphasis of this book is more on voluntary contributions by communities than on centrally imposed taxes. However one cannot altogether exclude consideration of official policies, for some governments encourage communities to impose charges while others either totally prohibit fees or impose ceilings.

The first part of this chapter examines philosophical issues, therefore. Because governments are influenced by the views of international bodies, it begins at that level and comments on the outlooks first of UN bodies and then of the World Bank. The third section of the first part turns specifically to government perspectives, and the last looks at some community views. The second part of the chapter comments on operational questions, concentrating on who should set fees, how high they should be, and what they cost to collect.

1. Philosophical Issues

(a) The Views of United Nations Bodies

One of the best known UN statements on education is the 1948 Declaration of Human Rights. Article 26 of the Declaration (UN, 1973, p.3) states that:

> Everyone has the right to education. Education shall be free, at least in the elementary and fundamental stages. Elementary education shall be compulsory. . . .

The specialist branches of the UN have also made important pronouncements. Thus Principle 7 of the 1959 Declaration of the Rights of the Child (UN, 1973, p.94) states that:

> The child is entitled to receive education, which shall be free and compulsory, at least in the elementary stages.

And Article 13 of the 1966 International Covenant on Economic, Social and Cultural Rights (UN, 1973, p.5) states that:

(a) Primary education shall be compulsory and available free to all,
(b) Secondary education in its different forms, including technical and vocational secondary education, shall be made generally available and accessible to all by every appropriate means, and in particular by the progressive introduction of free education.
(c) Higher education shall be made equally accessible to all, on the basis of capacity, by every appropriate means, and in particular by the progressive introduction of free education.

Similar statements have been made at various conferences of Ministers of Education convened by Unesco, notably the 1960 conference of Asian ministers in Karachi, the 1961 conference of African ministers in Addis Ababa, the 1962 conference of Latin American ministers in Santiago, and the 1966 conference of Arab States ministers in Tripoli (Unesco, 1960, 1961, 1962, 1966). They have also been repeated in more recent Unesco documents.

These statements are chiefly based on the arguments that education is a critical component in personal fulfilment and in individual and group social mobility, and thus that it is unfair that individuals can be denied access to education simply because their families are unable to pay fees, In addition, it is argued that charges may keep talented individuals out of school and thus waste national resources.

It is, however, worth noting that the statements seem to give education a special status. If education is a basic human need, one might ask, are not clothing and food even more basic? Yet nobody seems to advocate the distribution of free clothes and free food. Free health services are more commonly advocated, but they were not recommended in the 1948 Declaration of Human Rights. Some would assert that expanded education is itself a mechanism for improving health (e.g. Colclough *et al.*, 1985). However, the number of well educated people who smoke cigarettes is simple evidence that correlations are not straightforward, and direct methods for both prevention and cure of ill health often appear more effective than indirect ones. And the fact that medical charges also discriminate against poorer classes and that this also causes loss of national talent and production seems to have weighed less heavily in the minds of those who framed the 1948 Declaration, of their successors, and of the public in general.

(b) The World Bank's Perspective

The views of the World Bank are particularly important because it has considerable influence on educational policies in the Third World. Indeed, with the crisis of confidence that Unesco faced in the mid-1980s, in many respects the Bank has taken over as the leading international body concerned with education. In recent years the Bank's philosophy in respect of fees (or 'user charges', which seems to be a preferred euphemism) has undergone a major shift.

Much of the Bank's philosophy is set out in a series of education sector policy papers. Chapter 3 of the 1980 paper was entitled 'Expanding and Equalizing Education Opportunities'. It commenced (p.23) by quoting Article 26 of the Universal Declaration on Human Rights, including the clause that education should be free. Nowhere did the chapter contradict this statement. A subsequent chapter suggested (pp.71–2) that 'a system of fees and loans, balanced by scholarships, can be introduced at the post-elementary levels when sociopolitical conditions are favorable', and that 'in communities where most people are not wage earners, fees will be collected in kind'. However, the implication was still that the Bank favoured fee-free elementary education.

Within only three years, however, documents produced by Bank staff had begun to suggest contrary stands (e.g. Birdsall, 1983, Birdsall *et al.*, 1983; Thobani, 1983, 1984a, 1984b; Tan *et al.*, 1984; Jimenez, 1986). Prefaces usually stated that the documents contained the views of the authors which did not necessarily coincide with those of the Bank itself. However, to many readers the distinction may not have been clear. Moreover, in 1981 one government (see below) was formally advised by a World Bank mission to raise its school fees, and followed that advice.

Nancy Birdsall's work is to some extent representative of the new outlook. Her 1983 paper challenged the conventional wisdom that fees are necessarily inquitable. She argued that fees could produce an extra source of government revenue which in turn could make the system more equitable, provided that (a) the money was used to improve quality and to build schools nearer children's homes, (b) the elasticity of demand of the 'rich' was sufficiently low to ensure increased revenues, (c) the positive effect on the poor's demand of the increase in quality and/or the lowering of distance was stronger in absolute terms than the negative effect of the increase in fee, and (d) the increased revenue was sufficient to improve the quality *and* to provide a larger number of school seats.

Eicher (1984, p.140) commented that Birdsall's conditions were 'very stringent indeed', and that specific circumstances would have to be investigated very carefully before policy makers could act confidently on the model. However, Thobani's analysis was similar to Birdsall's, and led to policy changes in Malawi.

Using an economic framework, Thobani (1984a, pp.403–12) first showed that social services usually need to be subsidised from both an efficiency and an equity viewpoint. However, he suggested that it was not clear that the low prices usually charged for such services were necessarily optimal, particularly in situations of financial stringency. Turning specifically to the primary school sector in Malawi, Thobani argued (1984a, p.417):

> There is some evidence that it will not be the poorest students that drop out [when fees are imposed]. The highest enrollment rates (about 100 percent) are in the northern region of Malawi which also happens to be the poorest. The richer central and southern regions had enrollment rates of 51.5 percent and 56.2 percent respectively in 1977. Thus there are other factors in Malawi that counter the expected positive relationship between income and enrollment. . . . The higher tuition fee proposed is likely to discourage those with a low expectation of gaining significantly from education and those whose opportunity cost of time is high—not necessarily the poorest. In fact, the effect of higher returns due to higher quality could conceivably outweigh the lower private returns due to higher fees and could lead to increased enrollment.

He continued:

> Another benefit of higher fees is that, once the initial impact on enrolment settles down, the higher fees will lead to fewer drop-outs. . . . The higher fee may well discourage some people from entering school, but those who do enter would be more likely to stay because of the higher returns from improved quality. In addition, they will form a better pool of potential entrants to secondary school. Finally, if fees are not raised, quality will continue to deteriorate, and . . . we know that it is the poorest who stand to lose most from a deterioration in quality.
>
> Even if primary education were free, UPE could not be achieved until the quality of the service was improved and people perceived education to be privately beneficial—that is, until returns to schooling

are increased. To achieve UPE on a voluntary basis, the quality of education must be improved. Therefore, UPE and a smaller class size, coupled with more books and supplies, go hand in hand. Similary, given the limitation on the government budget, improved quality and higher school fees go hand in hand.

Thobani's paper has been heavily criticised. Klees (1984, p.424) commenced by congratulating Thobabi on presenting 'a plausible rationale for the counterintuitive argument that raising the tuition charges for schooling will advance the interests of the disadvantaged, poorer segments of the population'. However, he was far from convinced by Thobani's arguments, and accused him of being more interested in efficiency than equity. He added (p.439); 'the very real danger of the neoclassical perspective, so clearly embodied in Thobani's paper is that it covers with a technical veneer what are really a complex set of political, social, cultural and economic issues'.

In part because it wanted a World Bank loan, the Malawi government decided to accept the thrust of Thobani's arguments, raising primary school fees by 25 per cent and secondary school charges by 50 per cent. Primary school enrolments duly fell in most districts (Malawi, 1984, p.17), a result that was viewed with considerable misgivings by at least some staff in the Ministry of Education. At the time of writing, however, longer term assessment had not yet been conducted.

Meanwhile, the view of senior World Bank staff Psacharopoulos, Tan and Jimenez (1986, p.23) was that 'in general, increased private financing at the primary level is not recommended as it might interfere with universal coverage'. However, they added that:

> when resource transfers between levels of education and from other sectors are impossible for administrative or political reasons, increased user charges for primary education could increase efficiency within schools, especially if that revenue stays with the school where it was raised.

Their paper commented positively on the policies in Lesotho, in which primary school fees were used to purchase textbooks, and specifically recommended reconsideration of policies that favoured free secondary education (p.19). The Bank is an influential organisation, and its stand is likely to make national governments more sympathetic to schools which charge fees.

(c) The Views of Individual Governments

The Malawi case is unusual in so far as it has been the testing ground for a new World Bank strategy. However, the economic stringency behind that strategy is not unusual. Many governments simply cannot afford to operate education systems without fees. Schooling is a highly labour intensive activity, and is therefore expensive. Education is already the largest item in many public budgets, particularly in Africa, but enrolment rates remain low. If governments wish to expand systems, they have to find ways to spread the financial burden.

Most governments still keep fees as low as possible, however. Nowhere do public schools charge what might be described as a full-cost fee, and even right-wing governments usually temper economic policies with social concern.

One reason for this is that most governments also have to operate within a highly charged political framework. Because of the perceived importance of education to individual and group social mobility, politicians are usually under strong pressure to abolish school fees. Policies with this objective are generally greeted with acclaim, both on philanthropic grounds and for reasons of individual self-interest. The fact that there is no such thing as free education in the sense of education that does not have to be paid for by somebody is often overlooked. Parents who are offered the choice of paying or not paying fees usually opt for the latter without asking where the money will come from instead. And if parents do ask, they are still likely to opt for abolition of fees—for then education will be paid out of everybody's taxes, whether they have children in school or not, and those who actually do have children in school will only have to pay part of the total cost.

The political framework often requires leaders to ignore revenue considerations. In Eastern Nigeria, for example, fees have already been abolished twice and could soon be abolished again. The first occasion was in 1957, when the regional government launched a campaign for Universal Primary Education (UPE). For financial and logistic reasons the scheme collapsed within a matter of months, and fees were reintroduced in 1958 (Abernethy 1969, p.181). In 1976 the Federal Government of Nigeria launched a national UPE scheme. Again it rapidly encountered financial and logistic problems, and again it was found necessary to reintroduce fees (Igwe, *infra*). Sometimes the fees were disguised as levies—for enrolments, textbooks, buildings, uniforms, etc.—but often they were specifically named fees, and even when they were called levies it is arguable that the difference was merely semantic.

The Nigerian experience has many parallels elsewhere. The Ghanaian government abolished fees in 1961, but encountered a financial crisis and allowed them to creep back within a few months (Fiah, 1979). The Kenyan government abolished them in 1974, but had a similar experience (Court and Kinyanjui, 1980, p.348; Lillis and Ayot, *infra*), and shortly after Tanzanian parents had been told about a fee-free UPE campaign in 1977, they found themselves being required to pay substantial registration charges (Omari *et al.*, 1983, p.42). Kaluba's chapter (*infra*) shows further parallels in Zambia.

The Nigerian experience also shows that even military governments are not immune to popular pressure. The 1976 UPE campaign was launched by a military government, and in 1985 the Military Governor of Oyo State announced yet again that newly introduced primary school levies would soon be abolished (*West Africa*, 1 July 1985, p.1343).

In many cases, however, primary and secondary school pupils receive harsher treatment than university students. Thus while in such countries as Nigeria and Papua New Guinea primary and secondary school children have to pay fees, university students have received handsome scholarships. This is a reversal of the priorities of the UN, and seems particularly inegalitarian in view of the much higher life-time earnings that tertiary students are likely to secure as a result of their studies. Policies are usually justified by reference to national needs for highly trained manpower and to the sacrifices of earning that students have to make when they engage in full time study. Often, however, more powerful factors are the forces of tradition and of politics. Systems were made free of charge when numbers were small and when trained manpower was urgently required, and university students and staff generally constitute a powerful political body. Even though primary school pupils and their parents are much more numerous, it is rare for their voices to be stronger than those of the students and the élite.

One final point is that although general taxes have the advantage that they can be spent on anything, school fees have the advantage of specificity. Parents are often more willing to pay school fees, from which they can perceive a specific benefit, than to pay equivalent taxes.

To summarise the dominant force, however, most governments are under considerable pressure to eliminate fees. Because of inadequate alternative tax bases it is often impossible to eliminate fees altogether, but most governments would like to do so if they could.

(d) *Community Perspectives*

Most communities must be more pragmatic than governments or international agencies: if they want to have schools, they must charge fees. To those who suggest that the fees infringe a basic human right, the communities would reply that denial of an education (or a suitable education, in the case of those communities offering an alternative model) is a much more serious denial.

Occasionally, community and government views come into direct conflict. As noted above, one response may simply be to call payments levies rather than fees. Kaluba's chapter notes that this has happened in Zambia, and other examples may be found in Kenya and Nigeria. Alternatively, communities with strong power bases may actively challenge the government.

One instance of the latter occurred in Nigeria in 1979, when the Catholic Archbishop took the Lagos State government to court, questioning the legal basis for the latter's decision to abolish fees (Alabi, 1985, p.48). Similar queries were raised in Papua New Guinea when the national government tried to abolish fees in 1982 (Bray, 1983a). In the Lagos case, the archbishop's opposition was chiefly based on the feeling that Catholic (and other) schools were being starved of resources. The same issue was raised in Papua New Guinea, though a point raised more strongly by some churches, and by provincial governments which opposed the national government's action, was that it can be desirable to have at least small fees so that parents and children value their schools more highly.

2. Operational Issues

Among the problematic questions, three of the most important are who should set fees, how high they should be, and how much they cost to collect. These questions are addressed in this section.

(a) Who should set Fees?

It has already been pointed out that fees may be imposed either by governments or by communities themselves. At the community level, there may be several fee-setting agencies. In the primary schools of Papua New Guinea, for example, pupils commonly have to pay up to four types of fee. The first, paid to the government, is known as the School Equipment Trust Account (SETA) fee, and is intended to defray the cost of materials. The second is set by individual Boards of Management and covers the costs of buildings and other Board projects. The third is set by individual Parents' and Citizens (P&C) Associations and covers similar projects (in the process, as Chapter 13 points out, leading to frequent confusion). The fourth, in church schools, is set by the agency running the school, and helps pay the salaries of Church Education Secretaries.

This general situation is common—there may be an official fee payable to the government, but school committees impose fees determined in the light of advice from their head teachers, the projects they wish to accomplish, government regulations, and the incomes of the people served by their schools. Agency fees are set by broader bodies as a further additional fee. The existence of so many fees can be confusing, but the system enables parents to see where their money is going more clearly, and may enhance their willingness to pay.

(b) How High should Fees Be?

Hill (1974, p.15) reports that in Kenya so-called Harambee schools are occasionally profit-making institutions. In this case, one may assume that the proprietors set fees at the highest level that they think the market will bear, while being cautious not to attract too much attention and criticism.

However, the schools with which this book is mainly concerned do not seek to make a profit. They have to meet recurrent and capital costs, and may also try to maintain a comfortable reserve fund; but within these constraints they seek to keep fees as low as possible.

Nevertheless, fees can still cause considerable strain. For example, Putsoa (1985) reports on a survey of building levies in Swaziland, which in 1984 were found in 69 per cent of primary schools and 76 per cent of secondary schools. Their sizes are indicated in Table 4.1, and the extent of the burden is emphasised by the fact that per capita incomes in rural areas were estimated at only E425–75, and in urban areas at E830.

Fees can also cause major problems of equity. The following quotation is taken from a case-study of Kenya in the mid-1970s, and the situation has not greatly changed:

> Ultimately both Bware and Uriri schools were completed and are now being run as secondary schools. . . . But in both instances the villagers who had helped to put them up have been dismayed by the high school fees charged when the schools started to operate. The fees have been so high that only the very prosperous can now send their children to them. The majority of the people, who are living more or less below the poverty line, have therefore to suffer the agony of watching children from all over the district . . . receive the 'precious' education in 'their' schools for which they had sold their only chickens and crops in order to raise funds at the time of building. Education, for them, has become the domain of the rich, and since some of them are already aware that

TABLE 4.1. *Building Levies, Swaziland, 1983 and 1984*

Building Fund Charge (Emalangeni per Pupil)	Number of Schools	
	1983	1984
20–29	52	41
30–39	17	11
40–49	12	5
50–59	13	8
60–69	7	4
70–79	0	2
80–89	3	2
90–99	2	0
over 99	4	4

Sources: Putsoa (1985, p.6).

education is the key to a better life in the future, they feel cheated and robbed. This is borne out by the fact that in 1974 the fees at each of these schools were K.Shs.990 per annum, without uniform, bedding, utensils and most of the textbooks, in an area where the average per capita income for a year is less than K.Shs.400. (Bray, Dondo and Moemeka, 1976, p.232)

Chapter 7 enlarges on this point, and presents additional evidence from Tanzania.

In many cases it is impossible to avoid these problems altogether. However, governments may set ceilings on the fees that schools can charge. Also, it is not uncommon for communities to operate scholarship schemes for needy individuals, and to give fee reductions to families with more than one child in an institution. Many schools also allow flexibility in payment of fees. They may permit payments by instalment, or they may wait until the harvesting season when money is more plentiful. This type of flexibility can only be achieved in the case of fees which are set within the communities themselves, since governments are not usually able to devote sufficient attention to individual circumstances.

(c) The Cost of Collection

One factor which should influence both the size of fees and the overall decision about whether to impose them at all is the cost of collection. When governments impose fees the cost may be considerable, for they have to establish mechanisms to receive the money from head teachers and to check whether every child has been accounted for. The costs of collection may be so high that they bring into question the benefits from having the fee at all.

The fact that Psacharopoulos *et al.* (1986) and many other World Bank authors ignore this point is unfortunate, for it may be particularly important at the primary school level. Primary school fees are not usually very large, and many institutions are so remote that the cost of collection by the central authorities may be particularly high. When head teachers are required to bring the money to a central location, they incur travelling expenses and may have to neglect their classes. Systems which are properly managed also require government officers to check on school enrolments to see how many pupils should have paid. If governments prohibit fees, on the other hand, they avoid those needs and also avoid the danger of fees being stolen or embezzled. It is unfortunate that no data on the costs of collection in systems of centrally imposed fees are readily available, for they would help governments to gain a clearer view of appropriate policies.

Where communities set their own fees, costs of collection are much lower. They are not non-existent, for receipts should still be issued, money should still be banked, accounts should still be audited, and the head teachers' time is still taken away from other activities. However, the machinery for collection and checking does not have to be so elaborate. This provides governments with a strong argument for devolution of responsibility for fees to the school level.

In this light, the system of 'Assumed Local Contributions' operated in Eastern Nigeria (Igwe, *infra*) seems attractive. The government sets clear guidelines on what schools ought to provide, and leaves the institutions to raise the money in ways that they consider fit. It is true that many teachers in Eastern Nigeria found themselves underpaid because their communities failed to make up the required balance (Abernethy, 1969, pp.227–32), and that similar criticisms have been made in India where a comparable system has been operated (Nayar and Virmani, 1978, p.16). The arrangement may also increase differences between schools. From the official viewpoint, however, the fact that communities which fail to collect adequate funds are likely to be penalised by their inability to attract staff could be a further point in favour of the scheme.

Summary

This chapter has highlighted a series of United Nations resolutions which advocate policies of fee-free education. The resolutions are still widely quoted and supported, and politicians who abolish fees generally win considerable approval. Recently, however, the World Bank has changed its outlook, and its new policies are likely to encourage governments to revise their views. Not all governments will follow the Malawi example of increasing centrally imposed fees, but many will be more tolerant of fees imposed by communities.

The second part of the chapter turned to operational issues. It pointed out that a number of agencies may impose fees at the community level, and highlighted the roles of Boards of Governors, PTAs and religious agencies. It then turned to questions on the size of fees. It is hard to draw up any general rules, but most non-profit-making institutions try to keep fees as low as possible, and may alleviate hardship through scholarships and other schemes. The final section stressed the need to offset the costs of collection against the revenue from fees, and pointed out the influence that this may have on overall policies.

CHAPTER 5

Construction and Maintenance

MARK BRAY

Issues relating to school design can arouse strong passions. Questions arise, for example, on the extent to which governments should impose minimum construction standards when communities are providing the resources, on the extent to which external agencies can facilitate community initiatives without stifling them, on the costs of government-constructed buildings as opposed to ones built by contractors or village labour, and on the maintenance of buildings. These questions should be addressed at both the government and community levels. This chapter is concerned specifically with buildings, though most of the points apply equally to furniture and other facilities.

1. Appropriate Government Policies

While some governments insist that communities should construct according to minimum building standards, others adopt a laissez faire approach. Both policies encounter difficulties, however, so some governments seek to obtain the best of both worlds with a hybrid policy. This section discusses the three strategies in turn, and highlights the attractive and problematic features of each.

(a) Insistence on Minimum Standards?

Many governments impose strict regulations on the types of school buildings that communities may erect. For example, Chapter 9 in this book points out that the government of Imo State in Nigeria provides standard plans. It expects communities to follow these plans, and inspects facilities before it agrees to take over schools. Other governments may not insist on standard designs, but nevertheless lay down minimum criteria for building construction. Chapter 16 indicates that this is the practice in Guyana, for example.

These policies are usually based on arguments about necessary learning conditions. Thus, governments may point out that village building styles often allow insufficient ventilation for large numbers of children, and may

67

exclude too much daylight for prolonged reading and writing. They may add that in round buildings it is hard to position chalkboards in places that do not attract glare, and that villagers often lack the technical expertise for good design even of rectangular buildings. Authorities may be concerned that buildings are dangerous, or that they are unable to prevent children from getting wet during storms.

Governments may also be concerned about inefficient use of resources. For example, although some buildings may be cheap to construct they may have such high maintenance costs and short life-spans that it is wiser to build more expensive but sturdy ones. In addition, governments point out the need for good buildings to protect furniture, books and equipment from rain, termites and thieves. And finally, governments may argue that smart buildings can be a source of pride, and can raise the prestige of education.

(b) Acceptance and Encouragement of Local Designs?

Although these arguments may be powerful, equally strong ones suggest that governments should be flexible, and should be careful to avoid imposing standards on communities. Thus it can be argued that local cultures should be encouraged and respected, and that building designs are a prominent part of such cultures. Indeed, because of the status and role of the school, it may be especially desirable for it to be built in a local style. In addition, as Weeks (1975, p.20) has suggested:

> If it is built out of local materials, in keeping with local construction, and built by the people of the community, the school may have a good start in the community. A community centre of permanent materials but imposed from outside may go unused while one less pretentious built by the people may be fully used.

Perhaps of even greater importance, buildings constructed out of local materials may be much cheaper. And in many remote areas such construction is the *only* way that schools can be built, for it may be impossible to carry zinc sheets, metal windows and cement to difficult locations. Moreover, villagers often find it easier to maintain buildings when they are familiar with the designs and materials.

In addition, government standard designs do not always have the merits that are claimed. Kennedy (1979, p.103) quotes an example from Yemen:

> Out of ignorance, lack of imagination and contempt for Yemeni culture, . . . architects and engineers have been building structures completely inadequate in regard to the climate, cultural background and economic conditions of the Yemen Arab Republic. . . . It took some time for the Yemenis to realise that they had been shortchanged and that in fact those shiny, bright-coloured, oddly shaped buildings

were soon full of cracks, with their paint and cement coatings crumbling away. Besides, those new buildings were cold in winter and hot in summer.

In Yemen, the study added, the buildings also had a disastrous effect on the economy. By discouraging people from using local building methods and materials, the advocates of the so-called 'modern' architecture transformed skilled craftsmen into unskilled labourers.

(c) Try to Achieve the Best of Both Worlds?

In the light of these opposing arguments, many governments feel that the best approach is to compromise. This can be achieved in two main ways:

(i) Work sharing.

Some governments combine their own work with self-help. In Peru, for example, the government has assembled prefabricated lightweight steel structures with aluminium roofs, and communities have built the walls and partitions (Kennedy, 1979, p.102). A similar project has been operated in Swaziland (Putsoa, 1985). The arrangement can encourage communities by giving them 'head starts' in construction and making their efforts go further.

However, the projects do not always work well. For example, under the third International Development Agency project in Malawi, approximately 500 classrooms and 100 teachers' houses were built on a government design with the government providing all materials except labour, sand, water and bricks. Williamson's (1983) report on the project is very critical. It says that the project was too large, poorly planned and poorly managed, and that technical problems arose from the fact that villagers were unfamiliar with the techniques of roofing construction. Materials were also poorly handled, which caused metal window frames and other items to be damaged in transit.

In contrast to this project, one in Nepal has been much more successful— but only because it was run independently of the government and was able to avoid many of the problems which most governments face. In the late 1970s and early 1980s, Unesco, Unicef and the UNDP combined to run the Seti Project in the far west of the country. The organisers made contracts with the School Management Committees of individual institutions, agreeing to provide essential materials and 40 per cent of the total costs if the communities provided the other materials and labour. The project was successful and by the end of 1985 had led to construction of 80 new schools, 40 compound walls, 19 playgrounds and 36 water supply systems (Young and Aarons, 1986, p.1).

To help achieve their objectives, the project organisers only made retroactive payments once sites had been visited by overseers, and always paid promptly. This was said to have greatly helped community morale. The tight system of control was possible only because the project was externally financed. In the mid-1980s the government proposed a similar but larger project, using its own resources. Young and Aarons were not optimistic about its success, indicating (p.2) that it was much less tightly managed:

> Budgets are often not approved until half way through the year; flexible accounting procedures are anathema to the bureaucratic system; and corrupt practices are far harder to control.

They felt that it would be much harder to operate a large project, and particularly stressed the point about corruption:

> The Seti system works in Seti because it is seen to be incorruptible: the people in the community know that their labour and their money are going to be a worthwhile cause, that their children will benefit; morale can be sustained. Once corruption is suspected or known, the commitment of the community inevitably wanes rapidly.

Other governments may suffer less from corruption; but most still suffer from inflexible budgeting and management procedures.

(ii) Technical advice.

Nevertheless, there have been successful projects, both of joint ventures and of more narrowly conceived technical advice. For example, in Aghanistan the authorities noted that traditional mud roofs sometimes leaked or collapsed during heavy rain and recommended insertion of a thin sheet of plastic to solve the problem (Vickery, 1985, p.18). In Northern Nigeria, brushing a silicone-based liquid on the roofs was also found to be effective, and in Bangladesh plastic resins were mixed with jute for improved roofs and walls (Kennedy, 1979, p.103).

Other examples are also worth citing. Thus in parts of Angola, government advisers have arranged for the thatch on round mud school buildings, to be replaced by hollow, burned clay tiles which form a waterproof dome (Vickery, 1985, p.18). And in Pakistan, architects have successfully recommended designs that are more resistant to earthquakes than are normal classrooms (Heneveld and Karim, 1985, p.6).

However, experience also stresses the need for caution. Vickery (1985, p.19) points out that in one country a government architect once insisted on parapet construction to prevent the feet of walls wearing away because water splashed from an overhanging roof. His design worked well to begin with, but in the spring, water from melting snow could not escape over the edge of the roofs, and the buildings collapsed. Again, sometimes government designs are so complex that either buildings are not put up properly or skilled labour has had to be hired from outside (Williamson, 1983, p.49; Heneveld and Karim, 1984, p.6).

Among the ways to reduce the problems of complex designs, two are particularly worth noting. Firstly, governments can accompany building materials with simple and well illustrated booklets. This strategy has been used in Peru, Burma and Nepal. Secondly, governments can employ technical advisers, whose job is to travel round communities and work with villagers. The advisers require salaries and travelling allowances, but this money can be a good investment. It is important, however, for them to have appropriate attitudes as well as skills. Vickery (1985, p.18) stresses that the adviser:

> should be a skilled and highly energetic and sympathetic, local person, speaking the local language/dialect. The advocate's role will be to attend the planning meetings in the village and to remain silent until a useful opportunity occurs to intervene with a specific suggestion that might lead to an improvement in the facility to be planned. There is no place in such meetings for what, in one country, are known as 'trousered gentlemen' who arrive in large cars and expect to be listened to. The advocate in a successful project will be no more than one in a village team.

Good officers would also offer advice on contracts between communities and local contractors, to help ensure that buildings are reasonably priced, are of an adequate standard, and are completed on time. The officers could also help with advice on probable enrolment by grades based on local population projections and probable drop-out rates, (so that buildings are not unnecessarily large in the senior grades), the number of teachers for whom housing will be needed, and aspects of the planned curriculum that have implications for stores, laboratories, etc.

(b) Comparative Costs

It is important for governments to be quite clear about the objectives, costs and benefits of their schemes. Sometimes it is better to use contractors rather than to ask villagers to do the work themselves, even when village labour is unpaid. This is because the quality of work done by contractors may be better, and the buildings may last longer. For instance, Williamson (1983, p.35) calculated alternative costs of buildings in Malawi as follows:

	Villager-Built Units	Contractor-Built Units
Capital cost	K7,000,000	K10,500,000
Life expectancy	25 years	50 years
Maintenance costs	K150,000 p.a.	K100,000 p.a.

Although the villager-built units had a lower initial cost, their life expectancy was shorter and their maintenance costs higher. Because of this, it was arguable that the contractor-built units were a better investment.

This view only assesses the situation from one angle, and project designers may feel that the benefits from involvement of villagers outweigh the costs of inefficiency. It is also questionable whether classrooms *should* have a life expectancy of 50 years. Nevertheless, the costing cautions against the assumption that unpaid village labour is necessarily cheaper than commercial contracting.

The costing also emphasises the need for attention to maintenance. Both governments and communities often neglect maintenance. Sometimes this is for political reasons, for governments like to be seen as innovative and progressive, and may be more keen on their own building programmes than on maintenance of their predecessors' projects. Likewise it is often easier for community leaders to raise large sums for new projects than to secure smaller sums to maintain existing buildings, even when maintenance would in fact be a better investment. In Lesotho, maintenance of buildings designed by the government and erected jointly by the government and churches under a World Bank project has become a major problem which was not anticipated when the project was first developed (Motanyane, 1985, p.11). This problem, it would appear, is far from uncommon.

2. Community Perspectives

Many of the points raised in connection with governments, as was specifically pointed out with reference to maintenance, also apply to communities. In general, however, communities have less room to manoeuvre. First they must work within the constraints of government policy—or at least, they ignore official regulations at their peril—and second it is rare for communities to have access to comparable resources. Nevertheless, several policy options are again worth considering from the community angle.

(a) Use of Traditional or Modern Designs?

On the one hand communities may be keen for their school buildings to match traditional designs, for as already pointed out, the school is often a focus of pride. Also, villagers are already well acquainted with methods of construction of their traditional buildings. However, just because the school is a focus of pride, many villagers prefer their schools to be 'modern', i.e. to be built out of cement, with an aluminium roof and in the familiar rectangular shape. Nimpuno (1976, p.195) points out that although in Tanzania:

almost all rural construction uses traditional technology, constituting over 70% of the total construction volume in the country . . . educational institutions do not try to develop and improve this important sector; instead they ignore it completely. At most it is accepted as a second or third best solution to be used only when western technology is too expensive.

Many communities thus look askance at external efforts to persuade them to use traditional designs. They have an idea what a good school should look like, and they want the best for their children. 'Modern' schools require costly materials, and may do little to improve pupils' learning; but these facts do not carry great weight.

However, it is not necessarily the custom for communities to construct all buildings from the same materials. Kennedy (1979, p.102) comments on a Panamanian practice to erect school offices in modern materials but the dormitories in traditional ones. Other communities give priority to teachers' houses. Schools in most Third World countries are responsible for housing their own teachers, and the nature of housing is a major cause of teacher dissatisfaction. Communities which can provide good houses (which to the teachers usually means cement ones with aluminium roofs) usually have a better chance of attracting qualified staff and of persuading the staff to stay for a number of years.

(b) Use of Village Labour or of Contractors?

Survey of community practice reveals that some choose to put up their own buildings themselves, while others prefer to employ contractors. To some extent, the choice depends on the design and thus on factors mentioned above. There are, however, additional considerations.

One factor, of course, is availability of cash in the community. Preston and Khambu (1986, p.30) report that communities in one part of Papua New Guinea now employ people more often than they used to, and are able to do so because the economy is becoming increasingly monetised. A similar pattern has been reported in Kenya by Mbithi and Rasmusson (1977, p.113). At least in theory, paid employment allows communities to demand work of a particular quality and on a specific time scale, and it avoids the considerable difficulties of organising communal labour.

With regard to the latter, Preston and Khambu highlight problems in securing labour contributions because of poor leadership and inter-village strife. It is particularly hard to motivate people to contribute labour if they live far from the schools, and those who live nearby may be unsympathetic to the fact that others have to travel to reach the school. As a result, the researchers indicate (p.30), 'teachers frequently commented that villagers would arrive late, achieve little and depart early, leading to undue protraction of building work'. It seems probable that other communities in the Third World are also moving from communal to paid labour as soon as they can afford it.

However, it is not always possible for communities to find contractors with local support who are trustworthy and competent, and stories of communities being exploited by contractors are common. The contractors may do poor work, skimp on cement or other materials, charge excessive prices, and fail to keep to agreed time schedules. Sometimes contractors come from neighbouring communities, and the people who finance the schools may resent seeing their money go into other people's pockets.

Summary

Clearly there is no 'right' policy on buildings that should be adopted either by governments or by communities. Strong arguments suggest that governments should closely control building standards, but equally strong arguments favour more laissez faire policies. Similarly, at the community level powerful arguments favour local designs which support local cultures and can easily be constructed, while equally powerful arguments favour imported designs. Because of this, many programmes attempt to achieve the best of both worlds. The Malawi and Nepal experiences show that even these are sometimes hard to operate, however, and are not simple solutions to policy dilemmas.

CHAPTER 6

Issues of Quality

KEVIN LILLIS

This chapter examines issues associated with the quality of systems which receive community support. Quality is a complex topic, and discussion must focus on the inputs and processes of school systems as well as on their outputs.

It is again necessary to recall the diversity of systems with which this book is concerned. As the Introduction pointed out, at the one end of the spectrum the book covers community support for government schools, but at the other end it includes schools wholly financed by communities. In the former case, one may assume that community resources supplement government ones and therefore only improve quality. The chief concerns of educational planners in this type of system are to maximise community inputs and to ensure that they are allocated to the most effective use.

Different concerns arise at the other end of the spectrum, however. Schools which operate entirely outside the government system or which only receive small government grants are sometimes excellent in quality, but are more likely to present serious problems. Questions arise about the extent to which these institutions should be allowed to operate at all.

Although the quality of education has been widely commented on, few judgements in developing countries are based on hard data. Once again, this chapter relies heavily on data from Kenya, where research has been relatively detailed. It is able to make comparative comments from other countries, however. The chapter looks in turn at the quality of intakes, facilities, teachers, curriculum and attainment.

1. Quality of Intakes

Quality of education achievement cannot be properly assessed without first assessing the quality of initial intake. This becomes particularly important in the case of self-help systems which operate parallel to government ones and are accused of inferior standards.

Questions about the nature of intakes are important even at the primary school level. One would not expect comparison of primary school intakes in independent church systems, such as those run by the Seventh-day Advent-

75

ists, to reveal sharp differences in either ability levels of socio-economic background from the cohorts entering government schools. However, subsequent attainment may indeed differ, which implies that the educational process may also differ.

Likewise, in some countries schools are sponsored by universities or by commercial firms for the children of their senior staff. In these cases attainment is often superior to that in the government system, but it is a function of input as well as process. Children of senior staff are likely to have much more supportive backgrounds than average.

In most countries, however, the major watershed is at the secondary level. Thus in Kenya, for example, the intakes of harambee schools are selected by default: the only pupils attending harambee schools are ones who have failed to gain places in government ones (Wellings, 1983, pp.19–20). A similar situation exists in Botswana (Simon, 1984, p.106), and criticisms of the output of self-help schools should take this into account.

2. Quality of Facilities

Where communities are entirely responsible for capital works and receive little or no government support, their facilities are likely to be poor. Institutions run by prosperous foundations and schools with a substantial input from overseas churches or from commercial enterprises would be exceptions to this, but the general picture seems to be valid.

Again, statistical evidence on this may be found in Kenya, where total responsibility for primary school construction now lies with communities. A 1980 survey showed that only 8 per cent of primary schools in Eastern Province had permanent walls; in Nyanza only 46 per cent had permanent roofs; and in Western Province only 24 per cent had permanent floors (Unicef, 1984, pp.82–3). Qualitative problems were exacerbated in 1985 and 1986 when the government restructured the education system and extended the length of the primary cycle by one year. Many of the new classrooms and workshops were very flimsy, and a large number soon lost their roofs in high winds (Lillis and Ayot, *infra*).

Similarly, it has been said of Lesotho's church primary schools, which comprise the majority of institutions in the country, that:

> the majority of children have no seats and no desks to write on. Overall, 65 per cent sit on the floor. This accounts for almost all the children in the lower standards. Many pupils do not have a proper set of books or materials. (Lesotho, 1985, p. 14.)

The situation in Papua New Guinea seems better, for a 1977 survey found that 55 per cent of primary school classrooms were in good condition and 36 per cent were in fair condition (Cayago, 1979, p.12). However, one could argue that even in Kenya and Lesotho the primary school facilities would be much worse without the community inputs.

Issues at the secondary level may be different, however, because countries are more likely to have parallel government and community tracks with different levels of resources. The Ministry of Education in Kenya used to grade the infrastructure of secondary schools from A to D. Of the 416 institutions inspected by 1978, 27 per cent of maintained schools were graded A, but only one harambee school was accorded this rank. At the other extreme only 7 per cent of maintained schools were graded D, compared with 84 per cent of unaided schools (Unicef, 1984). Furthermore, this grading did not embrace all unaided institutions, for only schools offering candidates for the East African Certificate of Education were included. Many unaided schools either were too young to have an examination class or had such poor facilities that they decided against even entering for the examination.

A different situation exists where communities supplement government support, however. Okoye (1983, p.272) presents an interesting case from Anambra State of Nigeria where communities became so enthusiastic about building secondary schools that they also took over construction of thirteen new government schools when the state was unable to continue beyond the first stage. In this case, as in the Kenyan and Lesotho primary schools, community self-help helped reduce a crisis rather than create it.

3. Qualifications of Teachers

While it is recognised that qualifications are not necessarily reliable indicators of the performance of individual teachers, qualifications do indicate teachers' general educational levels and their training for specific jobs. Statistics on teacher qualifications may therefore act as another indicator of quality.

Presenting data from Kenya once again, it may be observed that harambee schools have poorly qualified staffs compared with government institutions. In 1982 87.3 per cent of unaided harambee school teachers were unqualified, compared with 15.4 per cent of government schools. Though it was actually against the law, some harambee schools even employed staff with only the Kenya Certificate of Education (Lillis and Ayot, *infra*).

Particularly important in most schools are the qualities of the head teachers, for whatever the influences from outside may be, the enduring problems of day-to-day operation and control fall directly on them. Head teachers also play crucial roles in schools committees, and therefore need appropriate professional backgrounds and personalities.

With these points in mind, Anderson (1975, pp.382–4) collected data on the qualifications of heads in 214 harambee secondary schools. The survey was conducted in 1967, and covered 83 per cent of the schools then existing.

Anderson's findings are reproduced in Table 6.1, and they indicate the difficulties schools had in obtaining well qualified heads at that time.

Anderson notes that most of the trained graduates shown in Table 6.1 were Europeans, though there was one Asian, and nearly all were employed through missionary organisations. Where well-qualified Africans were found, they either had 'unrecognised' degrees, e.g. from India or Eastern Europe, or had some 'defect'. An example of the latter was a trained graduate who had been a head teacher in a government school but who had been imprisoned for embezzlement. In most cases, therefore, it was the lesser qualified teachers, often with little more than basic secondary education themselves, and often with experience only of primary schools, who took the brunt of the initial harambee secondary school development.

These figures were collected during the main expansionary phase of Harambee, and pressures since then have been reduced. On the one hand, the growth of the harambee sector has showed down, and on the other hand the supply of educated personnel available for such posts has expanded. However, the figures on staff qualifications presented by Lillis and Ayot do not suggest that problems have been solved altogether.

In addition, although Kenya may have grown beyond the worst phase, other countries may only be entering it. For example, the main growth in Community Junior Secondary Schools (CJSSs) in Botswana has only occurred in the 1980s. Simon (1984, p.106) indicates that in 1983, most government/aided secondary school teachers were qualified with a Diploma in Secondary Education or better. In contrast, over half the CJSS teachers had qualifications no higher than School Certificate.

Two factors explain this type of situation. First, because self-help schools are usually short of money, they find it difficult even to pay teachers *any* salaries, let alone competitive ones, and they are unable to offer either pension rights or security of tenure. Their cash constraints also make it hard to supply books, teaching aids and good housing. The intakes, as has been

TABLE 6.1. *Qualifications of Head Teachers in Harambee Secondary Schools, Kenya, 1967*

P2 (2 years' secondary + 2 years' teacher training	15
School Certificate (no training)	25
P1 (School Certificate + 2 years' teacher training)	106
Higher School Certificate (no training)	11
S1 (High School Certificate + 1 or 2 years' training)	17
Graduate (no training)	7
Graduate (with training)	26
Professional or technical qualification (no teacher training)	3
No response to questionnaire	4
Total	214

Source: Anderson (1975, p.384).

noted, are likely to be academically weak, and all these combine to make the institutions unattractive to teachers who are sufficiently qualified to go elsewhere.

Secondly, local self-help schools also suffer from their inability to recruit staff from a nationwide catchment area. Although in theory it is possible for institutions to advertise in national newspapers, few do so. Most recruitment is done by word of mouth, and the institutions lack either the expertise or resources to select the best staff that the market can offer.

In some cases, however, problems can be alleviated. Firstly, significant help is often given by foreign volunteer agencies. These bodies actively seek to place their workers in disadvantaged schools, and can do a lot to raise standards and general morale. Secondly, as implied by Anderson's comments, church schools may have an advantage over those run by village development associations because they are more likely to be tied into national and even international networks. Many dedicated and competent teachers work in church schools, and in some countries many foreign teachers may still be found in secondary schools.

In connection with the latter point, however, use of foreign staff can be precarious. In Malawi, Seventh-day Adventist (SDA) schools used to have a reputation for high quality work. Yet the other churches had foresight to localise staffing more rapidly than the SDAs, so when localisation was finally made compulsory the SDA schools found themselves in difficult circumstances. Their teachers still have a reputation for discipline, but not for academic competence (information from B. Chawani, 1985).

Finally, it must again be emphasised that where community resources are *supplementing* government ones, their overall effect is likely to be positive. Communities which construct good teachers' houses and which are able to make staff feel valued and productive by giving them a high level of support are more likely to be able to attract and retain well qualified staff than are other communities.

4. The Nature of Curricula

The factors of pupil intake, facilities and teacher availability combine to influence the curriculum. It is useful to contrast the outlooks of different voluntary agencies, and to highlight the special problems faced by harambee-type self-help groups.

In many countries, one can discern different atmospheres in schools sponsored by different agencies. Referring to Zaire, for example, Youdi (quoted in Sheline *et al.*, 1984, p.224) commented that school sponsorship was:

the one characteristic which primarily determines the internal 'culture' of the institution, and upon which most other factors seem to depend—

the quality and nationality of the teachers, the composition of the student body in terms of quality, religious affiliation and sex of pupils, the administrative style and teacher-student interaction, the origin of imported educational equipment, and even the architecture of school buildings.

In concrete terms, he said, Catholic secondary schools were segregated by sex, had large, well-kept buildings, were taught and administered by French-speaking Belgian priests and nuns, maintained strict discipline, and offered both academic and vocational courses. By contrast, Protestant schools had more modest buildings, were usually co-educational, were taught and administered by staff whose first languages were English or Swedish, were more relaxed in discipline, and tended to offer more academic courses.

Governments which tolerate or encourage strong voluntary agency participation in the education system have therefore to countenance the possibility that institutions will differ widely in cultures and curricula, both official and 'hidden'. In Zaire, the government was not prepared to tolerate this diversity, and in 1974 nationalised all institutions. In the event, the reform was a disaster and was partially reversed (Sheline *et al.*, 1984, p.233). The Zaire government, like most others, was faced by the reality that if it wanted voluntary agency contributions it would have to accept limitations on its control of the curriculum.

Similar forces have been evident in Kenya's harambee system. As has been pointed out, most harambee schools suffer from weak intakes, poor facilities and underqualified teachers, and inevitably their curriculum has suffered. Most harambee schools are mere shadows of government institutions. Many are unable to offer science subjects because they lack laboratories and qualified staff, and many of those which do have laboratories and staff only feel confident to offer general science and health science rather than chemistry, physics and biology.

In the Kenyan case, this is particularly disappointing because, as Wellings (1983, p.11) points puts, the early years were ones of great enthusiasm. Harambee was expected not only to expand educational opportunities but also to promote a revised, rural-oriented curriculum. Instead:

> Occupational relevant disciplines such as metalwork, carpentry, masonry, mechanics, agriculture and horticulture, requiring specialised facilities, equipment and staff but teaching the skills most desperately required in the rural areas, are to be found almost exclusively in the higher-grade government schools. As a result . . . the poorer the school the more formalised is the curriculum (Wellings, 1983, p. 17).

Harambee schools are usually unable to offer anything other than a weak academic curriculum. And even if they had more resources, they would still be unlikely to attempt a non-academic curriculum. Because of the nature of the labour market, students need academic qualifications, and anything else is seen as a second-best choice.

Similar observations have been made about countries in the Pacific. Hindson (1985, p.291), for example, documents the development of a parallel, self-help system in Kiribati during the late 1970s and early 1980s. The government was keen to develop rurally-oriented curricula in special Community High Schools, and to site the institutions on the outer islands. The thrust of popular demand, however, was for academic education on the mainland. Four church-sponsored institutions were opened, with varying amounts of resources. The well-provided Mormon school used syllabi and texts from Utah; the less well-endowed Catholic institution started with a more practical syllabus but later abandoned it, partly in response to market demand; and the Church of God and Seventh-day Adventist schools which opened in 1983 and 1984 looked unlikely to reverse the trend. As in Zaire, the government had to accept the limits on the extent to which it could control the curricula in voluntary agency schools.

5. Quality of Attainment

Within the academic framework, the previous section implies, some schools which operate through community support perform well, while others are very weak. Among the former are often church schools, as in Zaire, but among the latter are unaided harambee-type institutions. Once again, valuable information is worth reporting from Kenya.

Until recently, secondary Form IV students in Kenya sat the East African Certificate of Education (EACE) examination, and their results were graded 1, 2, 3, 4 and Fail. Wellings (1983, p.18) indicates that in 1978 there were 128 Grade A, 165 Grade B, 287 Grade C and 864 Grade D schools in the country. As pointed out above, most government schools are in the upper half of the scale, and most unaided schools are in the lower half.

Table 6.2 indicates the performance in each group in 1978. Wellings points out that the significance of the differences may be assessed by chi-square tests on the raw data. These show that students at Grade A schools are eight times more likely to obtain a Division 1 or 2 pass than their peers in Grade D schools.

Wellings also analysed differences in performance between school types within grade categories. Table 6.3 shows the EACE performance of Grade B, C and D schools, and confirms his analysis. Lillis and Ayot (*infra*) provide further evidence from the government's national league tables in 1983 and 1984 to show that the picture had barely changed.

Again, comparable figures may be quoted from Botswana. Simon (1984, p.106) indicates that in 1983 38 per cent of students in government and aided schools obtained first and second class passes in the school certificate

CFE—D

TABLE 6.2 *EACE School Performance by School Grade, Kenya, 1978 (%)*

School Type	Passing Division 1 or 2	Passing EACE
A	47.1	94.9
B	29.4	87.0
C	17.9	77.0
D	5.7	59.1

Reproduced from Wellings (1983, p.18), with permission from Manchester University Press.

TABLE 6.3. *EACE School Performance within School Types, Kenya, 1978 (%)*

School Type	Grade B		Grade C		Grade D	
	Passing Div 1 or 2	Passing EACE	Passing Div 1 or 2	Passing EACE	Passing Div 1 or 2	Passing EACE
Government	34.0	90.8	22.7	83.6	7.9	60.7
Private	11.3	72.0	9.0	54.1	3.6	51.1
Harambee	23.8	83.2	6.8	67.2	5.5	60.3

Reproduced from Wellings (1983, pp.19–21), with permission from Manchester University Press.

examinations, but the Community Junior Secondary Schools achieved only 6 per cent.

Important work on the factors behind the Kenyan picture has been conducted by Somerset (1984). He analysed the performance of pupils in the Certificate of Primary Education (CPE) examination and then their subsequent performance at EACE. His twin objectives were to test both the predictive validity of the primary school examination and the processes of secondary schooling.

As he expected, almost all primary school leavers who had a choice went to government rather than harambee secondary schools. Within high-quality government schools. Somerset found only a weak relationship between pupils' CPE grades and their subsequent EACE grades, and within unaided and low-quality government schools he found no relationship at all. However, Somerset did conclude:

> It seems that a pupil who enters a high-quality maintained school is likely to gain an EACE result 12–15 points better than another pupil with similar CPE marks who enters a low-quality maintained school. In the same way, an entrant to a low-quality maintained school is likely to perform 10–12 points better than a similarly-qualified entrant to an unaided school.

This evidence suggests that, at least in this context, pupils entering unaided secondary schools are doomed to be low attainers in their secondary school leaving examinations. Somerset concluded from his results that the quality of process in secondary schools was much more important for final success than the quality of intake.

To substantiate his conclusions, Somerset analysed the results from Starehe Boys' Centre, which at that time was the only high-quality secondary school that did not restrict its intake to pupils with high CPE scores. He found that Starehe was no more successful with the pupils who had scored highly at CPE than were other high-quality secondary institutions. However, Starehe pupils with lower marks were enormously advantaged. High-quality maintained schools did not accept any pupils with CPE marks below 180, but Starehe took fourteen. These pupils average 28.6 at EACE— 10 points better than their counterparts in low-quality maintained schools and 21 points better than those in unaided schools.

Somerset concluded:

> Teachers from schools which do not achieve good EACE results often explain their failure in terms of the quality of the recruits they receive from the primary schools. If the well-established schools take all the high-potential recruits, they argue, then the other schools can hardly be blamed if their EACE results are poor. Implicit in this argument is the assumption that the critical constraint is the shortage of pupils with the necessary abilities to do well in EACE. The results from both the Starehe and the Nyeri samples indicate quite clearly, however, that the quality of education provided at secondary schools is much the more important determinant of EACE success.

Welling's (1983) article asked whether unaided secondary education in Kenya was a blessing or blight, and firmly concluded that it was the latter. Somerset's work seems to confirm his view.

Finally, however, a contrast should be drawn with Tanzania. Government policies there have restricted growth of secondary schools very severely. As in Kenya, unaided schools have sought to meet unfulfilled demand, but in contrast to Kenya a large number have had better academic results than government institutions. Court and Kinyanjui (1980, p.392) report that the top five of the 118 schools entering candidates for the Form IV examination in 1975 were unaided schools; and in one region in 1976 the best unaided school sent twenty-five students to Form V and managed to place all other leavers in further training and employment.

This situation emphasises the fact that the Kenyan pattern may not apply in all countries. However, it does not necessarily suggest that the Tanzanian government should encourage the growth of unaided institutions. Because the government schools were so few, the unaided institutions were still taking the 'cream' of the country. As Chapter 7 will point out, they were also mainly in the more prosperous and educationally privileged parts of the country. Rapid growth of unaided institutions would severely strain the system, and would cause the Tanzanian picture to resemble the Kenyan one rather more closely.

Summary

This chapter has focused separately on pupil intakes, facilities, teacher qualifications, curriculum and academic attainment. Because of the range of institutions covered, it is hard to reach firm conclusions. Nevertheless, it is possible to make several general statements.

When community support supplements the existing government system, it may be assumed to improve quality. The facilities in Kenyan and Lesotho primary schools show that the quality may still be poor, but amenities are at least better than they would have been in the absence of community support.

Where communities run entirely separate systems, however, problems may arise. The chapter has used data on Kenya's harambee schools to show that quality may be poor on all counts. Moreover, Somerset's work indicates that harambee schools cannot escape blame for poor attainment by arguing that they have poor intakes. He agrees that intakes are one factor, but shows that the quality of teaching is even more important. Harambee schools in Kenya compound the problems of poor intakes by giving their pupils poor tuition. Robinson's comments on *minban* schools (*infra*) imply that similar factors operate in China, and one would expect them also to be common elsewhere.

It might still be argued that harambee schools extend opportunities, and that in a sense no education is even poorer in quality than a bad one. However, Wellings (1983) does not agree. He suggests the schools waste resources which could have been put to better use, and encourage unrealistic aspirations among communities and their children.

At the same time, this conclusion need not necessarily apply to all countries. Okoye's analysis of Nigeria's Anambra State (1986, p.273) points out that the policies of keeping community schools within the state system and of using the same teachers and management as older schools has avoided most of the problems of Kenya's harambee schools. And even where systems are separate, they are not necessarily of low quality. During the mid-1970s, unaided secondary schools in Tanzania were often better than government ones; and in several (though not all) countries, the Seventh-day Adventists run good quality schools, and only remain independent because they prefer to operate without the strings that accompany government grants.

CHAPTER 7

Geographic and Social Inequalities

KEVIN LILLIS

Although equality of opportunities is among the goals of most governments, the majority of education systems exhibit glaring inequalities. Community support for education is only one component of the picture, but it can be an important instrument both of increased and reduced inequalities.

To some extent, geographic and social inequalities overlap. Underprivileged groups may be concentrated in certain suburbs or regions, while their more privileged counterparts may be equally concentrated. This does not always happen, however, and the chapter will identify various inequalities within regions. All inequalities must be assessed in both the quantity and quality of provision, and this will be done here in four parts: regional, rural/urban, socio-economic and sexual.

1. Regional Inequalities

Geographic inequalities chiefly arise because communities in some areas are more interested and/or more able to embark on self-help projects. The problem has arisen in many countries, but data from Kenya and Tanzania are particularly clear.

Table 7.1 shows the provincial distribution of secondary school places in

TABLE 7.1. *Distribution of Secondary School Places, Kenya, 1979*

Province	% of Pop.	Aided Number	%	Assisted Number	%	Unaided Number	%
Central	15.3	35,795	24.6	29,942	35.0	24,203	17.6
Coast	8.8	8,249	5.7	4,067	4.8	7,426	5.4
Eastern	17.7	23,046	15.9	16,471	19.3	26,695	19.4
Nairobi	5.4	13,738	9.5	1,281	1.5	12,638	9.2
N. Eastern	2.4	792	0.5	224	0.3	—	—
Nyanza	17.3	21,634	14.9	11,879	13.9	29,920	21.8
Rift Valley	21.1	20,860	14.3	12,954	15.2	17,025	12.4
Western	12.0	21,243	14.6	8,667	10.1	19,560	14.2
KENYA	100.0	143,357	100.0	85,485	100.0	137,467	100.0

Source: Mwiria (1986, p.72).

85

Kenya in 1979. Central, Nyanza and Western Provinces were advantaged in some or all categories, while Coast and North Eastern Province were disadvantaged. The operation of self-help activities was a key factor in this imbalance, and comparable inequalities existed at the primary level. Unicef (1984, p.96) comments that 1981 primary school statistics are consistent with an analysis in the 1970s in which three types of district were identified as not having participated equally in educational development:
—arid and semi-arid districts, especially those with a pastoral economy,
—poorer and agricultural districts, several of which also had semi-arid portions and dispersed populations, and
—municipalities.

Table 7.2 takes analysis further by correlating the strength of harambee activities with district wealth. In the Unicef (1984) primary school data, six districts (Marsabit, Garissa, Mandera, Wajir, Samburu and Turkana) had gross enrolment rates below 50 per cent. While cultural and environmental factors have also influenced access to education, Table 7.2 shows the districts to have had both low incomes and low self-help activities.

The Tanzanian government has made even stronger efforts to combat regional inequalities, and has also been frustrated by self-help initiatives. Table 7.2 shows that private schools grew in a very uneven manner during the 1966–76 period. Demand for and supply of private education was concentrated in precisely those areas which had the best quality primary and secondary schools but which suffered from policies which restricted the expansion of government secondary schools.

By the mid-1980s, it was reported, the Kilimanjaro region had 20.1 per cent of the country's secondary schools but only 5.3 per cent of the nation's population, and 68.0 per cent of its secondary schools were unaided (Galabawa, 1985, p.17). Court and Kinyanjui (1980, p.392) point out that annual fees of TShs 2,000 per pupil can only be paid in relatively wealthy areas, and the fact that many private schools have close associations with long-established missions suggests another mechanism through which historical advantages are maintained. Moreover, whereas in Kenya the quality of unaided schools is frequently criticised, it was pointed out in Chapter 6 that some Tanzanian unaided schools are of very good quality.

Comparable forces have also been noted in Nigeria. During the self-help thrusts in Anambra State during the 1970s and 1980s, for example, patterns emerged in which:

> the parts of the State where education was first established showed the initial interest in the scheme, while other areas followed; a natural consequence since secondary education can only be useful to children who have completed their primary education. The disadvantage, however, is that in the less developed part of the state, where many children . . . do not reach Primary 6, the lack of secondary schools

TABLE 7.2. *District Rankings of Contributions to Harambee Projects and Wealth,*
Kenya, 1977

Harambee Contributions		Wealth
Kakamega	1	Mombasa
Kiambu	2	Nakuru
Murang'a	3	Kiambu
Meru	4	Kisumu
Nyeri	5	Kericho
Machakos	6	Machakos
Bungoma	7	Nyeri
Kisii	8	Kakamega
Nakuru	9	Uasin Gishu
Embu	10	Meru
Kajiado	11	Murang'a
Taita Taveta	12	Kisii
Laikipia	13	Trans-Nzoia
South Nyanza	14	Nandi
Kirinyaga	15	Bungoma
Kitui	16	South Nyanza
Baringo	17	Kilifi
Nyandarua	18	Embu
Kisumu	19	Nyandarua
Kericho	20	Kirinyaga
Siaya	21	Laikipia
Mombasa	22	Taita Taveta
Kilifi	23	Kitui
Busia	24	Kajiado
Kwale	25	Kwale
Narok	26	Siaya
Trans Nzoia	27	Baringo
Lamu	28	Busia
Elgeyo Marakwet	29	Elgeyo Marakwet
Turkana	30	Wajir
Nandi	31	Garissa
Uasin Gishu	32	Narok
Mandera	33	Marsabit
Samburu	34	Isiolo
Wajir	35	Tana River
Marsabit	36	West Pokot
Tana River	37	Lamu
West Pokot	38	Samburu
Isiolo	39	Turkana
Garissa	40	Mandera

Source: Unicef (1984, p.75).

continues, without the impetus of a local school to encourage parents to educate their children. (Okoye, 1986, p. 272).

The authorities did try to encourage less developed areas, both through public enlightenment campaigns and by relaxed requirements on the conditions for school establishment. They also limited the expansion of schools in

TABLE 7.3. Distribution of Secondary School Places, Tanzania, 1966 and 1976

Region	1966				1976			
	%	Aided	%	Unaided	%	Aided	%	Unaided
Arusha	2.9	685	5.4	203	3.3	1,310	8.8	1,513
Coast	20.3	4,842	28.0	1,062	4.5	1,810	—	—
Dar es Salaam	—	—	—	—	13.3	5,321	20.8	3,592
Dodoma	6.7	1,596	3.5	134	7.0	2,799	2.5	429
Iringa	7.1	1,702	1.0	40	8.4	3,365	4.0	679
Kigoma	1.2	276	—	—	1.1	431	0.8	141
Kilimanjaro	11.7	2,781	14.2	540	11.4	4,542	19.8	3,414
Lindi	—	—	—	—	1.1	427	2.7	466
Mara	2.4	562	4.2	167	3.6	1,417	2.0	349
Mbeya	4.3	1,013	5.1	194	4.1	1,619	3.7	665
Morogoro	5.9	1,399	4.0	150	4.5	1,788	7.6	1,317
Mtwara	6.0	1,430	0.7	25	5.0	1,961	—	—
Mwanza	7.3	1,742	14.9	563	6.2	2,463	8.2	1,421
Rukwa	—	—	—	—	0.9	341	1.1	194
Ruvuma	2.6	627	3.2	122	4.0	1,607	1.6	282
Shinyanga	1.2	288	—	—	1.6	639	2.6	453
Singida	—	—	0.6	23	2.1	844	0.7	125
Tabora	6.6	1,568	3.8	145	5.5	2,209	3.0	518
Tanga	8.4	1,997	4.8	181	7.4	2,973	3.8	663
West Lake	5.6	1,327	6.4	243	5.2	2,091	5.9	1,024
TANZANIA		23,836		3,792		39,947		17,245

Source: Court and Kinyanjui (1980, p.391).

the more developed areas. Okoye reports that little progress was made, however, and only a handful of less developed communities responded. Moreover, when the overall programme was suspended in the mid-1980s because resources were being stretched too far, inequalities, at least for the time being, were made more permanent.

Finally, Ota (1985, p.10) points out that when prosperous groups embark on self-help and recruit well qualified teachers, their recruitment may severely diminish the number of good teachers left for other schools. Moreover, although specific communities may decide that they can afford it, when they have small classes the scarce teacher resources may not be deployed to optimum advantage. Ota raises these points specifically in connection with the Zimbabwean experience, where they have given the authorities serious problems, but they are also applicable to other countries.

2. Rural/Urban Inequalities

Many commentators have also highlighted rural/urban inequalities. On the one hand, rural groups may find it easier to forge a sense of community identity. However, governments often exploit the income-generating capacity of rural groups and give larger grants to town schools; and the urban dwellers may be richer in the first place. Moreover where dual systems operate, the self-help schools may be primarily rural. Robinson (*infra*) indicates that this has been the case in China, and the Barrio High Schools in the Philippines were also conceived of primarily as rural institutions (Cruz and Calado, 1975, p.20). It is hard therefore to identify universal patterns, though it is possible to gather scattered evidence.

Beginning with the stronger bonds of rural communities, one may again refer to the study of PTAs conducted in Cameroon. Ashuntantang *et al.* (1977, pp.110–11) found that participation in large urban schools was much less than in smaller rural ones, in part because 'the social control over the individual member of the community [in urban schools] is nearly non-existent, and thus participation in meetings of school committees cannot be ensured or enforced'. This finding matches general experience in most countries. For instance, Igwe's account of fund-raising in Eastern Nigeria (*infra*) conveys a similar impression.

Table 7.4 provides statistics from Sudan. As well as showing regional disparities, they indicate that in Khartoum self-help provided a small proportion of funds while the government provided a large proportion. Further analysis of the factors behind these figures is needed, but they probably reflect both the difficulties of organising self-help among urban communities and the relative generosity of the government to urban dwellers.

Mbithi and Rasmusson (1977, p.113) add further evidence from Kenya. Two sublocations which the researchers identified as least successful in

TABLE 7.4. *Non-Salary Funds, by Source and Region, for Sudanese Secondary Schools, 1984 (%)*

	Government	Self-Help
Central	82.1	17.9
Darfur	90.2	9.8
Eastern	75.4	24.6
Kordufan	53.3	46.7
Northern	75.2	24.8
Khartoum	87.1	12.9
Total	76.5	23.5

Source: Salih (1986, p.6.10).

organising harambee projects were Kinoo and Dagoretti, outside Nairobi. The main factor in this was probably the plentiful supply of government resources, which reduced both the people's sense of relative deprivation and their inclination to embark on self-help projects.

Contrasting with this, however, is Mbithi and Rasmusson's (1977, pp.134–7) case study of Kenya's North Eastern Province. In this area, the rural population is scattered and largely nomadic. In these conditions it is hard to develop a strong sense of community, and the bulk of self-help projects were found in the town, Wajir.

In addition, one may note that activities of such organisations as the Rotary and Lions Clubs tend to be urban based. And Coombe and Lauvas (1984, p.78) note that Zambian self-help efforts seemed to have produced greater resources among the more prosperous communities in high-cost housing estates. When urban communities do embark on self-help initiatives, therefore, they usually have more resources at their disposal.

3. Socio-economic Inequalities

Socio-economic inequalities overlap with geographic ones, for poor people are often concentrated in particular regions and suburbs. However, inequalities also exist within geographic areas, and may be exacerbated by self-help activities. The main problematic factors are twofold: that richer groups can afford to help themselves and that this widens gaps, and that some community projects become mechanisms through which poor people create facilities which are then used by the relatively rich.

With reference to the first point, inequalities may become particularly visible when socio-economic status coincides with race. This has occurred in many parts of the world among minority Europeans, Asians and Chinese. Some examples were referred to in Chapter 1.

Turning to the second point, Galabawa (1985, p.18) has highlighted the situation in Tanzania. In some projects, he says, all community members are expected to contribute but only a minority benefit:

Only the rich bourgeois group can afford to send its children to private secondary school where fees exceed 2,000 TShs per year per pupil. The ordinary peasant in Tanzania cannot afford this amount. But many of the private schools are built with the help of the money or labour of the small peasant. . . . A striking example is that of the Omumwani Secondary School in Kagera region. . . . The school fees are exorbitant and yet the Kagera Region Co-operative Union was paying 600 TShs per annum for every pupil.

Similar comments, as was noted in Chapter 4, have been made about Kenya by Bray, Dondo and Moemeka (1976, p.232). Table 7.5 shows the range of different fees charged in typical Kenyan secondary schools. Even when schools do not create high direct costs, poor families are often excluded by opportunity costs.

4. Sexual Inequalities

Although the main forces for sexual stratification usually lie elsewhere, the nature of self-help schemes can also have implications for male–female imbalances. Self-help operations may reduce inequalities, but they can also increase them.

Taking again the example of Kenya, it is important to note that overall female enrolment rates have greatly improved during the last two decades. However, the majority of girls' places have been in harambee schools, and the government is not to be congratulated for its activities. In 1968 there were 143 maintained schools for boys, but only sixty-one for girls and twenty-eight for both sexes. This was already a discriminatory situation, but over the next six years the gap widened. By 1974 there were 235 government boys' schools but only eighty-two girls' schools and forty-seven co-educational ones (Krystall, 1980, p.9), and during the rest of the decade the picture barely improved. Table 7.6 shows that in 1979, boys comprised 68 per cent of enrolments in government schools, compared with 32 per cent for girls.

TABLE 7.5. *Mean Annual Fees Charged in Kenyan Secondary Schools, 1979 (KShs)*

Type of Fee	Maintained	Assisted	Unaided Harambee
Tuition/Boarding	1,085.0	2,352.9	2,852.6
Building	82.4	148.1	185.3
Uniform	168.4	111.1	73.2
Caution	44.3	34.2	37.9
Activity	43.5	33.2	31.9
Medical	7.8	9.9	4.7
Books/Equipment	6.6	44.1	42.8

Source: Unicef (1984, p.72).

TABLE 7.6. *Enrolment by Sex in Kenyan Secondary Schools, 1979 (%)*

	Maintained	Assisted	Unaided
Boys	68	50	55
Girls	32	50	45

Source: Unicef (1984, p.67).

In the light of these figures, Unicef (1984, p.68) points out that Kenyan girls' chances of having secondary schools to attend depend more than boys' on the socio-economic development of their communities. Because fees are much higher in harambee schools and because many families are still reluctant to invest in girls' education, many females still do not attend even when there is a harambee school in the neighbourhood. Drop-out rates for girls in harambee schools are much higher than those of either boys in harambee schools or girls in government schools. And Chapter 6 has demonstrated that harambee schools are qualitatively inferior to maintained ones, so even if they do attend school they do not gain access to the same resources as boys.

Thus although harambee institutions have alleviated sexual inequalities, they have not removed them. If girls receive a complete secondary education at all, it is likely to be inferior in quality and will probably not enable them to proceed to post-secondary education.

Unfortunately, comparable data from other countries are not readily available. Tan (1985) shows that private costs for education of girls in Tanzania are higher in both government and unaided schools than they are for boys, but she does not discuss either possible reasons for this or its implications. Okoye (1986, p.271) also makes passing reference to sexual stratification in Anambra State of Nigeria, indicating that mixed institutions had experienced disciplinary problems, that most communities preferred to build boys' schools than girls' schools, and that the government, in contrast to the Kenyan one, had sometimes insisted on communities making more provision for girls. These are isolated comments, however, and it would be useful to have more complete analysis from both these and other contexts.

Summary

In general, this chapter has highlighted the ways that community initiatives increase inequalities rather than the reverse. At the regional level, for example, it is common for gaps to widen. This is partly because advantaged groups already have resources, and partly because they have established traditions of self-help. Governments often find it difficult to formulate policies on communities who do not assist themselves. If the government fills the breach, it may reduce incentives for communities to help themselves as well as penalising those who do. But if it fails to take action, the government may find that regional inequalities become steadily worse.

It is hard to generalise on the impact of self-help on rural/urban inequalities. Rural communities are often more cohesive and better able to apply sanctions to encourage contributions, but urban communities may be richer in the first place. Also, organisations such as the Rotary and Lions Clubs tend to be urban-based. More research in different settings is needed before one can confidently state whether a ban on self-help activities (or a campaign to boost them) would increase or decrease rural/urban inequalities.

Evidence from Tanzania and Kenya also suggests that self-help projects can sometimes increase socio-economic inequalities. Particularly poignant are instances in which poor people labour to build schools but then find that they cannot afford either the direct or the indirect costs to allow them to utilise the institutions.

Finally, evidence from Kenya suggests that harambee schools have provided more places for girls and so have reduced sexual inequalities. Girls remain disadvantaged, however. The fact that girls are not excluded altogether reduces pressure on the government to provide more spaces for girls in maintained schools, and harambee schools are generally poor in quality. Drop-out rates remain high among girls in harambee schools, and the poor quality of harambee secondary education reduces the chances of further education for those who do complete secondary school. These factors modify the impact of self-help in reducing inequalities.

CHAPTER 8

Central Guidance and Control

MARK BRAY

Several chapters have already mentioned the need for central guidance and control. Issues came particularly to the fore in Chapters 6 and 7 in connection with the quality of self-help education and the problems of social and regional inequalities. Yet when central control is too strong, there is a danger of local initiatives being stifled. Governments have to seek an appropriate balance, the locus of which may vary in different societies. In Eastern Nigeria, for example, the tradition of self-help is so strong that it seems to flourish under almost all circumstances. Bhutan, by contrast, has almost no comparable tradition, and projects would require much more careful nurture.

Government influence on community initiatives may be direct or indirect. Direct controls, which will be considered first in this chapter, take the form of regulations, e.g. on registration, class size, curriculum, teachers and fees. Indirect influences may be exerted through provision of grants, training programmes for teachers, and general advice through District Education Officers. These will be discussed in the second part of the chapter. The third part examines some constraints on the effectiveness of controls.

1. Direct Controls on Schools

Most governments require all schools to be registered, including ones that are independently managed and financed. They do this to facilitate enforcement of regulations on the quality of education and to help assess the geographical coverage of schooling.

In most systems, regulations lay down a series of steps which communities must follow before a school can gain full approval. They commonly have three stages: (1) approval in principle, which communities should obtain before they commence construction, (2) approval of facilities, which communities should obtain after they have built their schools but before they commence teaching, and (3) in some systems approval of teaching, which communities must obtain before their pupils can sit public examinations. The first step allows the government to check whether the location and nature of the school is satisfactory and matches its own priorities, and the second and third steps help it to regulate the quality of provision. Approval for examinations may last only for a specified period, and may have to be renewed every five years or so.

Although they may not be universally applicable, some additional features of the regulations in Imo State of Nigeria (1984a) are worth quoting. First, the government requires a community applying to build a school to have at least N50,000 in a bank account. Second, when the government has written to the community indicating that an application has been approved in principle, the community must accept the following conditions in writing:

(a) The government will not accept responsibilities for any school unless its phases have been completed in accordance with government specifications. Secondary schools must have at least 25 acres of land, and water supply within a kilometre. Recommendations are provided on the way that buildings might be grouped, and unless they have written permission to do otherwise, communities are required to use the Ministry's standard construction plans which indicate the materials to be used and the amount of floor space per pupil.
(b) Schools must be open to students from areas other than the places in which the institutions are sited.
(c) The government will not pay compensation when it takes over a school.
(d) The government shall be free to decide on the types of courses which the school will offer.
(e) The name of the school shall be subject to the approval of the Commissioner for Education.

Similar regulations apply in neighbouring Anambra State, where the authorities also decide whether schools shall be for girls or boys (Okoye, 1986, p.271), and in Tanzania. In the latter, the regulation on the names of school adds the clause that:

> the Commissioner shall not, save with the consent of the Minister, approve any name which contains the English word 'University' or the Kiswahili words 'Chuo Kihuu', or any similar word or combination of words in any language calculated to suggest that the school is a University. (Tanzania, 1982, p.11.)

The Tanzanian regulations go further than the Imo State ones by specifying that 20 per cent of the places in private secondary schools must be allocated to pupils from outside the region where the school is built (Tanzania, 1985, p.2). Such regulations are possible where community enthusiasm is very high. However, Okoye (1986, p.272) notes that they have had to be relaxed in less developed parts of Anambra State where community spirit has been less strong, and one may assume that this is also true in other contexts.

Governments may also require the managers of schools to be registered.

This is the practice in Botswana, Tanzania and Kenya, for example. It allows the governments to compile records on who the managers are, to ensure that the managers are individuals or bodies that the authorities consider suitable, and to encourage communities to become well organised, knowing who their managers are and what they are supposed to do.

Some governments also enforce regulations on fees and levies. It was pointed out in Chapter 4 that in a few systems they are totally prohibited, in others the policy is laissez faire, and in yet others the policy is intermediate. Complete prohibition assumes that the governments are able to provide all resources necessary. When governments are actually unable to do this, either the schools suffer or collections are made unofficially. One reason why so little information is available on community financing in many countries is that governments have an ideological objection to collection of money. This is partly because they do not wish to countenance the possibility that some children might be denied schooling because of inability to pay, and partly because the governments are reluctant to admit that they cannot meet all needs themselves. Because of the prohibition, communities are often unwilling to declare their collections.

The Imo State regulations on fees and levies fall in the intermediate category. Communities are permitted to collect PTA levies if they have the prior approval of the state Commissioner for Education, and to secure this approval they must furnish him in advance with (a) a copy of the circular notice summoning the meeting of the PTA, (b) a copy of the agenda of the meeting, (c) the attendance list of the PTA meeting, and (d) the signed minutes of the meeting (Imo State, 1984b). The regulations attempt to prevent exploitation of communities by corrupt or over-zealous individuals.

Governments may also set regulations on accounting procedures. Misuse of money, or allegations of misuse, is one of the most common causes of strife in community-funding projects. Even in Kenya, with its longstanding tradition of harambee, in 1985 the Minister of Finance and Planning still felt it necessary to state:

> As part of our effort to use resources more productively, we need greater accountability for harambee funds. Documentation of the collections and project expenditures must be prepared in order to maintain public confidence in harambee. (Saitoti, 1985, p.5.)

In almost all settings, improved record-keeping is desirable to discourage embezzlement funds and to protect the innocent. Even when individuals have not stolen school money, they often find it hard to demonstrate that fact when they have poor accounts, and the damage to community spirit in such circumstances can be just as severe as when theft has occurred.

With regard to centrally administered financial controls, small countries may have an advantage over larger ones. Putsoa (1985, p.13) states that in Swaziland:

During the month of February 1985 . . . the Ministry's audit department covered ten primary and secondary schools. If this is the normal
rate of auditing, and allowing for school holidays, it means that
approximately 100 schools or 17.8% of the total number of schools may
expect an auditor in the school year.

In turn, this would mean that the auditors could cover the whole system
within about six years. Likewise, the thirty-three Community Junior
Secondary Schools operating in Botswana in 1985 were required to present
annual accounts to the Ministry of Education (Makunga, 1985, p.3). The
accounts were checked carefully, and a Ministry officer helped with
methodological problems. Chapter 17 in this book indicates that a parallel
also exists in Guyana, where the Ministry has offered short courses in
accounting in collaboration with the Ministry of Finance. In these three
countries the relatively small number of schools makes the system easier to
manage.

In larger countries, however, it may be harder to supervise systems. Even
in Zambia, for example, which has a population of six million, the government finds itself unable to run routine checking procedures. Official auditors
go to schools only in a time of crisis, and the presence of an auditor is
therefore a sign of trouble.

Even within the constraints of size, however, in many countries a great
deal could be done to improve the situation. School accounts should be
readily comprehensible to ordinary laymen, and should not require the
services of professional auditors. In some settings much is done by District
Education Officers and by school inspectors. Even when these people do not
actually comb through the accounts of each school, a request for the records
on each visit encourages communities to give accounts more attention.

2. Indirect Influences

Governments can also shape the education sector through indirect
mechanisms. They may, for example, offer grants and technical advice,
provide training for teachers and workshops for managers, offer to take over
schools which are sited in the right places and have satisfactory facilities,
provide advice through District Education Officers and other personnel,
and influence the curriculum through their control of examinations.

Some examples of government grants were given in Chapter 3. It was
pointed out that as well as full grants, governments may provide partial
ones, perhaps on a matching dollar-for-dollar basis. The grants encourage
the communities to provide the facilities for which the money is intended,
and allow the government to set requirements on the types and nature of
facilities. Special grants may be made for disadvantaged communities in
order to reduce regional and social inequalities, and help may be in the form

of government-paid teachers and administrative personnel for churches and other voluntary organisations as well as in cash donations.

Indirect control may also be exercised through teacher training, which helps shape the outlook of teachers and provides a pool of trained staff from which communities may recruit. Ideally, governments can use training programmes to encourage teachers to think positively about community initiatives and to suggest ways in which staff can promote community self-help. These comments apply to both pre-service and in-service training.

Governments may also hold workshops for school Boards of Governors and PTA officials. This has been a strategy in India's Tamil Nadu State, for example (Nayar and Virmani, 1978, p.57) in Nepal (Young and Aarons, 1986, p.5), and in Papua New Guinea (Bray, *infra*). Experience has suggested that workshops need not be expensive, for communities are often willing to provide accommodation and travel expenses for their own nominees. Topics for discussion can include legal matters, accounting procedures, and fund-raising mechanisms, and the workshops can facilitate a two-way flow of ideas.

The offer by government to take-over community schools may also be an effective indirect influence. For instance, in 1967 the Government of Kenya announced that it would take over twenty-five to thirty Form I classes each year (Wellings, 1983, p.15; Lillis and Ayot, *infra*). Economic stringency later forced the government to modify the policy, but most Kenyan communities are very keen for the government to relieve them of a heavy burden by taking over their institutions, and hope of take-over remains a powerful influence on the nature of the schools. The government has clear criteria to help decide whether or not to take over a school, among which are the nature of the facilities and the standard of academic achievement. This procedure acts as a guideline and incentive for the communities.

Considerable influence may be wielded by District Education Officers, inspectors and similar personnel, who can be particularly valuable for stimulating the activity of poorly organised groups, and thus for reducing regional and social imbalances. They may also help with advice on the viability of projects, accounting procedures, building design, and procurement of supplies.

In Anambra State of Nigeria, the government has also been able to influence communities through its control of pupil admissions. Okoye (1986, p.268) has written:

> As the government could not compel communities to build schools, or to complete schools they had started, the only control available was not to allocate Class I students to the community school at the beginning of the year. . . . Warnings of this were given to both the community and the school at each stage, and well ahead of time, with conditions that were to be met if such a penalty was to be avoided. Community leaders

were often grateful to receive this notice in writing, as the letter could then be read out at the monthly Town Union meeting, and the necessary contributions or assistance would be forthcoming. . . . Spelling out the programme and drawing attention to needs in advance were therefore useful to the Government, the community leaders, and the schools.

Closure of schools when communities fail to construct toilets and other essential facilities is also a common strategy used in Papua New Guinea to jolt communities into action. However, the policy can backfire. Sometimes communities fail to take action, and the government then has to countenance falling enrolment rates and social deprivation.

Finally, the curricula offered by all schools are heavily influenced by the nature and requirements of the labour market. Governments often find that they do not have as much control over the labour market as they would like, but they do nevertheless have some influence. In most countries, governments also control the public examination systems, which in turn regulate entry to parts of the labour market. Even the communities which prefer to retain their independence and which reject government support because of the strings likely to accompany it still pay close attention to the demands of the examination system (see e.g. Keller, 1975, p.8; Okoye, 1986, p.273).

3. Constraints on the Operation of Controls

It must be recognised that many of these controls and guides are limited. Both central and local bureaucracies are frequently overworked and inadequately staffed, and it is hard to devote as much attention to these matters as many people would like. Governments often find it difficult to encourage communities which are fragmented and which do not have strong traditions of self-help. Sometimes, they also find it difficult to restrain eager communities whose activities have a detrimental effect on regional and social inequalities.

In some contexts, corruption is also a major problem. Young and Aarons (1986) stress its negative impact in Nepal. They note that although a joint Unicef, Unesco and UNDP project worked well, a similar government one was likely to founder because of general inertia, inflexibility and corruption. Similar difficulties are found in other systems, especially in Asia and Africa.

Political forces may also threaten careful bureaucratic operations. For example, Anderson (1973, p.27) describes the procedures laid down by the Kenyan Ministry of Education to regulate and direct the harambee schools into constructive channels. To some extent, he points out, these procedures were followed.

But as the elections of 1969 drew near, the political situation led politicians to become active once again in the education field. Further schools were encouraged, and the Ministry of Education was forced into making widespread commitments in the form of *ad hoc* aid and extra teachers, with little regard for the requirements of the education development plan.

Similar comments have been made by Keller (1975, p.6):

> although there is a legal basis for closing down or not registering harambee schools which do not meet certain specified standards, in some cases officials find it politically wise to surrender to local pressures for the recognition of a school even when it is not up to standard.

Keller (1980, p.52) adds that the politicians themselves may be unable to control the situation. He quotes the Kenyan Minister for Labour as saying:

> It is very hard to close harambee schools and reduce their production . . . *they are a political thing* and even though I am not very happy with what they are doing, I myself am building these schools . . . this is political and cannot be helped. (emphasis original)

This type of situation is not confined to Africa. Hindson (1985, pp.291–3) documents problems encountered by the government of Kiribati, which has been concerned both to promote balanced regional development and to limit investment in academic secondary education until it could be justified by expansion of the cash economy. Because the government refused to build new secondary schools in the main island, a number of communities decided to open their own. Between 1978 and 1984, schools were opened by the Mormons, the Catholics, adherents to the Church of God, and the Seventh-day Adventists. The schools clearly undermined official policy, but for political reasons the government felt unable to prohibit them, especially since they were entirely funded with non-government money. Similar comments have been made about schools in India by Nayar and Virmani (1978, p.46).

Some governments also operate through over-centralised and bureaucratic administrations. Hanson (1984, p.123), for example, comments on the Venezuelan Ministry of Education which, prior to a set of reforms in 1968, was responsible for all major and minor decisions about schools, personnel and instructional programmes. The Ministry, he says, became a huge bureaucratic job bank which often took nine to twelve months to reply even to simple requests on such matters as building repairs or payment of teachers in newly opened institutions. Clearly it would be hard in such a structure to encourage desirable community initiatives and to control undesirable ones.

Yet governments may also find that systems can become too

decentralised. In contrast to the Venezuelan situation, Hanson (1983, p.89) indicates that the Colombian situation in the late 1960s was one of excessive decentralisation in which the state education systems were 'functioning in a disorganized condition of semi-anarchy'. Simply because provincial governments are closer to the people, they often find it hard to resist short-term political pressures which may not be in the long-term interests of the region and its people. This suggests that an ideal structure for maximum flexibility and control might be a deconcentrated one in which provincial officers are employed by the central government but have enough authority to be able to deal efficiently with local circumstances. Yet even this relies on the existence of a competent and energetic cadre of officers at the local level—an ideal which in many countries remains distant.

Finally, well-intentioned attempts to improve the quality of teaching forces have sometimes been misconceived and counter-productive. Anderson (1975, p.386) documents one instance of this from Kenya. Table 6.1 pointed out that the academic qualifications of harambee school head teachers in the 1960s were very weak. The government became concerned about this, and sought to improve the situation by sending teachers to harambee schools and by taking a role in the teacher-appointment process. However, as Anderson points out, the qualities required of a good head teacher are not always reflected in academic qualifications. In particular, individuals are needed who have the confidence of school committees and their communities, and who are dedicated to their work. Anderson points out that government involvement sometimes *weakened* schools by replacing able and committed head teachers by 'better qualified' persons.

Summary

The chapter has highlighted a number of direct and indirect controls which governments may employ to regulate the number and quality of self-help institutions. Direct controls include regulations on registration of institutions and on the nature of their facilities, staffing, fees and curriculum. Indirect controls operate through grant systems, teacher training, workshops, and the examination system.

The chapter has also indicated a number of limitations on the effectiveness of controls. For example, governments may find that political pressures cause regulations to be by-passed, they may have inappropriate administrative hierarchies, and they may lack skilled personnel and information.

PART II

Case Studies

CHAPTER 9

Community Financing of Schools in Eastern Nigeria

S. O. IGWE

Among the people of Eastern Nigeria, community development through self-help has become almost a way of life. Few communities wait for governments to provide them with such amenities as pipe-borne water, hospitals, post offices, electricity and schools. Instead, communities take their own initiative, tax themselves, and later apply for government assistance. Communities have been particularly successful in the establishment and financing of schools.

Although Eastern Nigeria no longer exists as a political entity, the name is still commonly used as a collective reference to Imo, Anambra, Cross River and Rivers States. The peoples in these states have many common cultural features, and the comments of this paper are generally applicable throughout the region. Discussion focuses on Imo State, however, which is the author's home area.

The chapter has four main sections. The first examines the social and political structures of the area: the councils of elders, the village and clan improvement unions, and the age groups. The second discusses mechanisms for educational support before and after the government take-over of schools in 1970. The third section gives examples of the ways in which funds are raised today, and the final section draws strands together in conclusion.

1. Social and Political Organisation

Imo State is part of the homeland of the Ibo peoples, and it is useful to commence with comments on their social organisation. The basic social unit is the localised patrilineage known as *umunna*, which consists of individual families whose members are blood relations. The families occupy homesteads on defined areas of land, and each lineage group lives together under the moral authority of its oldest male member, known as *okpara*. A cluster of lineage groups makes up a village, and each village is closely knit: almost everybody knows everybody else.

Among the Ibo, competition between individuals, age groups, compounds, clans and villages is an established and cherished way of life. Every

105

community measures its progress in relation to the achievements of others. For this reason, when the acquisition of academic certificates became identified with personal achievements and salaried employment, the spirit of competition manifested itself in open rivalry for the establishment of schools and the highest enrolment rates. Ibos are aggressive, enterprising and individualistic, and are renowned both for their commercial prowess and for their receptiveness to new ideas.

(a) The Councils of Elders

Each village or clan in Ibo society is governed by a council of elders, and each lineage group is represented at the council by its oldest male member, the *okpara*. Members are regarded largely as equals, but age is highly revered, and council affairs are often dominated by wealthy individuals, title holders and men of great personal achievements. All matters affecting the general welfare of villages and clans are handled by their councils, which meet as often as is necessary.

(b) The Village and Clan Improvement Unions

Most villages and clans also have their own 'improvement unions', which generally originated in the 1930s or 1940s. It was during this period that people, particularly educated ones who had migrated from rural to urban centres, first realised that the best salaried jobs went to those with the highest educational qualifications. The new urban dwellers also realised that as individuals they could not influence events in their new communities, and that it was necessary to group together.

Although most unions started with the objective of improving conditions in the new urban environments, many soon turned their attention back to their homelands. They encouraged their kinspeople to join them in the towns, and they commenced projects to educate their peoples on the importance of schools (Abernethy, 1969, pp.105–11).

By the 1960s, many unions had become powerful and had branches in all the main urban centres. They built primary and secondary schools in their villages, and they awarded university scholarships to deserving sons and daughters. By 1964, for example, different village and clan improvement unions had established thirty-eight secondary schools throughout the region (Eastern Nigeria, 1967, p.70). Some of the more famous schools are Ibibio State College, founded in 1946 in the present Cross River State; Okerika Grammar School (1946) in the present Rivers State; Okongwu Memorial Grammar School at Newi (1949) in the present Anambra State; and Arondizuogu National High School (1951) in the present Imo State. The unions competed among each other to establish schools and to award scholarships.

(c) The Age Groups

Each village also has several age groups, which are informally started when their members are born. Groups are formalised when members reach the age of 15 to 20, and they choose a name and elect their leaders. Any person over the age of 20 who still does not belong to an age group is treated as a social outcast. In many areas of Eastern Nigeria, the formal launching of an age group is an occasion for elaborate ceremonies.

All public duties are shared among the different age groups in a village. For example, the groups act as market wardens, clear roads and playgrounds, cut forests for communal farming, and serve as village soldiers in times of crises. An age group can also be a powerful body for fund-raising once the council of elders at home and the improvement union 'abroad' (i.e. in other parts of Nigeria) have jointly decided on a development project. At the time of writing, the author paid a compulsory annual subscription of N100 (US$160) to his age group common fund. Sometimes, the subscriptions are increased to finance large projects. There is often keen rivalry among age groups to secure the highest contribution and to make the greatest development effort in the community.

2. Changes in the Patterns of Financing

(a) The Period up to 1970

From the mid-nineteenth century until 1900, the Christian churches were the only bodies concerned with formal education in Eastern Nigeria. In the early years, the schools were entirely financed from outside by the mission societies. Within a short time, however, the missions began to transfer the burden to local congregations in order to make them self-sufficient and to liberate funds for further evangelisation. Only at the turn of the century did the British colonial authorities begin to show an interest in education (Phillipson, 1948, pp.12ff).

To begin with, government action was restricted to grants-in-aid. The early grants were rather complex and were based on each school's average attendance, facilities, efficiency in administration, and examination results. Later the government opened its own schools, so that three categories of institutions existed: government, assisted and unassisted. Although some schools in the third category were private, profit-making bodies, the majority of assisted and unassisted institutions were run by the churches. Even in government schools the local chiefs or Native Administrations were responsible for buildings and for an annual 'subscription'. In all institutions, therefore, there remained a high degree of community financing.

Several detailed accounts of financing procedures in church schools in Eastern Nigeria were reproduced in the 1948 Phillipson Report. The account by Father J. Jordan of the Roman Catholic Mission is especially illuminating. He contrasted the pattern in Nsukka Division, which he described as 'probably the most backward Division in Iboland' with Newi, which he considered much more progressive.

Jordan categorised the unassisted schools in Nsukka into four groups. The Group A schools were in remote areas, and practically all of them, he said,

> developed from small rural churches which were accustomed to pay monthly and annual collections towards the support of a catechist responsible for keeping services, teaching religion and generally weaning catechumens from the pagan way of life. (Jordan, in Phillipson, 1948, p.114.)

They did not charge school fees because they did not wish to discourage potential converts. Instead, finance came from church levies and the church annual harvest. By contrast, schools in Group B charged fees. Their evolution from an A-type school took place 'when the local Church decides that the pagans are sufficiently interested in schooling to pay fees for their children'. Group C schools, which were said to be uncommon, existed where there were small communities in which the Christians were not numerous enough to finance schooling but where communal effort was easy. There were no fees, for the schools belonged equally to all the children of the village, and the parents' Education Fund defrayed the expenses. Such schools, however, often collapsed. Finally, Group D schools were an economic venture: 'The town puts money into education and looks forward to salaried employment for its children in return.' These schools were run by Christians and non-Christians in partnership, though usually under the umbrella of the church.

The Newi schools, Father Jordan suggested, all resembled the advanced schools in Nsukka. At least among boys, schooling was already practically universal. Fund-raising procedures were even more sophisticated than in Nsukka:

> At the beginning of the year the Manager distributes his teachers with an eye on the financial possibilities of each station. He knows exactly what he needs for salaries, estimates what he will get from school fees, and then imposes an assessment. The latter is rigidly collected by the Committee attached to each school. If there is a shortage at the close of the year or if the people decide to build a new school or to incur an unusual expense, a big general meeting of all influential Christians at home and abroad is held and a levy per head indicated. . . . [The schools all follow] the same procedure. One shilling per scholar, two per adult Christian woman and five per man. They will keep this up annually until the buildings are completed. The Mission will help them out before the end, but not until their own good will and organising talent have been clearly shown. (p.118.)

Jordan also commented on the power of the Committees, which, he suggested, was substantial:

> Many of the most influential members have lucrative employment abroad and keep in constant touch with the home front—and pay fees for many children in the home school. The members of the Committee domiciled in the town itself or in townships not far away write regularly to their senior fellow townsmen in Lagos, Burutu, etc., giving all relevant financial data and suggesting lines of action in concert with local effort. He at once calls together his 'brothers' in the distant township, explains the position and tells them what to pay! . . . There is no loose flinging around of money. Everything is in writing. Receipts are always issued and budgets from home examined. The men in Lagos know what their 'brothers' in Port Harcourt and Warri pay. Black sheep do not exist. Thus a network of communal effort is spreading all over Nigeria. (p.118.)

Phillipson's report led the government to capitalise further on this spirit of self-help. The incomes of all communities were assessed, and on each was imposed an Assumed Local Contribution (ALC). Communities were left to decide how to meet the ALC, but most did so through a combination of fees and other fund-raising measures. At times, the unions shared out the total amount among the age groups in the community. These in turn levied their individual members or paid en bloc from their common funds. Alternatively, the unions taxed all able-bodied adults, usually requiring the men to pay more than the women, or obtained the money by harvesting all individually and communally owned palm groves for a specified period of time.

During the 1950s the system changed with the launching in 1957 of a campaign to achieve Universal Primary Education (UPE). The campaign was partly based on philanthropic and economic motives, but was also heavily influenced by political rivalry with the Western Region, which had launched its own campaign in 1955. At the beginning of the Eastern Region scheme, the ALCs and all fees were abolished. By 1958 the scheme had run into major financial difficulties, however, and the ALC was reintroduced (Abernethy, 1969, p.181).

(b) Financing of Schools since 1970

Soon after the end of the Nigerian civil war in 1970, the governments of the three states which had previously comprised the Eastern Region took over all schools. They transferred the ownership, management and supervision of all schools to the states' Ministries of Education and to specially created school boards.

One of the outcomes of the state take-over was a further change in the system of grants-in-aid. In theory, from that date the state governments assumed full responsibility for both recurrent and capital school expenses. However, the payment of school fees continued at both primary and secondary levels, and because of the lack of government action many communities decided by themselves to rehabilitate schools that had been destroyed or damaged during the war. The communities did this through voluntary donations and compulsory levies on individuals and age groups (Eze, 1983, pp.121–2).

In September 1976 the Federal Government of Nigeria launched another UPE scheme, to cover the whole country. The federal authorities had announced that from that date they would be responsible for all finance, and the policy had been greeted with considerable acclaim. Under the scheme, a N40 grant was made in respect of every registered primary school pupil. In addition, before the scheme was launched the Federal Government provided huge sums of money to train the teachers who were to operate the programme (Nigeria, 1975, p.246).

However, in most parts of Nigeria the UPE scheme rapidly ran into major problems, reminiscent of the Eastern Region attempt 20 years earlier (Bray, 1981). Communities found that they were deprived of essential supplies, and in Eastern Nigeria they soon resorted to various levies to fill the gap. In January 1982 the annual grant of N40 per pupil was withdrawn. Federal authorities argued that under a new system of revenue allocation the states should be able to finance education without the grants.

Since 1970, competition among communities in Eastern Nigeria has shifted from the establishment of primary schools to the establishment of secondary schools. One reason for this has been that since the early 1970s almost every community has had its own primary school, and many have had more than one. The cutting edge of competition has therefore moved up a stage, and communities take pride in the fact if their children can attend secondary school in their own villages.

The growth of the secondary school system may be illustrated by the following statistics. When Imo State was created in 1976, 147 secondary schools existed. By 1984 there were 476, and all the new ones had been initiated and financed by the communities themselves. Today, very few villages have no secondary school, and some have more than one.

3. The Procedure for Launching and Maintaining a School

The first step in the establishment of a school is for members of the community to come together under the umbrellas of their council of elders and village improvement union to pass a resolution that they want to establish a school. They then identify a number of possible sites for the institution. Next, they make a formal application to the Commissioner for Education asking for approval to open the school, as required by law (Imo

State, 1980, Section 35). Communities are required to show that they have at least N50,000 in a bank account, with which they can commence building.

On receipt of an application from a community, a team of Ministry of Education officials is sent to investigate the request and make recommendations to the Commissioner. If its findings are favourable, written provisional approval is given for work to commence on construction, which must be undertaken according to Ministry plans. When the community has finished construction, it applies to the Ministry again. If the official recommendation is again favourable, the school is given final approval to open. The government then posts a principal and staff to the school.

Under this system, the government takes financial responsibility for staff salaries and other recurrent expenditure, and communities take responsibility for land and capital projects. Students are required to pay fees to the government, which in 1985 were N50 per term for secondary school tuition and N100 for boarding charges. Between 1976 and 1978 the Imo State government spent N14,802,000 on renovation and re-equipment of secondary schools. During the same period it was estimated that communities spent N12,939,000 on establishment of sixty-five new secondary schools. In addition to teachers' salaries, the state government spent N4,000,000 on vehicle advances for teachers in post-primary institutions. To balance that, secondary school fees yielded N3,200,000 in 1978 (Imo State Government, 1978, pp.4–5).

Communities raise funds in several ways, as follows:

(a) Voluntary Contributions through Launching Ceremonies

Whenever it is decided that there is to be a launching ceremony for fund-raising, the village improvement union issues a circular letter making it compulsory for all to attend. Special invitations are also issued to in-laws, relations, friends and well-wishers outside the village. Normally, the circular states that heavy fines will be imposed on any absent branch unions, age groups and individuals. Such fines range from N50 to N200 or more, and sanctions are enforced with a roll call.

In the village, a town crier goes round several times to announce the event and to invite people to decorate the venue before the date of the ceremony. All the village cultural dance, masquerade and other entertainment groups are invited to attend, and the women prepare food for the occasion. Public address systems are mounted, and each branch union and age group has a colourful stand. Sons and daughters who work in town charter buses to get to the village, and many arrive a few days earlier. The ceremonies are usually held at weekends to enable all public servants to attend and to prevent them from using their jobs as an excuse for absence.

At the ceremony, people compete to see who will donate the highest amount. There is a similar competition among the age groups. Everybody in the community endeavours to donate some amount, no matter how big or small, and each donation is announced over the public address system. By the general spirit of the people, it is better to be dead than to be alive and not be able to contribute to the development of one's village or clan. The ceremony lasts all day.

In Okoko-Item, the author's home village, the launching ceremony for its Comprehensive Secondary School was performed in August 1978. The President-General of the village Progressive Union 'opened the table' by donating N12,000, and further promised to put up a dormitory complex of four wings. Another wealthy individual donated N10,000 and also offered to build a dormitory complex of four wings. Someone else offered to finance the principal's quarters at a cost of N50,000. Another rich individual volunteered to build the assembly hall. The women's wing of the union offered to finance two staff quarters, provide the kitchen utensils for the boarding house, and feed the first batch of students free of charge for the first week. At the end of the day over N100,000 in cash had been collected, quite apart from the donations in kind and further promises. Soon after the ceremony, the money was put in a special bank account. Similar ceremonies are organised from time to time for other development purposes and for general up-keep.

Again in 1985, another rich man in the village singlehandedly built an N80,000 technical workshop for the school. The building was handed to the Imo State Ministry of Education in a special ceremony. This type of situation is typical of most parts of Eastern Nigeria.

(b) Compulsory Levies

There are three main types of non-financial levies. First, the land on which the school is established is often compulsorily acquired by the community. This is a type of obligatory levy on the owners of the land, whose compensation is usually in prestige rather than money. Second, the site is cleared by all able bodied men and women in the village. Some days in the week are set aside for the job, and participation is compulsory for all adults. Heavy fines are imposed on those who are absent without good reason. Members who live outside the village usually contribute cash in lieu of the labour which those at home contribute. Third, during the construction of the buildings such materials as sand, stones, gravel and water are compulsorily supplied by the women in the village.

In addition, community members pay a wide range of cash levies. Sometimes the levies are imposed directly on all members of the village, with men contributing more than women. However, it is usually easier to employ the age group system. Okoko-Item currently has 14 age groups. Whenever it is decided to impose a levy, the Central Executive Committee of the Union shares it among the age groups and gives them a date by which the money is to be paid. In turn, the age groups levy their members, who may pay in lump sums or by instalments. If time is short, an age group may pay its levy from central funds and later recover the money from the members. When this is not possible, a wealthy member of the group may pay the levy and later recover it when the others contribute. Age groups usually compete to pay the levy first. It is considered disgraceful for any age group to be unable to pay its levy or to be late in payment.

(c) Special Funding-Raising Activities

To illustrate the types of fund-raising for specific projects, the Okoko-Item Comprehensive Secondary School may again be used as an example. In 1982 the Principal reported to the Board of Governors that students' sporting activities were being hampered by lack of a school bus. He appealed to the Board to devise ways to provide one. The matter was later referred to the Executive Committee of the union for action. It was decided that a special fund-raising ceremony should be organised to coincide with the school's annual inter-house sports. Circular letters were immediately issued to all branch unions, age groups and individuals, inviting them to the twin occasion. Some important personalities from outside the village, including the State Commissioner for Education, were also invited.

At the fund-raising ceremony itself, the President-General of the union opened the table with a donation of N2,000. Many others followed in quick succession. In addition to cash donations, one wealthy individual offered to build and equip a standard tennis court for the school. Another donated two sets of table tennis equipment. The Lagos branch of the union offered to build and instal an iron gate at the school, and the State Commissioner donated 1,000 textbooks and some science equipment. By the end of the ceremony a total of N18,000 had been raised in cash, in addition to the donations in kind. The bus was bought within a week and delivered to the school.

Other forms of fund-raising include concerts, cultural dances, masquerades, film shows, fun fairs, and model football matches. For some of these activities, tickets are sold in advance. Communities may also decide to tax their market stalls, or to harvest all palm fruits in the village for a specified period of time.

(d) Loans from Wealthy Individuals

Loans from wealthy individuals are sought in times of emergency. For instance, in 1983 the Principal of Okoko-Item informed the Board of Governors that the school urgently needed a standard science laboratory block. Unless this was provided, he said, the first batch of students would not be allowed to enter for science subjects in the West African School

CFE—E

Certificate examinations the following year. This had been announced following an inspection of the school by the Ministry of Education. The Board of Governors referred the matter to the Central Executive Committee of the union, which decided to borrow the money and pay it back once it had been raised from normal levies and fund-raising ceremonies.

A loan was also required in Okoko-Item when strong winds blew off the roofs of some classrooms and teachers' houses in one of the village's primary schools in 1984. Because the need was urgent, several individuals, including the author, were asked to lend N100 each. The money was later repaid, following collections by the age groups.

(e) User Charges in the Form of Fees and Levies

In Imo State, per pupil fees have been fixed by the state schools management board at the following levels:

Primary:	Classes 1–3	N15 per term
	Classes 4–6	N20 per term
Secondary:	Tuition	N50 per term
	Boarding	N100 per term.

Parents and guardians are also responsible for desks, chairs, beds, books and uniforms. The items belong to individual students, who remove them when they leave the schools. In addition, head teachers are allowed to impose levies for specific school projects, provided they gain approval from the state Ministry of Education. These fees and levies are paid individually by parents and guardians, and are not collective in the way that the ALC payments had been.

(f) Parent–Teacher Association Levies

All schools are required to have Parent-Teacher Associations (PTAs), and their levies constitute a major source of revenue for projects like buses, buildings and fences. Before levies can be imposed, however, PTAs are supposed to get formal approval. The regulations require the Commissioner to have been furnished with (a) a copy of the circular notice summoning the PTA meeting, (b) a copy of the agenda for the meeting, (c) the attendance list from the meeting, and (d) the signed minutes of the meeting.

It was through the PTA that Okoko-Item raised funds to build its science laboratory in 1983. This was achieved through a levy of N10 per term for a period of six terms. With a student enrolment of 1,200, it will readily be seen that this provided a sizeable amount.

PTAs are particularly important in urban schools, where it is harder to mobilise the community as a whole. Whenever a PTA imposes a levy through the approved procedure, it ensures compliance by sending away students whose parents have not paid. This means that PTA levies are more or less compulsory on all parents and guardians.

(g) Alumni Associations

Another source of revenue, especially for older schools, is the Old Students', or Alumni, Association. For instance, in 1984 the author's former school decided to build and equip a new library block. Every member was levied N100 in the first instance, and invited to pay more. Some people paid N500 and promised to contribute even more in the future. However, alumni associations do not have the same armoury of sanctions as do PTAs and village bodies.

Conclusions

Community support for education in Eastern Nigeria is particularly impressive. It is a long-standing tradition which largely commenced because of the strategies employed by the missionaries, and which has flourished because of the Ibo peoples' strong spirit of rivalry and competition. Education has been perceived as an instrument for individual and collective advancement, and the Ibos are well known for their aggressive outlook in such matters. At various times the government has announced that it is taking over full responsibility for education. When it has found itself unable to meet this responsibility, communities have readily stepped in to bridge the gap. In many societies of northern Nigeria and other parts of the world the failure of governments to meet their responsibilities has met a very different response. There, communities are much more likely to continue to sit back and wait for external action.

The dominant philosophy in Eastern Nigeria may also be contrasted with that in Tanzania, for example. Whereas in Tanzania the official policy of socialism emphasises the equality of all citizens, and individuals may therefore be cautious about bragging about their wealth, in Eastern Nigeria the opposite is the case. People achieve respect through wealth and through their ability to finance projects. Moreover, donations of funds to community projects is itself often a good investment, for it brings publicity and often future contracts. Thus one cannot necessarily recommend other governments which want to increase community contributions to education to follow the Eastern Nigeria example. A great deal depends on the cultural context, and insensitive attempts to transfer fund-raising procedures could create major problems.

Although the present arrangement is a joint responsibility between government and local communities, the government is the senior partner. It controls standards, curriculum, examinations, and employment of teachers, and at least in legal terms can even control admission of students. In view of the fact that community inputs are at least as great as government ones, this might initially seem surprising. One might expect particularly strong demands for control over admissions and the curriculum. However, most communities seem to accept government control in these matters. The Ministry of Education does not abuse its powers over admissions, and communities realise that development of their own local curricula could restrict the mobility of their children in the labour market and in further education.

However, one aspect of official regulations does not operate so success-fully: the procedure for registration and control of the numbers of schools. On paper, the government is able to exercise considerable control. In particular, it has power to refuse to approve schools even when communities have met all the required conditions (Imo State Government, 1980). Yet in recent years planning has been poor. Many schools have been opened which are of questionable viability, and a financial crisis has developed. This has been the result of political forces, which have affected the military regimes as much as civilian ones. The government has found itself trying to control a very powerful force, and has only partly succeeded. In this respect there would seem to be strong parallels with the Kenyan experience (Lillis and Ayot, *infra*).

The situation in Eastern Nigeria largely arises out of the specific culture of the area, and neither governments nor communities elsewhere could be confident of successful imitation. Nevertheless, analysis is instructive, for it clearly shows what is possible when the conditions are right.

CHAPTER 10

Community Financing of Education in Kenya

KEVIN LILLIS AND HENRY AYOT

Kenya has become well known for the scale of community involvement in education, particularly in the secondary school sector. A key phenomenon since Independence in 1963 has been the development and growth of 'harambee'—a slogan meaning 'Let's pull together.' Harambee efforts, are capable of mobilising vast amounts of money, and have maintained their force despite severe economic pressures.

The harambee phenomenon is a two-edged sword, however. Many harambee schools suffer from severe qualitative problems, the movement increases at least some geographic and social inequalities, and it is arguable that harambee diverts resources from more productive uses. Some of the Kenyan experiences have already been indicated in Part I of this book (particularly Chapters 2, 6 and 7), and this chapter extends discussion.

Although the harambee movement has been particularly notable at the secondary level, the chapter also examines the primary sector. Before Independence, primary education was almost exclusively the responsibility of communities and churches. Parents, students and community members contributed labour and funds for buildings, teaching materials, equipment and furniture. In the last 20 years, the Kenyan authorities, like their counterparts in other African countries, have assumed a larger share of financing of primary education. However, a recent shift has caused partial return to the earlier position.

Before Independence, churches were also responsible for the majority of secondary schools. The government has now assumed greater responsibility in this sector, but harambee and other community contributions remain considerable. At the secondary level the issues are complicated by the existence of 'excess demand' for school places.

Even with strong community contributions, the central government continues to make substantial financial inputs to education. The sector received the largest allocation of total government expenditure in 1983–4. A stable 30 per cent of the nation's recurrent budget is allocated to formal education, compared with 18 per cent at the time of Independence (Kenya, 1984a, p.192). Government recurrent expenditure was approximately KShs 3,440 million in 1983–4, and an estimated KShs 200 million in

117

1983–4 was incurred on development expenditure. To a large extent community endeavours therefore seem to supplement rather than replace government efforts.

A full account of community financing of education in Kenya would have to discuss pre-schools, village polytechnics and harambee institutes of technology. Like the rest of the book, however, this paper focuses on formal primary and secondary schooling. For studies on other levels, readers are referred to Godfrey and Mutiso (1974), Keller (1974, 1980), Mbithi and Rasmusson (1977), and Ng'ethe (1978).

1. Categories of Schools

For the purposes of clarity, the different types of primary and secondary school need to be outlined. They are as follows:

(a) Primary Schools

The primary school system is fairly homogeneous. Most schools are in principle government institutions, though they depend on communities for provision of facilities. They are subject to curriculum control and inspection by the Ministry, and depend on the Teachers' Service Commission (TSC) for appointment and payment of staff.

A few private, profit-making schools exist, but the majority of non-government schools do not seek to make profits. Some of the latter are sponsored by such commercial companies as Brooke Bond Kenya Limited or by private bodies like the Aga Khan Foundation, and most employ teachers on TSC terms. Some schools employ private teachers, but they are subject to TSC screening.

Apart from these, some institutions cater for expatriates, offer foreign curricula and do not generally concern themselves with Kenyan development issues. It can be argued that they have a backwash effect on governments schools, but this matter is beyond the scope of this chapter.

(b) Secondary Schools

The Ministry of Education, Science and Technology recognises various types of secondary school: (i) maintained, (ii) assisted, (iii) unaided harambee, and (iv) unaided private.

(i) Maintained schools

The government itself provides maintained schools, and finances all capital and recurrent expenditure. Among the maintained schools are several prestigious institutions including nearly thirty 'national' schools drawing students with the highest primary school examination scores in the nation. In 1983, five of the 611 maintained institutions were 'high-cost' boarding schools, 219 were 'low-cost' boarding schools, fifteen were technical boarding schools and 372 were day schools.

Classification is confused by the fact that some maintained schools have harambee classes. Among all secondary school pupils in 1982, 34.2 per cent were in maintained streams but 15.0 per cent were in harambee streams attached to maintained schools.

(ii) Assisted schools

Assisted schools are either private institutions, many of them mission as in the case of the Loretto schools, or assisted harambee ones. The government provides some or all of their teachers, and pays a percentage of staff salaries. It also provides other grants, but the balance of operating costs is recovered from fees and private or community support.

Assisted schools range from those with only one teacher paid by the government to others whose staff are fully government-paid. Some harambee schools have the advantage of highly qualified local teachers, and others have foreign teachers recruited through missionary and volunteer bodies. Many, however, have serious staffing problems.

(iii) Unaided harambee schools

Most harambee secondary schools start with completely private or local funding. Many later gain government assistance, but there is always a large unaided group. In 1983 it comprised 49.6 per cent of all secondary institutions.

(iv) Unaided private schools

Unaided private schools vary from low quality, commercially-oriented profit-making organisations to non-commercial former European or Church schools with very high reputations. The good schools attract good pupils and highly qualified and motivated staff, and have excellent resources.

2. The Size of the System

The explosive growth of education since Kenya's Independence is well-known. It is important here to note the size of the system that demands community support.

Table 10.1 indicates the growth in primary school enrolments between 1979 and 1983. Just between these two years, enrolments grew by 16.9 per

TABLE 10.1. *Primary School Enrolments by Standard, Kenya, 1979–83*

	1979	1980	1981	1982	1983
Standard I	977,368	906,118	844,508	908,764	890,012
Standard II	579,620	722,286	704,999	695,211	710,661
Standard III	507,973	547,790	626,072	654,860	662,198
Standard IV	483,188	496,025	515,595	578,816	617,688
Standard V	450,940	456,650	460,997	484,869	537,293
Standard VI	417,468	446,353	460,498	490,557	520,670
Standard VII	281,689	351,407	368,493	371,525	385,300
Total	3,698,246	3,926,629	3,981,162	4,184,602	4,323,822

Source: Kenya (1984a, p.194).

cent. Comparison of the enrolments in Standard I with those in Standard VII gives an idea of further growth already in the pipeline.

Table 10.2 provides statistics on the secondary sector in 1983. Maintained schools represented 22.6 per cent of the total number of institutions, but had 44.7 per cent of the pupils. In contrast, unaided schools represented 56.0 per cent of the total number of institutions, but had only 33.0 per cent of the pupils. From this it is evident that maintained schools were generally larger than others. On both measures, however, the unaided sector is shown to be considerable.

3. The Notion of Harambee

Discussion on community financing in Kenya must take account of the nature and ideology of harambee. Kenya's version of self-help is a complex political, economic and sociological phenomenon.

Though not covering every aspect, a wide literature on this topic already exists. Anderson (1969, 1970), Heyman *et al.* (1972), Abreu (1982) and Mwiria (1985) have addressed the history of the harambee school movement. Mbithi and Rasmusson (1977) and Keino (1985) have examined its sociological significance. Holmquist (1979) and Ng'ethe (1979) have focused on the nature of popular participation. Keller (1975, 1980), Hill (1975) and

TABLE 10.2. *Secondary Schools and Enrolments, Kenya, 1983*

| | Schools | | Pupils | |
	Number	Per Cent	Number	Per Cent
Maintained	611	22.6	220,446	44.7
Assisted	580	21.4	108,637	22.0
Unaided Harambee	1,341	49.6 }	164,627 }	33.3
Unaided Private	173	6.4 }		
Total	2,705	100.0	493,710	100.0

Source: Kenya (1984a, p.194); Makau (1985, p.21).

Collins (1981) have studied the anthropology of harambee in the context of specific communities. And Wellings (1982, 1983), Keller (1980), Makau (1985) and Mwiria (1985, 1986) have addressed the qualititative implications of harambee and the social and occupational expectations that it fosters.

This literature suggests that harambee stems from local dynamics; that it originates from a need for an alternative to political organisation through conventional political parties; that it is associated with particular emergent classes and sub-culture; and that it originates through pre-emptive attempts to attract government aid and to compete for scarce resources. Harambee, the literature points out, evolved first as an unsystematic and *ad hoc* response to the problems of rural poverty, but was later formally adopted as a component within the government's development strategy. The movement has developed its own momentum from a political slogan used by Kenyatta in 1963 to become a nation-wide impetus providing cattle dips, access roads, bridges, pipelines, dams, wells, dispensaries and schools.

Government attitudes to the harambee movement have varied. On the one hand, the government has allowed loose and rapid expansion of projects, but, especially in the late 1960s, has also realised the danger of loss of control and the need to incorporate harambee projects into controlled central planning. In some cases the government has engaged in part-financing of self-help schemes. A 1985 party policy statement (Saitoti 1985) indicated the continued importance of harambee within the overall Kenyan development strategy.

4. Other Sources of Support

Several other sources of suppport at the school level should also be noted. For example, both domestic and foreign religious organisations continue to play a key role. Many schools employ foreign volunteer staff, and bodies like Kenya Charity Sweepstakes, the Lions' Clubs and Cooperative American Relief Everywhere (CARE) have often made significant inputs. In recent years the District Development Committees have played a strong role as part of a new thrust at district level development.

The role of commercial organisations should also be highlighted. Companies often assist their own employees, others in the communities in which the schools are located, and sometimes people from even wider catchment areas. For example, provision of educational facilities for the children of its employees has long been a priority of Brooke Bond Kenya (BBK) Limited. By the end of 1984 the company had established seventeen schools, thirteen of them in the Kericho area in which its main tea operations are located. The company provides the land and constructs the buildings, and hands them over to the government when they are completed. In 1984, BBK embarked on a KShs 3.5 million programme to construct thirty-four classrooms in the Kericho area to meet the need for new Standard VII and VIII classes. It also

built eight teachers' houses and a whole replacement school in Kericho, and
a twelve classroom school with staff housing at Kentmere coffee estate. In
addition, it assisted the relocation of the only government-aided school in
Kibwezi division, and funded construction of two hostels. This type of
provision is paralleled by the large sugar and coffee companies and by other
organisations.

5. Community Financing of Primary Schools

Parents have contributed resources for primary schools right from the
inception of formal education in Kenya (Olembo, 1985). Missionaries who
pioneered the schools for Africans were given land and building materials by
chiefs, and parents and other community members helped with construction. Full government involvement in the financing and administration of
primary education did not occur till 1970, but even then parents were
required to pay tuition and development fees. It was not until 1974 that
parents, by presidential decree, were relieved of government tuition fees for
pupils attending Standards I to IV. By 1978, only private schools charged
official tuition fees (Olembo, 1985).

Since schools were still short of resources, however, most institutions
imposed new fees to supplement government subventions. Because of these
fees, many parents found themselves paying more than before. In 1979 it
was felt necessary to issue another presidential directive prohibiting all
direct levies on parents.

Yet that directive also required the establishment of Parents' Associations in all schools, and instructed the associations to collect development
funds through voluntary harambee contributions. In some cases this meant
that the picture did not greatly change, for strong community pressures
made at least minimum contributions compulsory. The only costs which
communities did not have to meet were teachers' salaries and a small per-
student allocation for equipment and supplies.

One 1984 survey of 196 schools found that 189 had Parents' Associations.
The head teachers in these schools also indicated that contributions to
development funds were voluntary, as required by the presidential directive. Parental donations for development expenditure varied from district to
district, but most parents paid between KShs 150 and KShs 500.

However, evidence from Nandi indicates that parents have been required
to contribute a fixed amount towards development expenditure, and the
press has published many complaints that pupils have been excluded or
suspended from schools because their parents have failed to contribute. The
issue of compulsory contributions to development funds therefore remains a
matter of concern. Many head teachers find ways to levy charges, often in
contravention of official policy.

To tackle this problem, another presidential statement in 1985 ordered schools to stop collecting what had become known as 'activity fees'. Such fees, it said, should not be the responsibility of individual parents, but should be collected on a harambee basis 'because schools belong to the whole community' (*Daily Nation*, 7 February 1985). However, it is questionable whether this strategy can be realistically implemented in all cases, because some institutions are district schools with wide catchment areas. These schools cannot expect such a strong sense of community, and therefore have to rely more heavily on parents.

In January 1985 the picture was further complicated by the launch of a major structural and curricular reform. It is called the '8–4–4' system of education because in the new structure primary schooling lasts 8 years (instead of 7), secondary schooling 4 years and tertiary education 4 years (Kenya, 1984b).

The restructuring brought new demands on communities. For the intended 13,370 Standard VIII streams, a corresponding set of classrooms was required. Each of the 12,493 primary schools also needed home science rooms and practical skills workshops to permit changes in the curriculum, and most schools required extra teachers' houses.

It is too early to judge the impact of the restructuring, but widespread evidence has indicated that many communities have been unable to meet demands, at least in the short run. In February 1985, for example, the Mombasa Municipal Education Officer reported that ninety-eight workshops and home science rooms were needed in the Municipality, but that only ten had been completed in time. Five of those in one division (Mombasa Island) were furnished, but three in another division (Likoni) had no furniture. Eighty-six Standard VIII classrooms out of a required 138 had been completed in the district, but only thirty-five contained furniture. Other districts also found themselves incapable of launching the 8–4–4 successfully.

This situation highlighted the complexity of the relationship between community and official funding. The government has both encouraged and coerced community involvement as a necessary element in the 8–4–4 scheme. However, it has also prohibited communities from charging fees, which in turn has created financial problems and threatened the success of the whole scheme. Moreover, the restructuring coincided with a severe drought and consequent economic stringency. So extreme was the pressure for harambee contributions to a wide variety of sectors that the President called for a three-month moratorium on local harambees.

6. Harambee Secondary Schools

The 1970–4 development plan (Kenya, 1969, p.400) pointed out that 1968 enrolments in harambee secondary schools nearly equalled those in maintained and assisted schools. It suggested that several factors militated against continued rapid harambee school expansion during the plan period. It argued that many areas had sufficient schools of this type; that communities were discouraged by the costs; and that lack of employment opportunities for harambee school leavers was a disincentive.

In fact, the number of harambee schools grew from 483 in 1970 to 1,341 in 1983, and saturation point had still not been reached. Communities were prepared to continue expenditure, and employment difficulties were an incentive rather than the reverse. If communities felt that harambee pupils had problems in the labour market, they knew that youths with only primary education had no chance at all.

The 1970–4 plan also set out several government policies on the harambee movement. The government, it said, would assist harambee schools to improve quality, and would encourage amalgamation of institutions in order to achieve economies of scale. The plan also proposed to scrutinise school finances. In all these spheres, however, implementation fell far short of objectives. Ten years later there were many poor quality and small schools, and even maintained institutions had a two-year backlog of unaudited accounts. Little had changed, though the 1985 district focus strategy for rural development reiterated the need (Saitoti, 1985).

The chief strategy for qualitative improvement was a Secondary Schools Harambee Package Programme. Through the programme, fifty schools each year were to be offered qualified, government-paid teachers, audio visual equipment, and help from the inspectorate. The programme was designed to assist harambee schools in Forms I and II, i.e. up to the level of the Kenya Junior Secondary Examination (KJSE), according to opportunities for secondary education in the area, existing facilities, inspectorate reports, and the auditing of accounts.

In addition, various incentives were offered. If a school committee could purchase a KShs 2,000 science package from the Kenya Science Teachers' College, the government promised to supply a qualified science teacher. Likewise, if a committee constructed an industrial arts workshop, the government promised to provide a qualified industrial arts teacher.

Until the mid-1970s, the government also had a policy of taking over harambee schools. It usually did this by starting at Form I in particular institutions and then following that stream through the school, supporting the streams behind it and gradually phasing out the harambee section. In 1974 this policy was changed, and instead the government gave harambee pupils a second chance to enter maintained schools, after the KJSE at Form II. All the new Form II streams were supposed to be sited at well-established two or three stream maintained schools, and the government promised to provide up to two teachers for each one. The plan was to open twenty harambee Form III streams in government schools every year.

Several factors limited the effectiveness of these policies, however. The package was an interesting attempt to introduce curriculum change and improve quality, but science remained woefully weak and only two of the thirty-five institutions teaching industrial arts in 1986 were genuine harambee schools. Likewise, many maintained schools resisted the idea of having harambee sections 'grafted' on to them. They felt that it disrupted their traditions and lowered standards, argued that provision of extra teachers was not enough, and suggested that additional grants-in-aid should also have been provided.

7. Issues of Quality

Part I of this book has already indicated serious shortcomings in the quality of harambee schools, and the present chapter has outlined various measures that have been proposed—though not always effectively implemented—to remedy this problem. It is useful now to add some further discussion.

Chapter 6 indicated that criticisms of the quality of harambee schools often fail to distinguish between quality of attainment and quality of process. In practice, it is true, both are often disastrously low. However, the institutions which achieve a reasonable process are handicapped by their poor intakes and thus are still only capable of modest attainments.

Referring first to the quality of intakes, it is pertinent to restate that harambee schools are usually at the bottom of family choices. The majority of institutions only gain pupils who have failed to secure places in maintained schools, and admission is largely unselective. To compound this problem, harambee schools are also deficient in the educational process. Most of them have inadequate facilities, and because of the lack of laboratories and other equipment many are unable to offer science subjects. They also suffer from inferior teachers.

To assess attainment, it is useful to look at the rankings of school performance in the Kenya Certificate of Education (KCE) published each year by the Ministry of Education, Science and Technology. In 1983, the top harambee school was 118th out of 1,385. Each subject is graded one to nine, and its thirty-eight entrants gained an average grade of 6.57 in comparison with the top school's 3.53. The next harambee school was 148th, with a 6.79 average grade that bordered on a mere pass. Only thirteen harambee schools were rated in the top 300, achieving an average grade of 7.24 or better. Of the 1,385 schools, 734 scored better than 8.00 (i.e. the second lowest grade). Of those scoring below 8.00, 465 out of 559 were harambee schools.

Similarly, in 1984 the top harambee school was twenty-ninth in order of merit, achieving an average grade of 5.03 compared with the top school's 3.38. The next harambee school was fifty-eighth, with an average grade of 5.49. Only seventeen unaided harambee schools were in the top 300, achieving an average grade of 6.00 or better. Of the 1,736 schools entering

KCE in 1984, 1,403 scored better than 8.00. Of those scoring below, 246 out of 337 were harambee schools.

Examination scores are notoriously difficult to interpret, for they are a very blunt instrument even to measure cognitive achievement, let alone other aspects of quality. Nevertheless, performance in public examinations is the commonly accepted measure of quality in Kenya, and pupils' examination grades have considerable influence on the employment and further training open to them. The statistics quoted above and in Tables 10.3 and 10.4 do not show rigid boundaries between maintained, assisted, unaided harambee and unaided private schools, but they do show that unaided schools generally perform poorly.

The nature of the disparity in the teaching force may be indicated by a few additional statistics. From 1973 to 1977, almost 90 per cent of teachers in maintained schools were qualified. In unaided schools the proportion was only 30 per cent in 1973, and dropped to 25 per cent in 1977. In the latter year, graduates comprised 42.5 per cent of teachers in maintained schools but only 12.1 per cent in unaided schools. By 1982, as Table 10.5 indicates, disparities had become even greater.

TABLE 10.3. *Kenya Certificate of Education Results, 1980*

	Number of Schools Entering Candidates	Schools with Results of Mean Divison Four and Less*	
Maintained	499	394	(79.0%)
Assisted	272	65	(23.9%)
Unaided Harambee	526	68	(12.9%)
Unaided Private	174	41	(23.6%)
Total	1,471	568	(38.6%)

* KCE performance is aggregated into four divisions, Division 1 being the best and Division 4 the poorest. To calculate a school's mean performance, candidates with results below Division 4 were awarded hypothetical Division 5s.
Source: Makau (1985, p.22).

TABLE 10.4. *Schools in the Bottom Quarter of the Order of Merit, EACE 1978 and KCE 1980 Results, Kenya*

	Number in 1978	Number in 1980	% of all Schools in this Category, 1980
Maintained	9	8	1.6
Assisted	30	36	13.2
Unaided Harambee	149	227	43.2
Unaided Private	46	66	37.9

Notes: (a) EACE = East African Certificate of Education. It was the predecessor to the KCE. Both examinations were taken after 4 years of secondary school. (b) In 1978 the results of schools in the bottom quarter ranged from mean division 4.13 to 4.94. In 1980 the range was 4.42 to 5.00.
Source: Makau (1985, p.27).

TABLE 10.5. *Profile and Distribution of Secondary School Teachers, Kenya, 1982*

	Maintained	Assisted	Unaided Harambee	Private & Church	Total
Trained					
Graduate & Approved	3,550	347	99	107	4,103
Non-Graduate	2,583	1,010	754*	425	4,772
Total	6,133	1,357	853	532	8,875
Untrained					
Graduate	898	166	513	567	2,144
KACE	211	168	5,049	1,028	6,456
KCE	7	2	312	45	366
Total	1,116	336	5,874	1,640	8,966
Grand Total	7,249	1,693	6,727	2,172	17,841

* including 346 overseas teachers
KACE = Kenya Advanced Certificate of Education
KCE = Kenya Certificate of Education
Source: Planning Section, Ministry of Education, Science and Technology, Nairobi, 1984.

Several government strategies to improve this situation have already been mentioned. The harambee package is one, though it has not had the effect that had been originally hoped for. Like all other schools, harambee institutions are open to government inspection, but in practice the large number of schools and the limited number of government officers precludes close attention.

To maintain quality in physical facilities, the Ministry of Works has a directive on the specifications of buildings, and model plans are available free from the National Construction Corporation. Most government secondary schools adhere to the requirements, though some schools built under the auspices of external donors appear to infringe them. Urban self-help schools are also likely to adhere to the requirements, but rural institutions frequently ignore them and, again because of central government staffing constraints, are unrestrained. Roof sheeting is often of low quality, and roofs even of the recently constructed Standard VIII classrooms have already been blown off.

Basic criteria for legal registration were established by the 1968 Education Act. The government merely demands that schools be sponsored by a mission or recognised local committee, and managed by a responsible body. The harambee schools are required to register their management committees with the Ministry of Education, Science and Technology, which in 1979 established a unit to liaise with the unaided sector. Schools must have at least 30 acres of land, a KShs 40,000 capital fund, two classrooms, teachers' houses and latrines built according to public health requirements.

Before receiving approval from the Ministry, schools should satisfy the Local Authorities, the District or Municipal Education Officers, and the

Provincial Education Officers. Yet even with all these regulations, schools are rarely turned down. Usually, the combination of political patronage and lack of sufficiently zealous bureaucrats suffices to ensure registration, especially if communities are able to appoint a good manager. In sum, therefore, the qualitative safeguards do not seem very effective.

Conclusions

In the context of community financing of education, Kenya is best known for its harambee secondary schools. Harambee is an important but complex movement, and has been the chief focus both of this chapter and of the Kenyan material in Part I of this book. However, the chapter has also highlighted the considerable community resources that are poured into the primary sector, and has indicated that commercial companies, religious bodies and other voluntary associations also contribute to both levels.

Meanwhile, the government has expressed ambivalence on the nature of levies. On the one hand, communities are required by law to maintain primary school facilities; but on the other hand the government has been embarrassed by the fact that parents have had to pay fees. Again, on the one hand the government has decided to extend the length of primary schooling in the 8-4-4 reform; but on the other hand it has become embarrassed by the burden that this has placed on communities. A series of presidential directives has sought to prohibit fees, and at one point in 1985 the President declared a three month moratorium on harambee efforts. Neither of these actions is in consonance with other aspects of government policy. Moreover, the requirement that schools should rely on communities rather than parents fails to recognise the fact that institutions with wide catchment areas find it very hard to foster a sense of community.

At the secondary level, the harambee experience has proved to be a two-edged sword. On the one side, the movement has had an enormous quantitative impact. Enrolments in the unaided sector exceed those in maintained schools, and harambee has allowed Kenya's secondary school enrolment rate to reach 19 per cent (World Bank, 1984, p.23). Self-help contributions have been an essential ingredient in the 8-4-4 programme which, whatever its shortcomings, must be recognised as a major logistic achievement.

However, the reader will recall from Chapter 7 in this book that harambee projects have often accentuated both regional and social inequalities. The present chapter, expanding on analysis in Part I, has also shown that the quality of harambee education is often extremely low. Only in exceptional circumstances, related mostly to political patronage, can schools claim to offer much more than an educational façade. As such, although the anticipated reward may make them *appear* to be worthwhile investments, they are actually a burden on communities.

Yet despite this conclusion, it is clear that the sector will retain its momentum for the foreseeable future. The 1970–4 development plan was proved wrong in its prediction that costs and employment difficulties would restrict the growth of the movement, and there is no reason to anticipate a change in direction. As such, the challenge facing the authorities is how to harness the movement more effectively. It remains to be seen how effectively they will be able to meet the challenge.

CHAPTER 11

Education and Community Self-Help in Zambia

L. H. KALUBA

Community support for schools and educational programmes is not new in Zambia, but in recent years it has greatly increased in strength. Two factors account for the change. On the one hand, demand for education has greatly expanded because of population growth and the increased number of primary school leavers who aspire to proceed to secondary schools. On the other hand, the government is beset by economic crisis which threatens even the maintenance of existing services. Communities have realised that if they want educational facilities, then they must supplement government provision through their own efforts.

Under official policy, between 1964 and 1970 the government met at least 75 per cent of self-help project costs (Zambia, 1984, p.1). The main community inputs were labour and local materials, and the government provided other materials, teachers, transport and supervision. However, during the 1970s the government found it increasingly difficult to shoulder such a heavy load. A new policy in 1977 stated that the government expected communities to meet the full capital costs of their projects (Zambia, 1977, p.77), and this policy has continued to be necessary in the 1980s.

Despite these changes policies have suffered from ambiguities, and many community projects are poorly organised. Officially, for example, boarding fees have been reintroduced but other fees are still prohibited. In practice a wide range of fees may be found, but the existence of the policy dampens one mechanism for raising resources. The government also lacks information on the total number and needs of self-help projects, and communities have encountered technical and administrative problems, often arising from over-ambitious objectives. Even during the favourable conditions of the 1970s many self-help projects were under-resourced, poorly managed and short-lived, and the situation has not greatly improved.

The chief factor which precipitated the present economic crisis was a 40 per cent fall in the price of copper in 1974–5. The mining sector's contribution to GDP decreased from 27.4 per cent in 1970 to 7.5 per cent in 1981 (Fägerlind and Valdelin, 1983, p.17). Government revenue from minerals decreased from K50.9 million in 1974 to K10.5 million in 1981, and this sharply reduced the amount of money available for education. The capital budget for education decreased from an annual average of K13.5 million in the period 1966–74 to just K7.0 million in the period 1979–84; and total annual government spending on education, which had increased by 5.6 per cent in the first half of the 1970s, decreased by 6.9 per cent in the second half. The problems caused by the low price of copper were exacerbated by rising petroleum prices, population growth, and the liberation wars in Southern Africa. Between 1974 and 1980, GDP per head in Zambia declined by 52 per cent (International Labour Office, 1981, p.xxv.)

This situation has necessitated severe cuts in public investment and increased dependence on foreign loans and aid. However, the government remains committed to the goal of universal basic education and to expansion of secondary schooling. To achieve its objectives, the government places strong emphasis on community self-help.

1. Types of Community and Types of Support

Domestic ties which bind non-resident sons and daughters to their home areas are not as strong in Zambia as they are in many other African countries. A school has recently been built in the Bayombe area and has been partly financed by its sons and daughters who now reside on the Copperbelt and in Lusaka, but this is an isolated case. Mechanisms for collecting money are not so well developed as in Nigeria, for example, and contributions are voluntary rather than compulsory.

On the other hand, the role of churches in Zambia is quite significant, and Christian communities have provided educational facilities for many years. Many schools used to operate without government aid, but now the majority receive official grants. Table 11.1 shows the number of grant-aided secondary schools belonging to different churches in 1985.

TABLE 11.1. *Number of Church Grant-Aided Schools, Zambia, 1985*

	Primary	Secondary
Catholic	—	25
Anglican	—	1
United Church of Zambia	—	5
Church of Christ	—	2
Brethren in Christ	1	1
Evangelical Church in Zambia	—	1
Seventh-day Adventist	10	1
Salvation Army	—	1
Christian Mission in Many Lands	2	—
Total	13	37

Source: Development Planning and Research Unit, Ministry of General Education and Culture, Lusaka.

The majority of schools also have Parent–Teacher Associations (PTAs). Where there is effective leadership, parents and general communities can be a tremendous support for their schools. Table 11.2 summarises the findings of a recent survey of forty-six self-help projects in four provinces conducted as part of the Education Reform Implementation Project (1985). Its conclusions are probably fairly typical, and indicate that PTA contributions generally provide the most important source of income. Recently, PTAs of some rural primary schools have combined to construct junior secondary schools. This has happened at Senga Hill and Ituna, in Northern Province, for example.

Although the law does not require schools to have PTAs, it does set out regulations on the composition of associations where they do exist. Their official functions (Zambia, 1966, p.64) are:

(a) to ensure, through regular contacts between parents and teachers, the welfare and best possible education of pupils, and enlightening of parents on all aspects of pupils' progress in school and an enlightening of teachers on the home background of their pupils so as to enable teachers to see their pupils as full individual personalities and thus cater the better for their individual needs;

(b) any other functions approved by the Minister;

(c) to raise and control funds.

Membership of PTAs is restricted to teachers and to parents who have children in the schools. However, provision exists for membership of 'any local chief' and 'any other local dignitary', and in practice appeals to support school projects are usually made to all members of the community whether they have children in the school or not. As well as head teachers, church and party leaders often play a key role in mobilising people. Members of Parliament may play a key role in pressurising the government to recognise

TABLE 11.2. *Sources of Community Support for 46 School Projects, Zambia, 1985*

	% of Projects Receiving Funds
School PTAs	82.6
Church & Religious Organisations	10.9
Local Residents	15.2
Commercial & Industrial Companies	8.7
Local Villagers & Farmers	19.6
PTAs of Feeder Schools	15.2

Note: The word 'project' has been used rather than 'school' because although many of the organisations visited were fully fledged institutions, some called themselves schools but were in fact merely additional classes in existing schools.
Source: Education Reform Implementation Project, 1985.

institutions and to provide assistance (e.g. *Zambia Daily Mail*, 23 January 1986).

In urban areas, charities such as the Rotary, Lions, Jaycees, Hindu and Muslim associations have also supported specific projects. In 1984 and 1985, for example, the Rotary Club of Livingstone contributed K1,306 to pay the examination fees of fourteen poor pupils, and in 1985 Lusaka's Rotary Club of Maluba donated K24,000 to build and furnish two classrooms in Bauleni Primary School (*Zambia Daily Mail*, 23 January 1986). This kind of support is usually *ad hoc*, and is generally tied to specific requests.

Although information on self-help projects in Zambia is scattered and no comprehensive surveys have been conducted, some impressions can be gleaned from District Education Officers' reports and from newspapers. Table 11.3 reproduces information from the former source on capital projects in primary schools in the years 1979–84. The fact that few reports mentioned toilets and other facilities should not be interpreted to imply that they were not provided, but the table clearly indicates prominent activity in construction of classrooms and teachers' houses.

The survey for Table 11.3 also requested respondents to identify other forms of common community support. Service on school PTAs was identified as one of the most prominent, followed by provision of building materials and labour. The increased spread of primary schools has reduced the need for boarding and lodging, but this form of help was mentioned in 17.4 per cent of cases (Table 11.4). Preparation of meals was mentioned in only 2.2 per cent of cases, and in no schools were communities said to have helped with teaching or supervision. Contributions of building materials

TABLE 11.3. *Numbers and Types of Self-Help Primary School Projects, by Region, Zambia, 1979–84*

	Classrooms	Teachers' Houses	Toilets	Practical Rooms	Desks	Others
Central*	10	14	x	x	x	x
Lusaka	x	x	x	x	x	x
Eastern	129	28	10	4	x	x
Luapula	54	15	x	x	x	x
Northern	348	132	x	x	120	x
North-Western	x	x	x	x	x	x
Copperbelt	x	x	x	x	x	K214,000+
Southern	224	169	19	x	x	x
Western*	14	11	x	x	x	x
Total	769	369	29	4	120	K214,000

* data from one district only.
x information not available
+ money raised by various communities for building teachers' houses.
Source: Compiled from Ministry of General Education, District Officers' Reports to the Mobile Education Planning Team, Lusaka, 1985.

TABLE 11.4. *Type of Support for Self-Help Primary School Projects, Zambia*

	% of Projects Receiving
Voluntary Cash	43.5
Compulsory Cash Levies	41.2
Skilled & Unskilled Labour	50.0
Building Plans	21.7
Building Materials	52.2
Teaching & Learning Materials	17.4
Land	39.1
Teaching & Supervision	0.0
Lodging Facilities for Boarders	17.4
Cooking Meals for Pupils	2.2
Serving on School Committees	58.7

Source: as for Table 11.3.

were much more prominent than gifts of teaching/learning materials, chiefly, it may be assumed, because the former could be supplied by villagers relatively easily whereas the latter had to be purchased from special stores and agencies.

Some commercial companies also assist with education projects. Zambia Consolidated Copper Mines Ltd. is one prominent example. The company supports eight primary schools and one prestigious secondary school in Copperbelt province, and during the recent thrust for junior secondary education the company donated buildings for two schools on Luanshya and one in Chililabombwe. The company handed over the properties to the government, but the schools still enjoy recurrent assistance in water and electricity.

Finally, a few schools, through their own initiatives, gain support from overseas. For example, Sikalongo junior secondary school in Southern Province recently raised K45,000 from appeals to two overseas organisations in North America and Europe; and Kabunda junior secondary school in Luapula Province was assisted by an expatriate who had been associated with the beginning of the institution. This type of support is more common at the secondary than at the primary level because the former schools are more likely to have overseas links.

2. Regional Differences

Table 11.3 has already provided some figures on regional differences, and Table 11.5 provides further information on the overall number and distribution of schools. Regional disparities have complex causes, and analysis is hindered by lack of complete data. Nevertheless, it is evident that regional diversity is marked (Mehra, 1985).

The outlooks of different education officers are one cause of this diversity. Regional and district officers are supposed to approve all self-help projects

L. H. Kaluba

TABLE 11.5. *Number and Distribution of Schools, by Agency, Zambia, 1985*

Region	Primary				Secondary				
	Govt*	Aided	Private	Total	Govt	Aided	Self-Help†	Private	Total
Copperbelt	256	0	14	270	24	3	7	13	47
Central	293	1	2	296	7	3	8	5	22
Eastern	454	2	0	456	10	2	4	1	17
Luapula	253	0	0	253	7	2	7	1	17
Lusaka	156	0	11	167	26	4	4	4	38
Northern	543	1	0	544	11	3	26	1	41
North-Western	274	1	1	276	6	1	8	1	16
Southern	488	3	0	491	8	15	9	4	33
Western	337	5	0	342	6	4	4	0	14
Total	3,054	13	28	3,095	105	37	77	30	245

* Includes schools constructed on a self-help basis.
† Schools started through self-help efforts. They are now government controlled and managed.
Source: Development, Research and Planning Unit, Ministry of General Education & Culture, Lusaka, 1986.

before they commence, and in some cases they initiate projects. Thus Tables 11.3 and 11.5 both show strong activity in Northern Province, for example. This partly reflects the province's size, but it also reflects the zeal of the province's Chief Education Officer. In contrast, other education officers may have less active personalities or may be wary of the impact of self-help construction on recurrent costs and demand for teachers. The latter fear has been voiced in Luapula, for example.

General prosperity is a further cause of disparities. Individuals in Copperbelt Province, for example, are relatively wealthy and thus are in a better position to contribute funds. As has already been mentioned, the mining companies themselves also often assist. Bodies like the Rotary and Lions Clubs are also supported by relatively wealthy groups. In general, though, community spirit is stronger among rural than among urban people, and the activities of the Rotary Club and similar organisations only help reduce the imbalance.

At the same time, the spirit of self-help has not been accepted completely. Some communities still maintain that it is the responsibility of the government to provide facilities. In other cases, parents have lost enthusiasm for junior secondary projects when they have found that their children have not qualified for Grade 8. And because of the general lack of resources, good teachers are often unwilling to work in self-help schools. More detailed information on these matters is urgently required, and it is unfortunate that it has not yet been collected.

Conclusions

Although many communities have provided substantial support for schools, comprehensive evaluation has not yet been undertaken. At the national level, evaluation would be a complex exercise requiring considerable data, and the government has not made it a priority. Like many other programmes, self-help schemes have often been embarked upon without careful assessment of their feasibility and implications. It is only now that the Ministry of Education, with encouragement from the Swedish International Development Authority, is considering a comprehensive evaluation exercise.

Even without detailed evaluation, however, the need for coordination is clear. Most projects are embarked upon in an *ad hoc* way when the need arises, and efforts are never part of an organised district, regional and national plan. Frequently, communities initiate projects without proper guidance and consent from the Ministry of Education. It is not uncommon for projects to commence with unrealistic cost estimates, which later requires work to be abandoned. Communities also often suffer from unavailability of cement and roofing sheets, from inappropriate building designs and project locations, from lack of transport, and from shortage of experienced builders.

The Ministry of Education has recognised some of these problems, and has initiated some corrective measures, for example by relaxing regulations on building standards in some areas, and decentralising aspects of control to the district level. In conjunction with the Public Works Department, the Ministry of Education also provides the services of qualified construction supervisors, and it assists with textbooks and qualified teachers on full government pay. In addition, workshops have been held in all regional centres to instruct District Education Officers on matters that relate to initiation and management of self-help projects.

However, the major policy and resource constraints are far from being solved. The wish to involve communities in the management of their institutions has been severely weakened by the lack of a clear policy on legal ownership and control of schools, and the decentralisation programme has suffered from considerable confusion (Coombe and Lauvas, 1984, p.85). Although the decision in 1985 to allow schools to charge boarding fees was a step in the right direction, schools are still officially prohibited from charging other fees—even though almost all do so, and have to do so in order to survive. It might also be worth considering amendment to the law to encourage all community members to join PTAs, changing the title of the associations if necessary.

CHAPTER 12

Community Financing of Schools in Botswana

J. R. SWARTLAND AND D. C. TAYLOR

'We ask that we may be enabled to give our children that learning which your children get.' So demanded Khama the Great, speaking in England in 1895 (Parsons, 1972, p.12). The thirst for schooling in Botswana thus has a long history, and it has not only been manifest in pleas of this sort to government authorities. There is also a long tradition of community initiative and self-reliance in the attempt to secure education for Batswana children.

As in other African states, a wide range of bodies has been involved in establishment of schools in Botswana. Some institutions have been founded by Christian missions; some were operated by local communities; some have been created from the start as government schools; some have been founded by chiefs as 'tribal colleges' catering for particular ethnic groups; and some have been started by pioneering individuals with visions of secondary schools as focal points for development, as American-style community colleges, or as multi-racial examples to neighbouring South Africa.

Many of the these schools, whatever their origins, have since been incorporated into the state system, either as government schools or as almost fully-funded aided schools. Some of those which were founded by the local community and which were once an embarrassment to the government are now recognised as Community Junior Secondary Schools, along with a new generation of schools being built in partnership between government and community. Current policy requires Community Junior Secondary Schools to provide two years of secondary education, which will later be extended to three years. On completion of their Junior Certificate courses, a minority of pupils will proceed to senior secondary ᵕ hools for a three year course leading to the Cambridge Overseas School Certificate examination.

This chapter concentrates on the secondary school sector, but includes some analysis of the primary sector. It begins with a brief explanation of the context within which schools operate in Botswana, and then outlines the historical development of the system, placing particular emphasis on the role of the community and giving examples of especially interesting schools.

Thirdly, the chapter examines current policy and mechanisms for community management and financing. The final section addresses problems which are currently experienced or anticipated, and draws some conclusions. The authors are officers of the Ministry of Education in Botswana who have previously taught in local secondary schools, but they write in a personal capacity. Their views should not be taken as official statements of policy.

1. Background

Botswana has an area of 582,000 square kilometres and a population of 1,132,000 (1986 estimate). This gives an average population density of two persons per square kilometre, which is one of the lowest in the world. This fact has implications for the locations and catchment areas of schools, and creates requirements for transport and boarding provision.

Botswana is also very dry, and most of the country is occupied by what is known to the outside world as the Kalahari Desert. Only in the northern and eastern parts is water available in sufficient quantities to make arable agriculture viable. Traditionally, the main source of income for the peoples has been their cattle. Botswana has a large modern abattoir, and beef is one of the country's main exports.

The absence of any obvious natural resources for commercial exploitation saved Botswana from the worst aspects of colonialism, but turned it into an imperial backwater which became increasingly integrated with the economy of neighbouring South Africa. However, the economic climate was transformed soon after Independence in 1966, when diamonds, copper, nickel and coal were discovered. Exploitation of these resources has led to rapid economic growth since 1970, in marked contrast to the widespread stagnation elsewhere in Africa. Mining now accounts for about half of government revenue, one-quarter of GDP and one-tenth of formal sector employment in the country (Botswana, 1985, pp.218–19, 225). The annual rate of growth of GDP *per capita* has been estimated at 6 to 7 per cent over the past decade.

Botswana is usually seen as a political success story. It has maintained a multi-party parliamentary democracy, a relatively efficient system of public administration, and a degree of personal freedom unknown in many parts of Africa. It has also maintained a principled and consistent foreign policy which has prevented the country from becoming too closely embroiled in the turmoils of neighbouring South Africa, Zimbabwe and Namibia. And it has established a system of development planning and financial management which permits frequent re-assessment of priorities and close co-ordination of recurrent and capital expenditure. The combination of political stability, economic growth and financial rectitude have made Botswana an attractive target for both foreign private investment and aid agencies.

The consequences of all this for education are considerable. Firstly, colonial neglect and economic integration with South Africa meant that the colonial administration had neither the means nor the inclination to spend much on education. People who wanted schools for their children had little choice but to take the initiative and find the money themselves; and they apparently did so willingly and enthusiastically in many places. With the advent of independence and mineral-led growth, the resources available to government have expanded enormously, both directly from domestic revenues and indirectly from external grants and loans. This has enabled a rapid expansion of government activities, particularly in economic infrastructure and social services, including education. But it has also increased expectations of what government can and should do with these resources, so that the spirit of self-reliance and community participation is not as strong as before. This is evident not so much in the number of projects initiated outside the sphere of government as in the limited willingness to contribute financially, despite much higher levels of personal income than were widespread in colonial times. The phenomenon is also linked to decline in the powers of the chiefs, and to decreased local and ethnic loyalties.

Secondly, the relatively late development of secondary education and the rapid growth of funds for investment have meant that in recent years inadequacy of human capital has been a more serious constraint on development than has been shortage of finance. Those who possess skills have considerable scarcity value, which raises their income levels, reinforces inequality in income distribution, heightens the aspirations of the young, and exaggerates the significance of educational qualifications. It also nurtures expectations of what schooling is for and what it can achieve, which in the long run must be unrealistic. Utilitarian perceptions of the functions of secondary schools in terms of access to modern sector jobs give the current expansion great popularity and considerable momentum. But the rate of employment creation is likely to slow down in the absence of any new mining projects. The number of secondary school leavers is therefore likely to grow much faster than the number of wage-earning jobs, creating new problems of unfulfilled expectations. This is all part of the present context, which is very different from the past and within which current policy must be assessed.

2. History

(a) Primary Schools

Although no secondary schools were established within the borders of present-day Botswana until the end of the Second World War, the first Western-style primary school was established by David Livingstone of the London Missionary Society (LMS) at Kolobeng in 1847. Further schools were opened in 1857 and 1860 by German Lutheran missionaries, and the

LMS later added others (Parsons, 1984, p.24; Townsend-Coles, 1985, pp.2–3).

These early schools aimed at Christian proselytisation, and the curriculum emphasised reading and writing. By the end of the nineteenth century, most Batswana chiefs had embraced Christianity and each Tswana state had what amounted to a state church. In most cases the church concerned was the LMS (Congregationalist), but in one state it was Lutheran and in another Dutch Reformed. Relationships between rulers, people and missionaries were complex, but by the end of the century there was widespread dissatisfaction in many Tswana states with missionary control of schools and with the nature of the instruction provided. Schooling was considered too restricted when it concentrated on scripture and literacy in Setswana, and there was strong demand for other academic skills, particularly English (Parsons, 1984, pp.24–31).

In addition, by the turn of the century demand for schools had been fuelled by contact with travellers, traders and colonial administrators. These pressures led to the creation of a number of independent tribal schools, which became known as 'national' schools. The initiative for them came from the chiefs and people rather than missionaries or the colonial authorities (Tlou and Campbell, 1984, pp.136–41). Referring to one specific institution, Parsons (1984, p.31) has explained:

> The independent tribal school at Kanye can trace its origins to 1889, when a new white missionary divided the local school into two—one free, for the masses, under Mothowagae, and the other fee-paying for children who wanted instruction in English, under the missionary Edwin Lloyd. In 1900 Lloyd, an indifferent teacher, was replaced by a local graduate of Lovedale, Kgosikobo, who was in the direct employ of Chief Bathoen I. Bathoen financed Kgosikobo's salary by an extra one shilling levy collected with the Hut Tax in 1900. . . . In effect, Bathoen had founded Botswana's first 'national' school, based on independent finance, and the other colonial paramount chiefs followed suit. Within a few years, based on similar levies, there were 'national' schools with instruction in English attached to the royal kgotlas at Mochudi, Molepolole, and Serowe.

The first colonial government grant for education was made to the LMS in 1904. However, primary education was increasingly financed from the tribal educational levies rather than general government revenue. Although these levies were at first a form of community financing, they were co-opted by the colonial government and formalised in 1919 as a Native Tax, to be collected along with the already existing Hut Tax. Revenue from the Native Tax was not spent exclusively on education, but much of it was channelled to schools through the Tribal School Committees which were established after 1910. This system of administration and financing remained much the same until just before independence in 1966, when many of the functions of the chiefs and tribal administrations were taken over by elected District and Town Councils. Since independence, primary education has been the dual responsibility of these local Councils and the Ministry of Education. The latter deals with the employment of teachers and with professional issues like the curriculum, while the Councils are responsible for routine administration and for the construction and maintenance of primary school buildings.

One of the most spectacular examples of community financing of primary school construction occurred in Mochudi in 1921. The Chief and the Tribal School Committee organised the building of a new Bakgatla National School on top of a hill with a commanding view over the village. Funds were raised principally by sending young men to work in the mines of South Africa; labour was provided by various age regiments of the Bakgatla nation; and all the building materials required were laboriously carried up the hill in a genuine community project which took three years to come to fruition (Grant, 1976). The building was abandoned as a school in the mid-1970s, apparently because of increasing maintenance costs and difficulties of access, but is now used as a local museum.

(b) Secondary Schools

Various attempts to start secondary school classes in the 1930s were resisted by the colonial government, which believed students from Bechu-analand would be better educated at schools in South Africa or Southern Rhodesia. The government particularly favoured the Tiger Kloof Institu-tion, which had been established by the LMS near Vryburg in South Africa in 1904 to cater for the needs of the Batswana peoples.

The first real secondary school within Bechuanaland, therefore, was not opened until 1944. It was called St. Joseph's College, and was established by the Roman Catholic Church at Kgale. Being a voluntary agency institution it was the result of one sort of community funding. However, the second institution to be established has become more famous as an example of large scale but entirely local community financing. Moeng College was the brainchild of Tshekedi Khama, who was Regent of the Bangwato nation while his nephew, Seretse Khama, was a minor and a student. Tshekedi Khama gained colonial government approval to open a school in 1946, and raised the necessary resources through cattle levies on his people. Most of the construction work was undertaken by the age regiments of the Bangwato nation. The site was a beautiful but remote valley away from the distractions of town and village life. The total cost of the project is usually put at £100,000, excluding the cost of direct labour. The school was originally called Bamangwato College, and opened in 1948. However, it ran into administrative and financial problems, and was taken over in 1956 by the government. It was re-named Moeng College, and whereas it was originally intended only for Bangwato students, in its new form it was open to all ethnic groups (Thema, 1970).

Similar 'tribal colleges', as they were usually called, were opened in Kanye, Molepolole and Mochudi in the 1950s, all with community rather than government or missionary initiative, and all named after an appropriate chief. But it is easier to mobilize community resources to build a school than it is to generate recurrent income to sustain it, and these three schools found it hard to recruit and pay trained teachers. Like Moeng, they were all taken over by the government, and in 1967 became part of the public system of secondary education.

The sixth secondary school to be established in Botswana was Moeding College, founded at Otse in 1961 by the LMS as a direct replacement for the Tiger Kloof Institution, which had been closed after the introduction of 'Bantu education' in South Africa in 1953. Tiger Kloof is still held in high nostalgic respect by older citizens of Botswana. For 40 years it provided the main opportunity for bright and rich Batswana to continue their schooling beyond primary level, and it sought to combine academic studies, industrial training and teacher education in a way that many still see as a model of 'relevant' education. Many hoped that Moeding would continue this tradition within the boundaries of Botswana, and it has certainly produced good examination results. However, it has never acquired the same broad reputation.

Two more schools were opened in 1963. Mater Spei College in Francistown was the second Roman Catholic Secondary School, and Swaneng Hill School in Serowe was a private school. The latter soon became world-famous for its diversified curriculum, practical work, community orientation and, above all, the vocational training 'brigades' which were at first an integral part of the same institution but soon grew apart. Swaneng was a product of individual rather than community initiative. Its founder, Patrick van Rensburg, was a white South African refugee who became a Botswana citizen and raised funds from a very wide range of supporters, including large and small aid agencies, religious and political groups, and the government. Although Swaneng Hill School could legitimately claim to be a community school, it could do so only in the sense that it was closely involved with various projects in the community and indeed itself initiated many such projects. The community was never much involved in financing or running the school (van Rensburg, 1974).

The colonial government of Bechuanaland belatedly realised that independence was inevitable, that an independent country would require a capital (the colonial administration was itself based across the border in South Africa), and that a capital city would require a secondary school. Hence Gaborone Secondary School was founded in 1965, the ninth in the country but the first to be established by the government. Colonial officials believed that the new school would make some of the others redundant, and they suggested the closure of Moeng at least. However, the people would have none of it, and Bechuanaland became the independent Republic of Botswana in 1966 with nine secondary schools—four founded by the chiefs and people as 'tribal colleges', three mission schools, one private but community-oriented school, and one school newly established by the departing colonial administration. The four 'tribal colleges' had been built with locally-generated funds and direct contributions of labour, but they were unable to maintain community financing on a scale large enough to meet long-run recurrent costs and had either become or were about to become fully-funded government secondary schools.

3. The Growth of Secondary Education Since Independence

Over the first fifteen years of independence, fourteen more regular secondary schools were established. Ten of these were government schools from the start, and one is a Methodist mission school. The remaining three started, like Swaneng Hill School, under an independent Board of Governors with a strong involvement in the local community. However, they were taken over by government when they ran into administrative or financial problems. Thus by 1986 there were nineteen fully funded government secondary schools plus four government-aided mission schools. The latter received a large proportion of their capital and recurrent resources from government and were subject to a high degree of government control despite being nominally private.

Despite this increase in the number of schools, demand for school places has remained greater than supply. Private, entirely unaided schools have appeared in many communities, often starting as night schools in borrowed premises.

One of the early unaided community schools was built at Mahalapye and provides a good example of the process which became common in many places. The school started in response to pressure from parents whose children had not been able to secure a place in one of the government or aided schools. A meeting was held at the Mahalapye *kgotla* (traditional meeting place), and was attended by three local Members of Parliament who subsequently requested permission from the Ministry of Education to start a private school. Evening classes began in 1969, and were held in a local primary school. The first teachers were bank clerks and primary school teachers. But the District Council did not favour the use of primary school classrooms for secondary classes, and the banks did not want their employees to work as teachers. In its second year, therefore, the school operated in a church hall and two community halls during the day, with staff moving between three sites and timetables drawn up to allow for this, and the Board was able to recruit full-time teachers using fee income. Among

CFE—F

the teachers were refugees from Lesotho who were willing to work for salaries below those paid by government. Many schools also hired Zimbabwean refugees on similar terms over the next ten years.

In 1972 Mahalapye Community Hall was completed and all the classes moved into it. At the same time, the Board of Governors acquired a site from the Land Board and organised construction of classrooms. Staff, students and parents worked together in the afternoons and at weekends to mould bricks and build classrooms, under the supervision of a master builder. Ten classrooms were ready by the end of 1972, and the school moved into them in 1973 when a further five classrooms were added. The fund-raising and building work was co-ordinated by a Development Committee of the Board of Governors, which was able to add a library in 1977 and a laboratory in 1978. The costs involved are not known because record-keeping has been weak in community schools and because it is difficult to assess the value of voluntary labour. But this example illustrates both the realisation of the Mahalapye community that public funds were inadequate to meet the demand for secondary education, and the commitment of the people to the principle of self-reliance (Makunga, 1985).

Tshegetsang Community School in Molepolole had similar origins in 1966. Teachers from the nearby, well-established 'tribal' school, including one of the present writers (JRS), offered classes in the evenings using the premises of a primary school. These teachers surreptitiously subsidised the new school from the resources of their regular school, taking paper, chalk and mathematical instruments from the established school to eke out the minimal supplies of the fledgling institution.

Itireleng Secondary School in Lobatse was founded in 1970 and operated until 1977 in old primary school classrooms borrowed from the Town Council and in a local church hall. Financial mismanagement in the early years, a common occurrence in schools lacking experienced managers, led to non-payment of teachers, misappropriation of funds, and heavy debt. But a new Board of Governors rescued the situation in 1973, and embarked on a fund-raising and building programme. Some of the income from school fees was reserved for capital expenditure, donations were solicited from the American Embassy, the International University Exchange Fund, and the Botswana Christian Council, and one-off events to raise funds were held within the local community. As a result of these endeavours, six classrooms were built on a permanent site, with toilet blocks and three more classrooms added after further fund-raising by the community. The Board financed recurrent expenditure almost entirely from fee income, and recruited a variety of teachers, including local citizens without professional qualifications, expatriate volunteers, and refugees from South Africa and Zimbabwe.

By 1975, fourteen of these private, unaided, community schools had sprung up, and they were admitting into Form I 15 per cent of those in

Standard 7 the previous year, on top of the 20 per cent which government and aided schools were able to admit (Botswana, 1977a, p.87). At first, the government had entirely ignored these schools. Although they were required to be registered by law, their existence was not recorded in the education statistics. When the government could no longer ignore them, it became embarrassed because they dramatised the inadequacy of the government's provision in relation to demand. Also, the fees were so high in these schools and the standards so low in comparison with government schools that the contrast seemed grossly inequitable.

4. New Policies

These issues were addressed by the National Commission on Education, which was appointed in 1975 and reported in 1977. The Commission was asked to conduct a broad-ranging review of the system, including 'secondary education, essentially public education but including private schools and continuation classes as they affect public policy' (Botswana, 1977a, p.3).

Current policy is derived from the recommendations of the Commission, and it is necessary to spell out the team's findings on these issues. The Commission, consisting of two very experienced Batswana and four internationally renowned foreigners, noted that the unaided community schools were regarded with 'contempt' and 'derision' in many quarters. 'The Government has tended to consider these unaided schools as part of the problem of planning the expansion of the system, we consider them part of the solution' (Botswana, 1977a, p.96). The Commission recommended that:

> Government should immediately review its policy towards the unaided schools and in the short term should be prepared to offer professional help to any school that is neither individually owned nor profit-making, and which puts itself under the management of a properly constituted board of governors.
>
> As resources permit, Government should develop in the medium term a programme of gradually increasing assistance, in the form of money and teachers to the presently unaided secondary schools. In the longer term these schools should be completely absorbed, mainly at the junior secondary level, into the public system. (Botswana, 1977a, p.98.)

The Commission also recommended restructuring of the entire schooling system from the 7–3–2 year cycles of primary, junior secondary and senior secondary courses to a 6–3–3 pattern. It argued that it ought to be possible with qualitative improvement in primary education to achieve basic literacy and numeracy in 6 years, and that adequate courses at both junior and senior secondary level would require 3 year programmes.

This was seen as part of a strategy of moving from a 7-year cycle of basic education (in primary school) to 9 years' basic education for all, with 6 years in primary school and 3 years in junior secondary school. The Commission felt that Botswana would soon be able to afford an extension of schooling opportunities for many more of each age group. It advocated moves towards universal junior secondary education, though pointed out that this would only be feasible within resource constraints if the costs of junior secondary provision were kept much lower than those of regular established government schools. To avoid the inequitable divide between low-cost junior secondary schools and relatively high-cost prestigious secondary schools offering the full junior and senior cycles, the Commission envisaged that the twenty-three government and aided (mission) schools should become exclusively senior secondary schools offering a three-year course preparatory to the Cambridge Overseas School Certificate examination. The junior secondary cycle would be provided in a new generation of small day schools, of which the existing unaided community schools would be the nucleus. This would require steadily increasing official support for these schools, and government stimulus or initiative to establish many more in the future.

The government accepted most of the Commission's recommendations, and published a policy paper in 1977 which stated:

> The unaided secondary schools will receive gradually increasing public assistance. This will begin with professional advice and eventually include increasing amounts of financial aid. Partial financial aid will begin to be provided after 1980 and will be increased until the private schools are fully absorbed into the public intermediate system. The Ministry of Education will begin planning immediately to absorb these schools into the public system as intermediate schools during the 1980s. An officer will be appointed in the Ministry of Education to be responsible for liaison with the unaided secondary schools. (Botswana 1977b, p.7.)

The Commission was re-convened briefly in 1979 to advise on the transition to the new structure (Botswana, 1979), and the National Development Plan which appeared in the same year incorporated many of the policy changes (Botswana, 1980). But progress towards the new structure and towards universal access to junior secondary schooling was slow until 1982, when there were significant personnel changes in the Ministry of Education. A major effort was made to provide more places in Form I, and enrolment jumped from 7,417 in 1983 to 10,835 in 1984. This was achieved partly by more intensive utilisation of existing facilities in government and aided schools, and partly by opening of new schools. The Minister of Education, K. P. Morake, toured the country in 1983 to urge local councils to make primary school classrooms available to newly-formed secondary schools, which were controlled by Boards of Governors drawn from the local communities and assisted by the Ministry of Education.

Hence was developed the notion of a 'partnership' between government and people in the opening and running of the Community Junior Secondary Schools (as they are now officially termed, though the name Intermediate Schools was used at one stage). By January 1986, forty-five such schools existed, and for the first time they enrolled between them more Form I students than all the government and aided schools. There are plans for 150 more institutions to be established, for the proportion of primary school leavers gaining entry to Form I to double to 70 per cent, and for the conversion of the government and aided institutions to senior secondary schools only. This is projected for 1991, the end of the current plan period. Whether such optimistic targets can be met remains to be seen, but growth in Botswana, both economic and educational, is not to be under-estimated.

Significantly, many of the schools established in the mid-1980s owed more to government initiative than to genuine community origins. In order to ensure more effective coverage, the Ministry of Education took the lead in determining the locations of new schools. And much of the funding comes not from community levies and self-help activities but from large government-organised loans from the World Bank and African Development Bank.

However, they can claim to be community schools in three respects. Firstly, they are owned and managed by Boards of Governors consisting of *ex-officio* and elected members of their local communities. Secondly, although many of the capital and recurrent costs are now borne by government, the communities are still expected to make some financial contribution, especially for the provision of teachers' accommodation. Thirdly, as small day schools they serve the communities of local catchment areas, unlike the government and aided schools which are mostly larger and at least partially boarding.

The National Commission had recommended that the unaided community schools should receive steadily increasing government support in professional advice, qualified teachers and financial subsidies. A *per capita* subsidy of P20 was introduced in 1980, subsequently raised to P40 and, from 1986, to P80. Most teachers in the Community Junior Secondary Schools are now recruited, employed and paid by the Unified Teaching Service with the community having little say in the process. This of course covers the largest element in recurrent costs. The schools themselves charge fees to cover the remainder of their running costs. Fees have varied from school to school in the past, but with effect from 1986 have been standardised at P170 per student.

Two sample statements of school income are given below to indicate the range of sources and magnitude of funds available in 1984. It will be immediately apparent that if user fees are excluded from consideration, the

TABLE 12.1. *Income of Ramotswa Community Junior Secondary School, Botswana, 1984*

School Fees	P75,628
Government Grant	16,260
Sales of Garden Produce/Poultry	1,964
House Rental	820
Fund-Raising/Donations	446
Telephone (private calls)	259
Miscellaneous	9
	P95,386

TABLE 12.2. *Income of Maunatlala Community Junior Secondary School, Botswana, 1984*

School Fees (net of Refunds)	P15,707
Government Grant	4,000
Donations	3,733
Feeding Fees	842
Rent	90
Garden Produce Sales	70
Other	9
	P24,451

extent of genuine community financing of recurrent costs is now very limited.

5. Problems

Many practical difficulties are associated with these community schools. In the 1970s, their problems were those of gaining acceptance from the government, though not from the people who were supportive from the beginning, and of finding adequate resources, particularly to recruit and pay qualified teachers. These problems have largely been overcome as a result of the National Commissioner's Report and the policy measures which have followed it, particularly the per student subsidies and availability of teachers at government expense.

New problems have emerged, however. It is difficult to know what to do with the older, experienced but unqualified teachers as younger qualified staff become available. Some Boards of Governors are inexperienced and ineffective, and are dominated by individuals. It is hard to identify locations for schools where there are sufficient children within walking distance to make a school viable in such a sparsely populated country. Until the network of Community Junior Secondary Schools is sufficiently complete to provide a school within reach of most children's homes, there is strong pressure for the provision of costly boarding accommodation; and there is the reality that students have to rent accommodation in nearby villages, with attendant problems of financial and other exploitation by landlords.

Even more important are the problems associated with increasing government involvement, particularly in the financing of these schools. What was originally seen as government support for community initiative is fast becoming a government programme with community support. Communities identify less closely with buildings provided for them by the government and the World Bank than they do with ones they have worked long and hard to build themselves. Similarly, the recent standardisation of school fees in all secondary schools, motivated by a desire to avoid inequitable differences between government and community schools, also has the effect of removing the freedom of a Board of Governors to fix its own fees in the light of its own needs. One of the strengths of a system of local control in education is the diversity and flexibility which is possible, and the responsiveness to locally perceived needs. Increasing government support too easily turns into conformity and control. It also heightens expectations of what government can and should do, and reinforces a dependent mentality rather than one of self-reliance. Having got subsidies, teachers and buildings from the government, the schools are now asking for film-projectors, security fences, 'official-free' stamps, school vehicles, and graders to level their sports fields. There is no easy escape from the dilemma that the more government is able to do, the more government is expected to do, and the less the community expects to do for itself.

The Community Junior Secondary School policy has also been criticised from other angles. Complaints have focused on the proportion of national resources going into schools, the quality of instruction, and the motives behind the programme. The government is sometimes accused of simply doing what is politically popular without regard for the consequences. Thus the schools have been dubbed 'Morake schools' (after the Minister of Education), and some communities in which opposition parties are dominant want no part in them.

There are also complaints, mostly from the expatriate and elite elements of Botswana society, that what Botswana needs is more 'practical', 'relevant' or 'vocational' education rather than more general secondary education. Such criticism ignores the realities that a practical approach to all teaching and learning is more fundamental than manual skills training, that what the majority of Batswana parents perceive as 'relevant' is that which enables their children to acquire credentials for selection purposes, and that the actual job opportunities and rewards have often been greater for those with 'academic' education than those with 'vocational' skills. These complexities make it far from clear that more agricultural or technical education would be more relevant to the real needs or the perceived needs of the majority of the population. There is often an unstated assumption that such types of education will themselves generate jobs; but unemployment is essentially an economic rather than an educational problem and cannot be solved just by more 'relevant' curricula. There is clearly no virtue in being impractical or irrelevant, but there is a strong case for providing a solid base of general education rather than a narrow range of manual skills in community schools. Equally clearly, the proper balance to be struck in the curriculum of these schools is still problematic.

The plans for rapid expansion in secondary education cannot be justified by manpower needs in the narrow sense. There will not be jobs for many, perhaps most, of those who complete two or three years in a Community Junior Secondary School. The modern economy will not require the services of the large numbers of children who will soon be completing junior secondary education.

The justification must therefore be different. It can be argued that Batswana children have a right to a longer period of schooling than hitherto, given the wealth of their country. It can be argued that secondary school places are in very great demand and that it is democratic to let people have what they want. It can be argued that expansion at this level will increase the pool of candidates for selection into senior education and employment. Or it can be argued that education is 'a good thing', and that more of it must be a better thing. There is, however, a danger that utilitarian perceptions of the function of schooling, and high employment aspirations, will lead to frustration and disillusionment when the modern sector jobs are not available.

A similar problem is the almost certain pressure which will arise for more places in senior secondary schools when the expanded intakes into Community Junior Secondary Schools work their way through the cycle. The nine-year basic education is intended to be the limit of formal educational opportunity for most Batswana, but it will be very difficult to persuade the majority that this is the terminal point.

Finally, the National Commission's recommendation for a strategy of universal junior secondary education was based on an assumption that this could be provided at low cost compared with existing secondary schools. Only if this assumption were satisfied, it was suggested, would Botswana be able to afford such apparently generous provision by comparison with other African states. But this has been largely forgotten. The concern has been rather to show that Community Junior Secondary Schools are equal to government schools in standards, teachers, fees, etc., and consequent unit costs have been very similar. This suggests that the recurrent costs of operating the expanded system will be prohibitive, and that the goal of universal secondary education will not be attained in anything like the time scale originally envisaged.

Conclusion

The Community Junior Secondary Schools owe their origin to the spirit of self-sacrifice amongst Batswana parents so that their children should have a better life. In many communities, people have contributed cash, cattle and labour in order that new schools could be built and more children have the opportunity of secondary education. There is a long tradition of such endeavour in Botswana and a few spectacular examples of large-scale community financing in the colonial era. More recently, the number of community initiatives of this sort has been greater but the extent of local fund-raising and genuine community participation in school building has been less. Despite high rates of economic growth and big increases in personal incomes, collective mobilisation of local community resources is now more difficult, especially in the new urban areas where community loyalties are relatively weak.

Instead, people look increasingly to central government and other sources external to the community. Local fund-raising for capital costs now often takes the form of local appeals to private companies, church organisations and foreign aid agencies, large and small. But even such external sources can only meet a fraction of the real costs of building and running schools, so that the government has been pushed into taking over the main burden of financial responsibility. Whether this will result in complete government control and eventual incorporation of community schools into the public system remains to be seen, but the spirit of self-reliance with which these schools started and their independence as community-managed institutions are clearly at risk.

CHAPTER 13

Community Management and Financing of Schools in Papua New Guinea

MARK BRAY

As in many other systems, schools in Papua New Guinea are required to have formally constituted governing bodies which, among other functions, act as a focus for fund-raising and community control. Many schools also have separate bodies called Parents' and Citizens' (P&C) Associations. This term implies a slightly broader membership than that of the Parent–Teacher Associations (PTAs) in other systems, but the P&C Associations serve much the same purpose as PTAs.

Primary schools in Papua New Guinea are officially called community schools. This follows an attempt at reform in the early 1970s, when the government proposed major curriculum changes and envisaged that schools would become open to adults as well as children (Kemelfield, 1972; Papua New Guinea, 1974; Bray, 1983b). In the event, little changed except the name. However, the new name does emphasise that in the primary sector it is often easier to define the specific community served by a school and to generate community support for that school.

Although it is possible to identify avenues of support for secondary schools, this paper concentrates on the community schools and focuses particularly on the roles of school Boards of Management and P&C Associations. Where they work well, these bodies can improve the running of the schools and provide a valuable channel for popular participation. Neither of these outcomes can be taken for granted, however.

For reasons of length and data availability, the paper does not examine such topics as the correlation between community involvement and pupils' academic achievement or the extent to which community involvement is in practice uneven. However it does provide information on the composition of Boards of Management and P&C Associations, on the legal definition of their functions, and on the extent to which these legal provisions are actually implemented.

155

1. Papua New Guinea and its Education System

With just three million people, Papua New Guinea is a relatively small nation. Before Independence from Australia in 1975, little economic development took place. Only in the 1930s were the highlands first penetrated by outsiders, and only since the 1950s have roads been widely constructed and the cash economy developed.

As in many parts of Africa and Asia, formal schooling was introduced to Papua New Guinea during the second half of the nineteenth century by Christian missionaries. The model for the education system is Western, and children are separated into grades, spend most of their time in straight rows facing their teachers, and utilise the familiar paraphernalia of blackboards, texts and exercise books. There are considerable variations within the country, but the overall enrolment rate of primary school children is estimated at 64 per cent and of secondary school children at 16 per cent (Papua New Guinea, 1985, pp.32, 42).

As in many other countries, the school system in Papua New Guinea grew in a haphazard way during the colonial era. The churches were largely left to develop their own systems independently of each other and of the government. Although this permitted the various agencies to pursue their own philosophies, it also created problems. Curricula varied widely between schools belonging to different agencies, and this made it hard for pupils and teachers to transfer between systems. Teachers' conditions of service also varied widely (Weeden *et al.*, 1969, p.15).

To avoid the problems that arose from this diversity, a national education system was created in 1970. Under the new rules the government agreed to pay the salaries of all teachers provided that it could also determine their conditions of service. The 1970 Education Act also introduced a legal framework for the creation of a common curriculum and for transferability of pupils and teachers between schools of different agencies. The majority of churches operating schools joined the system, and within the national education system today about half the children attend church schools, among which the Roman Catholic, Lutheran, Anglican and United Church institutions are the most prominent. A group of smaller churches has combined for educational purposes into an Evangelical Alliance. Although the churches can no longer determine conditions of service for teachers, in liaison with provincial authorities they can contribute to decisions on teacher appointment. They are also responsible for the physical facilities of their schools. The educational functions are generally overseen by Church Education Secretaries, who operate at the diocesan and provincial levels and help guide the Boards of Management and P&C Associations.

The only church which was operating schools in 1970 but which decided to retain its independence and refused to join the national education system was that of the Seventh-day Adventists (SDAs). Today SDA schools educate only 1.2 per cent of the primary school aged population and 0.4 per cent of the high school aged population, but the system is run efficiently and is a clear example of community support for education. A large portion of the resources for the secondary schools and for the tertiary college in Port Moresby comes from overseas, but the primary schools are mostly supported by local congregations.

The 1970 Education Act was supplanted in 1983. The greatest change in the new law was provision for the recently created provincial governments, but the new act was closely modelled on its predecessor. Provincial governments are empowered to change their laws on Boards of Management and P&C Associations, but to date only one provincial act has been passed and there is little drive among provincial governments to alter at least this part of the law (Bray, 1984, p.127). The 1983 national education act therefore provides a framework for analysis which is applicable to the whole country.

2. Boards of Management

(a) The Legal Framework

Boards of Management were first created in 1970 following the passage of the education act. In the newly formed national education system each school was required to have a Board comprising at least five members and 'broadly representative of the community served by the school'. Each Board was required to include the head teacher and another teachers' representative, and could include direct representatives of the agency owning the school provided they did not form a majority. The law also required Boards to meet once a term (Papua and New Guinea, 1970, Section 71.1).

These provisions were largely repeated in the 1983 Education Act, which also laid down the functions of Boards. They were made responsible for planning, provision and maintenance of school buildings, teachers' houses and ancillary facilities; for enrolment of pupils; for discipline of students, including punishment by suspension or expulsion; and 'within the general framework of policy established under this Act and the philosophy of the education agency conducting the . . . school, . . . for determining the aims and goals of that school . . . and for supervising the achievement of those aims and goals' (Papua New Guinea, 1983, Section 62.1).

(b) Boards of Management in Practice

In a sense, the legal provision for Boards of Management provides the theory which may be judged against the practice. To make this possible, an extensive survey was conducted during 1984. Postcard questionnaires seeking basic factual information were sent to head teachers of 1,077 primary schools, which comprised about half the schools in the country. The

TABLE 13.1. *Average Size of Boards of Management, by Province, Papua New Guinea (%)*

No. of members	Western	Oro	SHP	WHP	Morobe	ESP	ENBP	NSP	NCD	Total
Up to 4	3.1	2.1	0	1.7	1.1	0	3.8	3.8	0	1.6
5–6	9.4	2.1	1.2	5.0	3.3	7.8	1.9	8.9	0	5.0
7–8	46.9	48.9	23.5	28.3	24.2	28.4	30.2	19.0	83.3	29.2
9–10	31.3	27.7	34.6	40.0	42.9	37.0	34.0	40.5	16.7	36.8
11–12	6.2	12.8	24.7	18.3	20.9	15.5	24.5	22.8	0	18.9
13–14	3.1	2.1	11.1	1.7	4.4	9.5	1.9	1.3	0	5.1
15–16	0	4.3	3.7	1.7	3.3	1.7	1.9	2.5	0	2.5
Over 16	0	0	1.2	3.3	0	0	1.9	1.3	0	0.9
N	32	47	81	60	91	116	53	79	6	565

Abbreviations: SHP = Southern Highlands Province, WHP = Western Highlands Province, ESP = East Sepik Province, ENBP = East New Britain Province, NSP = North Solomons Province, NCD = National Capital District.

TABLE 13.2. *Average Number of Female Board Members, by Province, Papua New Guinea (%)*

No. of female members	Western	Oro	SHP	WHP	Morobe	ESP	ENBP	NSP	NCD	Total
0	84.4	67.4	69.6	67.2	72.7	74.8	44.2	44.7	50.0	65.4
1	9.4	27.9	15.2	22.4	21.6	14.0	28.8	32.9	50.0	21.6
2	0	2.3	8.9	6.9	3.4	7.5	13.5	17.1	0	7.6
3	3.1	2.3	5.1	1.7	2.3	1.9	5.8	5.3	0	3.3
4	0	0	1.3	0	0	0.9	3.8	0	0	0.7
5	0	0	0	1.7	0	0	0	0	0	0.2
6 or more	3.1	0	0	0	0	1.9	3.8	0	0	0.7
N	32	43	79	58	88	107	52	76	6	541

For explanation of abbreviations, see Table 13.1.

questionnaires were sent to both government and church schools in each of the country's four main regions. Of the cards sent out, 591 or 54.9 per cent were returned. To supplement this information, some schools were studied in greater depth.

The first important finding of the survey was that many of the basic legal requirements were barely adhered to. Although every school was supposed to have a Board of Management, some seemed not to do so and others had Boards which were dormant. One would expect the proportion with non-existent or dormant Boards to be greater among those which did not respond to the questionnaire than among those which did, and even among those which did respond some major organisational weaknesses were apparent. Nevertheless, some strong and encouraging features also emerged from the study.

(i) The composition of Boards of Management

The answers to the question about the size of the Boards are summarised in Table 13.1. In only 1.6 per cent of cases were Boards said to have less than five members, and 27.4 per cent were said to have more than ten. The larger Boards usually operated through sub-committees for buildings, finance, and enrolment.

The requirement that Boards should be 'broadly representative of their communities' did not always seem to be followed. The precise interpretation of the phrase is open to question, but four dimensions could include gender, occupational, residential, and ethnic representation. Tables 13.2 and 13.3 show that there were few female Board members, and that 65.4 per cent of schools which responded had none at all. In general, this reflected traditional patterns in Papua New Guinea in which women are ascribed few decision-making roles of this type. The percentage of schools with female

TABLE 13.3. *Average Number of Female Board Members, by Agency, Papua New Guinea (%)*

No. of female members	Govt.	Anglican	EA	Lutheran	UC	RC	All Churches
0	67.5	72.4	91.8	77.4	52.2	50.6	63.9
1	18.6	24.1	4.1	15.1	26.1	32.7	23.9
2	8.2	0	4.1	3.8	13.0	10.9	7.7
3	3.0	3.4	0	1.9	8.7	4.5	3.5
4	0.9	0	0	0	0	1.3	0.6
5	0.4	0	0	0	0	0	0
6 or more	1.3	0	0	1.9	0	0	0.3
N	231	29	49	53	23	156	310

Abbreviations: EA = Evangelical Alliance, UC = United Church, RC = Roman Catholic.

Board members was higher in East New Britain Province, but was very low in Western Province. Explanations for this are not immediately apparent. On a church-by-church basis, the percentage of schools with some female Board members was relatively high in Roman Catholic schools but very low in Evangelical Alliance ones. This may arise from different church philosophies, or it may be accidental.

On the other hand, most schools did have a good range of occupations among their Board members. Table 13.4 shows the occupations of Board members in three schools which were broadly typical. In general, communities did not seem to consider it necessary for Board members to have attended school themselves, and a large percentage were illiterate. The proportion of members with wage-earning jobs, even excluding the head-teacher and the teachers' representative, was generally far higher than their proportion in the population as a whole, but Boards also often included subsistence farmers, some of whom were Chairmen. This suggested that the Boards were more representative of their communities than might otherwise have been expected. One suggestion of a 1972 handbook was that Boards might also include pupils (McKinnon, 1972, p.2). However no instances of this were encountered during the research, and the concept would not fit readily with most Papua New Guinean social patterns, which do not generally give youths decision-making roles of this kind.

Many Boards also made careful efforts to secure geographic representation. Where schools served several villages, for example, Board members were often selected to ensure that each location was represented. This did not always operate smoothly because it was not always possible to find interested individuals. Complaints were also frequently heard that representatives of distant villages did not attend meetings.

Urban schools sometimes made deliberate efforts to secure representatives of each of the main ethnic groups resident in the area served by the school. However, this tended to be organised less carefully. Whereas it was common for head teachers to have lists on their office walls indicating the

TABLE 13.4. *Occupations of Board Members in Three Schools, Papua New Guinea*

A rural school	A station school	An urban school
Storekeeper	Subsistence Farmer	Builder
Councillor	Subsistence Farmer	Subsistence Farmer
Councillor	Priest	Radio Technician
Subsistence Farmer	Subsistence Farmer	Clerk
Youth Leader	Subsistence Farmer	Driver
Youth Member	Aid Post Orderly	Miner
Subsistence Farmer	Aid Post Orderly	Clerk
Teacher	Teacher	Teacher
Crocodile Buyer	Housewife	Head teacher
Head teacher	Head teacher	

residential representation of Board members, it was uncommon to find lists showing ethnic representation.

Inevitably the most important member on most Boards is the head teacher, for his advice is usually the starting point for discussion, and by providing or witholding information he can greatly influence decisions. In general, the activity and effectiveness of Boards depends more than anything else on the outlook of the head teachers. However, it is not always the case that Boards deteriorate when faced by a poor head, and examples exist of Boards actually arranging for bad head teachers to be transferred out.

(ii) The activities of Boards of Management

Of the functions listed by the 1983 Education Act, the construction and maintenance of facilities are taken most seriously by the majority of Boards. Indeed many Board members are unaware of the other functions, and consider construction and maintenance to be their principal role. Table 13.5 indicates the breakdown of expenditure during 1983 of the schools which responded to the question in the survey. One reason why Boards are particularly aware of their responsibility for buildings and facilities is that they are reminded by the teachers. The school staff may be less enthusiastic about encouraging their Boards to assume responsibility for enrolment of pupils and discipline, for they may prefer to take on these duties themselves.

The decision to make Boards of Management responsible for buildings and facilities has several important consequences. First, it relieves the

TABLE 13.5. *Expenditure of Boards of Management, 1983 and First Term of 1984, Papua New Guinea*

Items	1983 Whole Year		1984 First Term	
	% of total expenditure	frequency of response*	% of total expenditure	frequency of response*
Teachers' Houses	34.0	205	44.6	193
Classrooms	26.1	473	20.4	68
Maintenance	9.4	143	7.0	116
Furniture for Teachers	2.4	89	2.5	45
Furniture for School	5.0	95	5.6	50
Radios etc.	1.9	138	2.0	73
Library Books	1.7	94	1.5	40
Lawn Mowers	4.6	121	3.5	68
Prizes	4.6	220	0.6	16
Tools	0.9	77	0.8	35
Sports Equipment	1.6	170	2.0	94
Other	7.8	139	9.5	103
Total expenditure	K651,574		K307,209	

The 'frequency of response' refers to the number of responses to this item in the questionnaire. Altogether, 591 schools responded to the questionnaire, so the maximum frequency is 591.

government of expenditure, and thus spreads the financial burden of education. Second, it increases diversity between schools, for some communities have more resources and some Boards take their duties more seriously than others. This diversity can cause discontent among teachers who may consider themselves poorly treated, and it also maintains imbalances between rural and urban schools. Third, the policy allows the physical plant of the schools to mirror the communities much more closely than would otherwise be the case. If governments were responsible for buildings, they would probably employ standard designs and take little account of the local availability of particular building materials or the traditions of specific areas. Because of the present policy, many classrooms are built of the same material as their neighbouring village houses, and they exhibit considerable variety around the country. Moreover the villagers can readily engage in construction, which is an area of their own expertise. Consultation with villagers on curriculum and textbooks is less easy or productive because they are not areas of local expertise.

Diversity also exists in the extent to which Boards exercise their powers to recruit children. Primary education in most parts of Papua New Guinea is still far from universal, and schools are not always able to satisfy demand for places. When there are more applicants than places, the Board of Management should be the body which decides how they are allocated. In practice a few Boards have broad policies, but more often the head teacher decides which children should be selected. Most heads operate a 'first-come-first-served' system, though many organise recruitment drives and some use Board of Management members to assist them (see also Preston and Khambu, 1986, pp.15–16).

Though not mentioned in the act, many Boards also play an important role in encouraging attendance and punctuality of children. Sometimes Board members are assigned to follow up cases of poor attendance by visiting the children in their own localities, and some Boards even impose fines for poor attendance or lateness. This is a useful role which cannot easily be undertaken by teachers, many of whom are transferred at frequent intervals and who thus lack background knowledge of their pupils. Since Board members often hold their positions longer than teachers, they can provide a valuable element of continuity.

In matters of student discipline the usual pattern, if Boards are involved at all, is for teachers to draw up school rules and then to request the Boards to approve them. It is, however, valuable for head teachers to have a higher and possibly more neutral authority to which matters may be referred in time of dispute, and it may also be important to avoid excessive concentration of power in the hands of the head teachers. Should pupils wish to appeal to yet higher authorities, they are permitted to bring grievances to their provincial governments.

The broadest function of Boards indicated by the Education Act is determination of the aims and goals of their schools. It is arguable that in practice this is not very meaningful, for most of the aims and goals are actually determined by educational traditions, by the social and economic framework, and by the national and provincial governments. Nevertheless, Boards can contribute in religious matters, for example. They can organise pastors to provide religious instruction, and they can request prayers to be held at the beginning and end of each day. Although they are not able to hire or fire teachers, they are allowed to indicate the types of individuals they would like to be appointed and to recommend specific persons. Examples are easy to find in which the Boards have requested teachers of particular religions, or have requested the removal of teachers who have abused their positions through drunkenness, fornication and other anti-social practices. Thus the Boards can discipline teachers and can perform a role which in isolated villages would be impossible for the provincial authorities.

Finally, one of the instruments through which the interest of the community in the education of their children is maintained is the imposition of Board of Management fees. The levels of fees recorded in the survey are shown in Table 13.6. Rarely do they cover more than one tenth of the true cost of schooling, but it is a widespread opinion in Papua New Guinea that community involvement would decline in the absence of these fees. Interest is also maintained by the common Board practice of raising funds through the sale of crops, sponsored walks, fêtes and so on. It is possible that the involvement that these activities generate also leads at least some villagers to pay more attention to what their children are learning, and to pick up some ideas themselves.

3. Parents' and Citizens' Associations

(a) The Legal Framework

P&C Associations have an older tradition than Boards of Management. Whereas the latter were created following the passage of the 1970 Education Act, the former have existed in many schools for several decades. The model for P&Cs was imported from Australia, and they were particularly common in government schools. When the 1970 Education Act was formulated, senior policy makers assumed that the P&C Associations would be subordinated to the Boards, that the Boards would take the place of P&C executives, and that if P&Cs continued to exist it would only be to implement the policies drawn up by the Boards (personal information from K. R. McKinnon, 1984). This has not happened in all schools, however.

The current law on P&C Associations is less detailed than that on Boards of Management, and provides fewer guidelines. Most importantly, whereas every school is required to have a Board of Management, P&C Associations are optional. The 1983 Education Act (Section 89) simply states (a) that

TABLE 13.6. *Board of Management Fees per Child, by Province, Papua New Guinea 1984 (%)*

Fee	Western	Oro	SHP	WHP	Morobe	ESP	ENBP	NSP	NCD	Total
Up to K1.00	50.0	2.6	64.0	2.0	16.7	36.4	32.5	9.8	0	21.6
K1.01–K2.00	35.0	20.5	24.0	10.2	13.9	11.4	10.0	6.6	0	13.8
K2.01–K3.00	5.0	25.6	4.0	10.2	13.9	4.5	12.5	1.6	0	9.4
K3.01–K4.00	0	10.3	0	12.2	11.1	6.8	2.5	3.3	0	6.3
K4.01–K5.00	5.0	28.2	0	10.2	27.7	15.9	2.5	4.9	0	11.9
K5.01–K8.00	0	5.1	0	30.6	5.6	6.8	10.0	8.2	60.0	10.7
K8.01–K10.0	5.0	5.1	4.0	22.4	11.1	9.1	27.5	21.3	40.0	15.4
K10.01–K15.00	0	2.6	0	2.0	0	6.8	2.5	44.3	0	10.3
Over K15.00	0	0	4.0	0	0	2.3	0	0	0	0.6
N	20	39	25	49	36	44	40	61	5	319

For explanation of abbreviations, see Table 13.1.

TABLE 13.7. *Boards of Management and P&C Associations, by Province, Papua New Guinea 1984 (%)*

	Western	Oro	SHP	WHP	ESP	Morobe	ENBP	NSP	NCD	Total
BoM only	40.0	59.2	66.7	76.2	49.5	50.4	50.8	72.2	66.7	58.8
P&C only	14.3	4.1	8.9	3.2	7.5	31.6	8.5	6.0	0	11.9
Neither	5.7	2.0	1.1	1.6	3.2	1.7	5.1	7.2	0	3.2
Both	40.0	34.7	23.3	19.0	39.8	16.2	35.6	14.6	33.3	26.1
N	35	49	90	63	93	117	59	83	6	595

For explanation of abbreviations, see Table 13.1.

education agencies may approve associations representing parents and other persons interested in the education and welfare of students at the school, (b) that their functions should be as set out in their constitutions, and (c) that, subject to direction of the agency, an association may arrange with the controlling authority to use the school facilities for holding fêtes and other activities for the benefit of the school.

(b) P&C Associations in Practice

Because the framework for P&C Associations is less clearly defined, it is harder to assess their role. In some cases, however, conflict arises between Boards of Management and P&C Associations. Often the conflict could be avoided by organisational changes and improved supervision by provincial government officers and Church Education Secretaries, and some administrative changes are worth consideration.

Table 13.7 shows the number of schools in each of the provinces surveyed which stated that they had a P&C Association with a separate executive. Some head teachers stated that they only had P&C Associations and no Boards of Management. These may have been cases of confusion of terminology, or the schools may have been failing to implement legal requirements. More significant in the present context, however, is the number of schools with both a Board of Management and a separate P&C executive, for these are the schools with the greatest potential for conflict.

(i) The composition of P&C Associations

One problem with P&C Associations in many schools is that they do not have written constitutions. Of the 230 head teachers who answered the question in the survey, 57.0 per cent stated that their Associations did not have written constitutions. Moreover the case studies showed that among the ones which did have constitutions, many of the documents were worded loosely and were not widely known about or understood.

Few P&C Associations have formal arrangements for membership. Meetings may be attended by any interested individuals, and no enrolment fees are charged. However, fees may be levied on school pupils and may be quite separate from Board of Management fees. P&C Associations may also raise money in similar ways to Boards, e.g. by arranging fêtes, selling crops, and organising sponsored walks. Usually these funds are kept in a separate bank account. Levels of P&C fees are shown in Table 13.8.

To distinguish them from the Board of Management Chairmen, the heads of P&C executives are usually called Presidents. The executives are generally smaller than Boards, and the 230 cases for which the survey gained data had an average size of 4.5. Whereas by law the head teacher and a teachers' representative must have places on Boards of Management, no

TABLE 13.8. *Average Level of P&C Association Fees, by Province, Papua New Guinea 1984 (%)*

Fee	Western	Oro	SHP	WHP	Morobe	ESP	ENBP	NSP	NCD	Total
Up to K1.00	46.2	13.5	42.9	16.7	4.6	13.2	25.0	9.5	0	15.7
K1.01–K2.00	15.4	37.8	28.6	33.3	13.8	12.2	20.0	4.8	0	17.5
K2.01–K3.00	19.2	18.9	0	0	31.5	14.4	10.0	4.8	50.0	15.4
K3.01–K4.00	3.8	8.1	0	8.3	9.2	7.8	20.0	4.8	0	8.2
K4.01–K5.00	7.7	13.5	14.3	8.3	29.2	20.0	10.0	14.3	0	17.9
K5.01–K8.00	3.8	0	0	33.3	7.7	18.9	5.0	9.5	0	11.1
K8.01–K10.00	3.8	8.1	14.3	0	12.3	7.8	10.0	14.3	50.0	8.9
Over K10.00	0	0	14.3	0	1.5	5.5	0	38.1	0	5.4
N	26	37	7	12	65	90	20	21	2	280

For explanation of abbreviations, see Table 13.1.

such provision is automatically made for P&C Associations. This is one reason why they are smaller, and it may lead to problems of liaison with the Boards and staff in each school. In some cases, however, the P&C President is a member of the Board. In other cases no separate P&C executive exists and instead the Board itself directs the activities of the parents and citizens.

(ii) The activities of P&C Associations

One head teacher who was interviewed during the research discussed here likened the roles of Boards of Management and P&C Associations to the structure of government. When the system works well, he suggested, the Boards of Management act like politicians and decision-makers, and the parents and citizens act like public servants who implement the Board's policies. P&C Associations are widely seen as labour forces to be mobilised when it is time to build classrooms, cut the grass, or repair toilets.

Where both Boards of Management and P&C Associations exist, however, and where they have separate funds, confusion is particularly likely to arise from the fact that both may see themselves as responsible for school facilities. The danger of confusion is especially great when coordination between the two bodies is poor.

Conclusions

The organisational structure of education in Papua New Guinea does not give wide powers to communities at the school level. Major decisions on the school calendar, curriculum, qualifications and conditions of service of teachers, and even the target populations for whom schools cater are taken by national and provincial governments. However, the powers that do rest with the communities can be significant and should not be ignored. Boards of Management are responsible for buildings, enrolment of pupils, student discipline, and ancillary aspects of the curriculum such as craft work and religion. The fact that these decisions are taken locally helps spread the financial burden of education, and it achieves some purposes which could not be achieved by the school inspectors, teachers and other government officers. Boards of Management which operate well may improve teachers' morale by providing facilities and by taking an interest in what their children do each day. Through their ability to report to provincial and church authorities, Boards may also provide a check on the behaviour of teachers.

The organisational framework in Papua New Guinea provides greater powers than is the case in many other countries. Elsewhere it is common to have P&C Associations or PTAs but less common to have Boards of Management, at least at the primary school level. Governments in other countries might find it worth considering creation of Boards similar to those in Papua New Guinea.

However, the chapter has also noted that in some Papua New Guinean schools confusion arises between the roles of the Boards of Management and the P&C Associations. This is clearly detrimental, and to avoid it provincial governments and church education secretaries should consider three strategies. First they should encourage both Boards and Associations to adopt written constitutions which should clearly indicate the separate functions of the two organisations. Second they should discourage the maintenance of separate bank accounts, and third they should encourage better coordination between the two bodies by insisting that at least the P&C President should also be a member of the Board of Management. Perhaps the tidiest framework is one in which the Board itself directs the parents and citizens and there is no separate P&C executive. Some schools may wish to retain an executive, however, either as a sub-committee of the Board or as a body in its own right. One advantage of a separate executive is that it provides another forum for involvement and for community members to act as specific functionaries.

To help both bodies with their roles, it would also be useful to have simple handbooks. A handbook for Boards of Management was written in 1972 in English, Motu and Pidgin English (McKinnon, 1972). The book needs to be regularly updated and redistributed, and a similar one should be produced for P&C Associations.

These handbooks could also be used during short workshops. A few enthusiastic individuals have already held workshops in some provinces, and the enterprises could be repeated and extended. The workshops do not need to be costly, for experience has shown that Board members are often prepared to sacrifice their time and to travel to central locations at their own expense. The most logical personnel to organise such workshops are the provincial nonformal education officers and the Church Education Secretaries. Several primary school inspectors have also expressed interest in workshops, and could assist.

One specific item on which workshops could usefully devote particular attention is the procedure for book-keeping. Experience indicates that accounts are generally kept poorly, and this defect causes considerable strife. Allegations of misappropriation of funds are common, and in the absence of careful records they are hard to prove one way or the other. Even if allegations are groundless, they can be very destructive and can be the greatest single obstacle to effective running of the system. Moreover, the fact that accounts are not kept must itself be a major cause of temptation to misappropriate.

The impact of participation on children's learning and the extent to which Boards and P&C Associations are dominated by specific types of individual are two aspects on which it would be valuable to conduct future research.

Likewise, while it is clear that good Boards and P&C Associations can greatly help the operation of schools, it would be valuable to know more about their role in promoting the impact of the schools on society. Meanwhile, it is evident that when it works well the Papua New Guinean model has many advantages. The data which are already available suggest that the model has features which other governments could usefully consider.

CHAPTER 14

Cultural Values and Community Financing of Education in Burma

ROBERT BIAK CIN AND GUY B. SCANDLEN

For religious and cultural reasons, community involvement has long been a strong feature of education in Burma. Buddhism, which is the religion of the majority, has been a major factor in this. It stresses the concept of *cetana* or 'loving kindness', and every Buddhist learns about the never repayable thanks which should be expressed to the Lord Buddha (*phaya*), the role of sermons (*taya*), and the importance of monks (*sangha*), teachers (*saya*), and parents (*meeba*).

Although monastery schools still operate and will be briefly referred to here, this chapter chiefly focuses on secular primary, middle and high schools. Attitudes which in the past supported religious schools now apply to secular schools as well. The chapter charts general features of the education system and its historical development before highlighting the activities of community bodies and the experiences of the recent Unicef-supported Primary School Improvement Programme.

As in other societies, schools in Burma are supported by a range of individuals and community bodies. Most institutions have Parent–Teacher Associations (PTAs), which, as their name implies, chiefly cater for parents and teachers. Many schools are also supported by philanthropic individuals who may or may not have children in the institutions. Communities often organise cultural bodies and self-help groups of various kinds, and political party members and government officers at the local level also usually play a key role. In state primary schools, local support is part of a joint effort between communities and government. In 'affiliated' primary schools, initiatives come entirely from the communities themselves.

Table 14.1 concentrates on the primary sector and shows the number of schools and pupils in each state/division in 1982–3. Community involvement is strong in both state and affiliated schools, but is particularly strong in the latter. In state primary schools, teachers and some stationery, teaching aids, furniture are provided by the government. In some cases communities appoint additional teachers since most schools are understaffed, though centrally-collected statistics on the number of community-paid teachers in

171

state primary schools are not available. Affiliated schools are so-called because they are attached to primary, middle or high schools. All resources in affiliated schools are provided by their communities, though the government retains control over their curriculum and many affiliated schools are eventually taken over by the government. In 1982–3 affiliated schools comprised 7.7 per cent of the total number of institutions but provided only 3.4 per cent of the total number of pupils. They were said to have 2,641 community-paid teachers.

1. Historical Perspectives

During the pre-colonial era, most formal education was imparted through the monasteries. Every village had at least one monastery, where children of all social classes could study. The monastery schools did not provide for girls, however. In some places philanthropic individuals established lay schools for girls and for boys who were too young to go to the monasteries, but the institutions tended to be qualitatively inferior. Statistics collected by the colonial authorities in 1870 suggested that in British Lower Burma there were 340 lay schools with 3,838 boys and 1,231 girls, and there were 3,438 monastery schools with 43,773 pupils. The population of the territory at that time was estimated at 2,487,000 (Kyi, 1977, p.7).

During the nineteenth century, a network of Christian schools also grew. The government assisted them with grants-in-aid, and required them to conform to various regulations. Later, the principle of grants-in-aid was extended to lay schools and to those monastery schools which were prepared

TABLE 14.1. *Primary Schools and Pupils by Province, Burma, 1982–3*

	Schools		Pupils	
	State	Affiliated	State	Affiliated
Kachin Division	770	—	136,790	—
Kayah State	184	—	24,217	—
Karen State	739	—	101,366	—
Chin State	638	29	55,899	1,026
Mon State	844	—	231,070	—
Rakhine State	1,567	117	232,808	4,960
Shan State	1,862	140	311,492	8,733
Sagaing Division	2,611	350	516,741	27,329
Tennasserim Division	686	65	130,461	4,309
Pegu Division	2,721	123	542,449	8,859
Magwe Division	2,521	393	436,213	37,559
Mandalay Division	2,762	193	634,561	18,381
Rangoon Division	1,783	1	549,647	61
Irrawaddy Division	3,765	533	634,076	50,321
Total	23,453	1,944	4,537,790	161,538

Source: Department of Basic Education, Rangoon.

to adhere to the government's regulations. The church schools were subsequently nationalised, though monastery schools were allowed to remain independent.

Many monastery schools wished to avoid government control, and refused to register. Official statistics show only 3,091 registered schools in 1916, and the figure declined to 928 in 1932. That this was a small proportion of the total number was indicated by a 1941 estimate that about 18,000 monastery schools existed. A publicity campaign during the 1950s raised the number of registered monastery schools to 5,545. During the next few years both registered and unregistered monastery schools declined in number, however, for they found it increasingly difficult to compete with secular schools teaching English and other 'modern' subjects (Biak Cin and Scandlen, 1985, pp.5–8).

Another significant development during the colonial period was the creation of 'national' schools. These were established in the 1920s and taught secular subjects, but for political reasons their founders rejected British support. All the schools of the Young Men's Buddhist Association (YMBA) voluntarily came under the jurisdiction of a specially created Council of National Education, and the new system was started through subscriptions which raised 1.5 million Rupees (Kyi, 1977, p.13). The movement has had parallels in east and central Africa, among other places (Ranger, 1965, pp.78ff; Anderson, 1973, p.18).

2. The Growth of PTAs

Before the Second World War, no government institutions had School Committees, and few had Parent–Teacher Associations. The first School Committee was formed by the Ministry of Education in 1948, the year of Independence. It had 11 members, of whom two were community representatives. Its task was to assist the qualitative improvement of education and to promote the moral development of the students. It was not empowered to deal with personnel, curriculum, examinations or financial matters.

In the early 1950s mechanisms for community participation were reshaped and extended. A Unesco mission to Burma travelled extensively in the country during 1950 and 1951, and commented critically on the lack of community involvement. The country's first 4-year education plan (Burma 1952) sought to remedy this situation. It instructed schools to form PTAs, and stressed the value of Youth Organisations and similar bodies.

In 1959 the School Committees were formally abolished and in most middle and high schools were officially replaced by PTAs. Each PTA was supposed to have thirteen members, including five community representatives. The Education Director's 1959 instructions stated that PTAs could collect funds as they saw fit, but no further instructions were issued and each PTA devised its own procedures.

The Education Ministry, under the Revolutionary Council, again revised procedures in 1963. Each high school PTA was to have eleven members, and each middle school to have ten. In every PTA, four members were to be community representatives. The bodies were directed to place their funds in bank or post office accounts.

Until the 1970s, PTAs were more common in middle and high schools than in primary schools. In 1973, however, this was changed with a new directive. Since that time, primary schools have also been required to form PTAs, each of which should have nine members and four community representatives. The head teacher should always be the chairperson, and the two vice-chairpersons should be a teacher and a community member. Regulations introduced in 1973 restricted annual PTA contributions to 20 Kyats per family.

3. The Activities of Community Bodies

The 1973 document declared the official objectives of PTAs to be:

1. to assist the school in matters relating to the all-round development of its students;
2. to help the school build character and instil discipline;
3. to exchange appropriate knowledge and experience between teachers and community members; and
4. to organise collective work to develop the school.

PTAs may give stipends to poor students, and prizes to deserving ones. They may assist in the work of the School Council and other educational organisations, and they should be concerned with general improvement of educational facilities. However, they have no official role in school administration, teaching methodology, curriculum, admission of students or supervision of teachers.

A major survey of the financial activities of PTAs and other community bodies was carried out in the 1972–3 academic year by the Burma Educational Research Bureau. No comparable surveys had been carried out before, and the exercise has not yet been repeated. It is therefore worth examining at some length. Although the report on the survey does not specifically indicate the number of schools covered, it does say that questionnaires were sent to all schools and that returns were 'quite complete' except for nine townships in two different states and three different divisions (Kyi, 1977, p.68).

Tables 14.2 to 14.5 summarise the quantitative findings of the survey and indicate the activities of PTAs separately from those of philanthropic individuals. The latter usually assist projects in order to provide memorials for departed relatives, or to increase their general merit and promote their standing in the communities. Table 14.3 shows that their contributions have been particularly important in state primary schools, but comparison of Tables 14.4 and 14.5 shows that donations for capital works are much more common than for recurrent expenditure.

Table 14.5 shows figures from some government sources but excludes normal government payments of teachers' salaries. As such, the impression portrayed both by this table and by the summary table (Table 14.2) is unbalanced. It is also regrettable that Table 14.5 obscures the picture by adding teachers' salaries to contingencies. Separate information in the text reveals that teachers' salaries only accounted for 25.7 per cent of the total shown here, and that co-curricular activities (29.6 per cent), physical training (11.1 per cent), school libraries (5.9 per cent) and other contingencies (27.7 per cent) accounted for the remainder.

Nevertheless, the strong community contributions to education are clearly apparent. PTAs provided 21.2 per cent of the costs of buildings (Table 14.2), 63.8 per cent of the costs of furniture and equipment, 63.4 per cent of the costs of repairs, and 87.7 per cent of general contingencies. Table 14.3 shows that the greatest PTA contributions were to state high schools, followed by state primary schools, with lowest contributions going to affiliated and monastery schools. These figures were presented without companion figures on the number of institutions in existence, however, which makes them harder to assess.

3. The Primary School Improvement Programme

With a rapidly increasing population and rising costs, during the early 1980s the government of Burma again voiced concern about the difficulties in meeting educational development goals. To assist the government, Unicef embarked on a joint development programme which placed strong reliance on community involvement. The 1982–6 plan for the Primary School Improvement Programme (PSIP) anticipated total investment of US$19.6 million. Of this, 41.5 per cent was to be contributed by the

TABLE 14.2. *Total Educational Expenditure, by Type, Burma, 1972–3*

Form of support	PTAs	Local support Individual comm. members	Govt. aid	Government support Community dev. funds	Total (Kyats)
Buildings	21.2%	39.9%	9.9%	28.9%	21,412,682
Furniture/Equip't	63.8%	21.2%	1.7%	13.3%	2,439,557
Repairs	63.4%	14.0%	—	22.6%	5,969,229
Contingencies	87.7%	8.3%	3.9%	0.1%	7,958,430
Teachers' Salaries	82.2%	3.9%			2,754,642
Total	48.1%	26.4%	6.1%	19.4%	40,534,540

Source: Kyi (1977, p.48).

TABLE 14.3. *Incomes by Type of School, Burma, 1972–3 (Kyats)*

	Local support		Government support		
Types of schools	PTAs	Individual comm. members	Govt. aid	Community dev. funds	Total
State High Schools	2,276,368	1,033,427	2,056,613	2,223	5,368,631
State Middle Schools	1,608,070	1,581,832	1,934,971	177,092	5,301,965
State Primary Schools	2,000,076	5,071,804	2,523,669	1,946,847	11,542,396
Affiliated Schools	191,512	1,220,814	2,500	25,860	1,440,686
Monastery Primary Schools	26,993	171,209	10	350	198,562
Total	6,103,019	9,079,086	6,517,763	2,152,372	23,852,240

Source: Kyi (1977, p.40).

TABLE 14.4. *Expenditure by Type of Activity, Burma, 1972–3 (Kyats)*

	Local support		Government support		
Types of activities	PTAs	Individual comm. members	Govt. aid	Community dev. funds	Total
New Schools	2,969,717	7,064,806	4,876,920	1,834,784	16,744,227
New Classrooms	738,827	654,780	996,572	155,355	2,545,534
New Gymnasia	234,362	1,965	34,000	117	272,444
New Libraries	31,889	39,489	6,200	409	77,987
Other Buildings	452,373	341,008	274,358	101,949	1,169,688
Cost of Voluntary Labour	120,434	457,634	4,623	18,110	600,801
New Furniture	1,307,495	425,469	271,920	25,054	2,029,938
New Equipment	247,922	93,935	53,170	16,594	411,621
Total	6,103,019	9,079,086	6,517,763	2,152,372	23,852,240

Source: Kyi (1977, p.42).

TABLE 14.5. *Local Support Costs of Contingencies & Teachers' Salaries, Burma, 1972–3 (Kyats)*

| Types of schools | Local support | | Government support | | Total |
	PTAs	Individual comm. members	Govt. aid	Community dev. funds	
State High Schools	3,649,430	92,755	405	53,420	3,796,010
State Middle Schools	1,943,519	110,143	—	60,636	2,114,298
State Primary Schools	3,263,711	236,657	4,475	126,184	3,631,027
Affiliated Schools	714,102	300,844	902	61,794	1,077,642
Monastery Primary Schools	61,542	27,392	—	5,090	94,024
Total	9,632,304	767,791	5,782	307,124	10,713,001

Source: Kyi (1977, p.46).

government, 22.8 per cent by Unicef, and 35.6 per cent by communities. In addition, communities were expected to provide land and labour. The programme envisaged construction of 434 new schools and repair of the same number of existing schools (Unicef, 1982, p.6).

A distinctive feature of this project was the incorporation of community participation into a specific plan of action rather than just relegating it to the background. To increase the effectiveness of community inputs, it was considered necessary to assist communities with technical advice and materials. Unicef appointed an architect specialising in Burmese public structures as a project officer, who, with the help of the Unesco Educational Facilities Unit in Bangkok, developed a manual to help communities improve or construct their own schools. The manual presents ideas on layout of compounds and on construction of buildings and latrines. Unicef also appointed fourteen civil engineer or architect Project Assistants, whose main responsibilities have been motivation of communities and assistance with implementation of the PSIP. In addition, Unicef supplied roofing sheets, materials for sanitary latrines, equipment for water supplies, and other necessary items that are rarely available locally.

The project leaders have found that participation of the Burma Socialist Programme Party Committees and the People's Councils at each level has been an important ingredient of success. The Party and the People's Councils have powerful political officials at the state/division, township and village tract levels. If no Party Unit or Council is actively interested in the scheme, construction tends to be slow and inefficient; but where there is active support, schedules are more likely to be met. Kyi (1977, p.21) also highlights the benefits of party support.

Unicef estimates that an average family in a 180 household village would have to contribute the equivalent of US$45 for the initial construction of a PSIP school. This is US$30 less than it would have been had community members had to purchase all the materials themselves. The annual *per capita* income in Burma is estimated at US$190, and an average family is thought to have six members of whom a maximum of three might be working. On this calculation, the family's annual income would be approximately US$570. Contributions might be spread over more than one year, but US$45 would represent 7.9 per cent of a family's annual income (Biak Cin and Scandlen, 1985, p.13).

Despite this high cost, by 1985 only one village in Karen State and two villages in Pegu Division out of the 551 communities selected for new or repaired schools had declined to be included in the programme. This fact indicates strong community commitment to education. It also shows that government and agency projects which plan to share costs with communities may be quite feasible.

Conclusions

Community participation in education has long roots in Burma. It has always been a powerful concept in the monastery education system, and in recent decades traditions have been transferred to the secular one. The 1972–3 survey provided statistics on the work of PTAs and philanthropic individuals, and though no comparable surveys have been conducted since that time, the general picture is probably unchanged.

While individual contributions are considered meritorious in themselves, they also arise out of necessity. When communities employ extra teachers in state schools or open their own affiliated schools, they are chiefly doing so to fill a resource gap. Similarly, although the planners of the PSIP might argue that community participation is traditional in Burma, the project was also based on the reality that government and Unicef funds were limited and that much more could be achieved with a strong self-help component. The PSIP also has the merit of coordinating community inputs and improving their effectiveness through specific materials and new streamlined architectural designs.

Despite the extent of their inputs, communities have relatively little control over resources. They provide facilities for their schools, but officially have no control over school administration, teaching methodology, curriculum, or admission of pupils. Even in affiliated schools, the government is officially in charge of overall curriculum and organisation.

Kyi (1977, p.69) underscores the cultural roots of community participation when she writes that Burmese people are 'by nature voluntary service minded'. Necessity arising from the shortage of government resources forces many communities which want schools to construct them themselves; but most communities consider family contributions to be a natural part of life rather than an imposition.

CHAPTER 15

State Control and Local Financing of Schools in China

JEAN C. ROBINSON

Minban xuexiao—people-run schools—have been alive, if not well, in China for the last 40 years. Starting as popular, voluntary village institutions in the 1940s, *minban xuexiao* today are low status, low quality schools. Whereas the earlier schools were guided by Communist Party (CCP) cadres but managed and financed at the local level, contemporary *minban xuexiao* are funded at the local level but controlled and guided by provincial and central education experts. This evolution reflects tensions in the Chinese policy between centralisation and decentralisation; it simultaneously exhibits the growing unease of the Chinese leadership with popular participation in the management of social institutions and, in particular, with populist solutions to the problem of educational development.

This study analyses the evolution of people-managed schools as a reflection of the CCP's incremental move away both from decentralised decision making to centralised state and Party control and from populist education to 'regular' education. These policy shifts uncover the PRC's negation of experiments that have been seen as models for development in poor societies. They represent continuing solidification of trends begun a decade ago. As Unger (1980) has pointed out, the 'diploma disease' has strongly influenced the course of Chinese educational development; people-managed schools are now even more subject to central control, urban bias, and conflict over educational goals. Concurrently, the value of decentralisation in education has been called into question, even though decision making in certain sectors of China's economy is developing to local levels.

Some scholars maintain that decentralisation can be a viable strategy when there is agreement between central authorities and local citizens over goals and structures (e.g. Grindle, 1980). Yet the problem of educational development in poor societies is particularly subject to conflict over objectives, financing, and control. The level of decentralisation in a developing society can tell us much about these conflicts as well as about the more general relationship between governments and citizens.

Decentralisation policies in general evolve across several functional and

181

hierarchical levels, depending on the perception of the central leadership (Smith, 1980). One level—that in which decentralisation extends over a whole policy area (e.g. education)—implies that the regime believes that a consensus exists between the leadership and the citizenry and that the expertise gap—at least in that particular policy area—will not have untoward consequences. A middle level of decentralisation, involving partial policy areas (e.g. primary education), implies that the leadership is content with sharing decision making and has some confidence that people at the local level share common agreement on policy directives. The third level of decentralisation, representing the largest concentration of central power, involves only token participation and grass-root decisions on low-level policies (e.g. the construction of school buildings). Agricultural policy in China during the 1980s reflects a move from the lowest to the middle level of decentralisation. The history of *minban xuexiao*, by contrast, is a gradual shift from the broader type of decentralisation to the very narrow. This suggests that as the gap between educational experts and masses has widened, and that the Chinese leadership has lost confidence in the capabilities of peasants and local officials to manage local schools.

Changes from one functional or hierarchical level to another elicit a consistent bureaucratic response. Time and time again, central bureaucrats and experts prove reluctant to relinquish control. Vivienne Shue's perceptive analysis of conflicts between centre and locality in peasant China is to the point here. When power and authority are perceived as finite, the political leadership becomes unwilling to share its authority. Local leaders—and even the 'masses'—are seen as 'active rivals to central state power' (Shue, 1980, p.343). The resolution in terms of people-managed schools has been a growing acceptance of 'controlled decentralisation' (Hadden, 1980) in order to ensure the dominance of regime objectives in education.

1. The Yan'an Years: Schools in the Wilderness

When the Communists first arrived in Yan'an, they tried to provide basic education through a centralised bureaucracy. Schools were consolidated; multi-subject curricula were imposed; uniform texts and requirements were formulated; teaching and administration were professionalised (Seybolt, 1971, 1973). It did not take the Party long to discover that standardisation created an over-reliance on bureaucracy and an education that was often irrelevant to the needs of the populace. In 1943 the Border Region government hailed the creation of mass-based schools and urged that 'we must take the majority or perhaps all of the primary schools and turn them over to the local masses to run by themselves' (*Chinese Education*, 1972, pp.269–70).

Minban xuexiao in Yan'an stressed self-reliance in funding and curriculum design and were structured to encourage popular initiative and participation in educational, social, and political development (see Table 15.1). Most teachers were not trained professionals; often labourers with practical skills and revolutionary heroes were invited to share their knowledge and exploits with pupils. These teachers were part of the Yan'an effort to make a conscious link between education and production, to connect schooling with life in the broader society. Learning materials—including political tracts and planting brochures—were relevant to the rural experience of the peasants. The schools performed a triple function by promoting economic development, literacy, and support for the CCP.

The administrative leadership of the schools was provided by local Party cadres, labour heroes, and village leaders. The CCP felt that this type of community control could better establish appropriate curricula and administration than could bureaucrats or education experts who were far removed from the lives of the peasants (ShenGanNing Bianchu Zhengfu Bangongting, 1944a, 1944b). Responsibility for staffing, financing, and defining courses of study shifted from the central education bureau in Yan'an to the local leaders. Although subsidised by local government revenues, the main burden of financing was shouldered by the villagers. Not surprisingly, the number of books, desks, chairs, pens, paper, and other items of equipment was quite sparse—villages were poverty-stricken, and most government resources were being used to fight the war.

The mix of government and popular contributions to the schools varied according to the wealth of the particular village and local government, but in all schools, CCP cadres and government leaders set educational goals,

TABLE 15.1. *National and Provincial Growth of* Minban Xuexiao, *China, 1957–8*

Date	Location	No. of schools	No. of pupils
National:			
9/57	National 1	50,000	3,380,000
2/58	National 2	75,600	4,990,000
Provincial:			
2/58	Guizhou 3	. . .	500,000
3/58	Fujian 4	2,000	. . .
3/58	Shaanxi 5	3,487	276,000
4/58	Heilongjiang 6	. . .	1,800,000
5/58	Jiangxi 7	19,000	. . .
6/58	Henan 8	37,438	2,300,979
6/58	Anhui 9	28,000	1,100,000
9/58	Shaanxi 5	39,568	1,046,000
10/58	Shandong 10	60,521	. . .

Sources: *Jiaoshi bao*, 10 September 1957; incomplete returns from 15 provinces and municipalities, *Renmin ribao*, 10 February 1958; *NCNA*, 15 February 1958 in *SCMP* no.1716, 21 February 1958; *NCNA*, 6 March 1958 in *SCMP* no.1729, 12 March 1958; *Shaanxi ribao*, 16 September 1958; *NCNA*, 27 April 1958 in *SCMP*, no.1762, 1 May 1958; *NCNA*, 30 June 1958 in *SCMP* no.1778, 23 May 1958; *Guangming ribao*, 8 June 1958; *NCNA*, 30 June 1958 in *SCMP* no.1806, 8 July 1958; and *Dazhong ribao*, 1 October 1958.

oversaw administration, guided teaching, and chose local leaders. The Party and the Border Region government made it clear that although voluntarism and 'people-manage, public-help' were the themes of the day, neither were the same as laissez-faire (Lindsay, 1950a). *Minban xuexiao* epitomised the mass line (*Qunzhong luxian*) in that they were to be started from the ideas and requests of the masses but directed by the Party (*Chinese Education*, 1972, pp.269–70).

One important element of Party direction was its anti-bureaucratic strain. The establishment of *minban* schools, coterminous with the 1942–4 Rectification Campaign, was part of the more general effort to find alternatives to costly and remote bureaucracies as the medium for providing governmental and social services (Lindsay, 1950b; Selden, 1971). As such, *minban xuexiao* became associated with the ascendency of politics over expertise and decentralisation over centralisation. This early association was to be remembered as *minban* schools became the site for conflicts in the 1950s and 1960s. In the 1940s, however, there was little opposition to *minban* schools. Establishing them obviated the need for taxation for education by the central government, and since taxation had been the bane of the peasants' existence, it made sense for the bureaucracy and Party to circumvent such methods of funding wherever possible. Second, all cadres were undergoing rectification so that the administrative machinery was not as autonomous from the Party as it was to become 10 years later and did not have the power (or perhaps the inclination) to oppose the people's management effort. Third, the resistance against Japan, the struggle with the Guomindang, and the overwhelming emphasis on mass politics during the Yan'an period made *minban* schools more acceptable as a development policy than they were to be in 1960 or 1980. In a very real way, power and authority were expanding for the CCP in the 1940s; there was no fear of decentralisation because it did not mean, in this revolutionary context, either loss of authority or conflict.

2. The People's Republic: Two Tracks, Two Legs, and Shifting Control

By 1949 the growth of *minban xuexiao* had lost steam. The consolidation of the new government presented additional problems to the CCP leadership. The enormous number of urban schools to be put under Party and government control and an additional group of schools that had been closed due to wartime conditions needed aid in reopening. Although this situation would have seemed appropriate for popular participation and assistance, insecurity about the level of support for the regime led political leaders to opt for more control over educational work.

Minban schools declined in number in this early period as villages in suburban areas benefited from the establishment or reopening of more 'normal' schools. But the reduction was also attributable to administrative centralisation and to experts' belief that the quality of schooling provided in *minban xuexiao* was abysmally low. In 1952 the Ministry of Education stipulated that people-run schools could be accredited only after three years of operation, during which time they had to fulfil the same guidelines and requirements as public schools. This ruling made it nearly impossible for *minban* schools to operate, since they had neither the funding nor the staff to adhere to the same standards as state-supported schools. Since *minban* schools could not get accreditation, families were loath to send their children to the schools, which meant that many children received no education because state-supported institutions were too expensive or too far from home. The centralisation exacerbated the existing educational inequality between rural and urban areas and highlighted the conflict between local and central interests and between those who argued for politicised mass education and those who favoured scientific, selective education.

Yet, while conventionally run schools increased in number and quality, the leadership relied on *minban xuexiao* as the only affordable means of literacy and basic education in the hinterlands. In addition, *minban* schools had won favour in a powerful corner of the Chinese élite. Mao Zedong's concern with the split between mental and manual workers, centre and locality, and leaders and masses led him to support people-run schools with increasing fervour. At the same time, the central education administration reversed its position on people-managed schools.

Reports in the winter of 1956 noted that schools were beset by great states of confusion and that there were too few primary and middle schools, especially in the countryside (*Shaanxi remin jiaoyu*, 9 December 1956; *Guangming ribao*, 20 November 1956; Zhai, 1957, pp.2–3). But according to the minister of education, Zhang Xiro, the state had funded education disproportionately when compared with other expenditures and could not spend more money on schools to appease peasants. The solution was to encourage the masses to operate their own schools (*Renmin ribao*, 22 March 1957; *Renmin jiaoyu*, January 1947, pp.4–7), and a special directive, issued in spring 1957, urged innovation in this effort (*Zhanghua renmin gonghe-guo*, 1958, pp.316–17). The primary rationale for the establishment of *minban xuexiao* was different for Maoists than for administrators. The Party, led by Mao, appears to have seen *minban* schools as a way to bypass bureaucratic and centralised expertise, but the educational administrators were concerned only with finances. There was no talk of bureaucratism, of who would run the schools or set policy. Furthermore, apparently there was very little guidance or assistance forthcoming from the central education ministry to villages and co-operatives that wanted to establish such schools. The 1957 directive superficially promoted *minban* education, but the result was that the central ministry absolved itself of all responsibility (*Guangming ribao*, 28 May 1957; *Jaioshi bao*, 24 May 1957; *Jaioshi bao*, 4 June 1957).

In the face of the central bureaucracy's inactivity with regard to *minban xuexiao*, the power of local and provincial education bureaus was enhanced, as was that of CCP cadres. Party cadres were appointed as principals of local schools, and CCP members were given a strong voice in decisions about school tuition, texts, and rules. Provincial education bureaus assumed what had formerly been the responsibility of the central ministry in setting broad guidelines. The emphasis was on relevance to local conditions and on avoiding bureaucratism while encouraging parents and cooperatives to share costs (e.g. *Xiaoxue jaioyu tongxun*, 20 June 1957).

By the end of 1957, supporters of the *minban* school system claimed that it had resulted in 100 per cent increases in the number of schools and pupils over the previous year (*Jiaoshi bao*, 10 September 1957; *New China News Agency* [*NCNA*], 27 August 1958; *Survey of China Mainland Press* [*SCMP*], no.1847, 5 September 1958). With formal approval of decentralisation, and thus growing Party and local control, an even greater increase in the number of *minban* schools occurred during the years of the Great Leap Forward (Kwong, 1979, pp.443–55). Over 330,000 primary schools were established in the first half of 1958, with a 21 per cent increase in enrolment. Most of this was attributed to the *minban* system (*NCNA*, 27 August 1958; *SCMP* no.1847, 5 September 1958). Yet the greater numbers did not mean greater levels of popular control. Rather, in the name of 'politics in command', Party leadership was strengthened over communities and over the schools that communities ran. Decentralisation signified a decrease in assistance from the central bureaucracy, a lessening of orders and control from Beijing, an increased emphasis on politicised primary education, and a greater reliance on popular financial support for education.

Indeed, what peasants lacked in administrative control they made up for in the provision of supplies, funds, and 'advice'. Parents contributed equipment and furniture; they refurbished still more warehouses, temples, and clubhouses for use as school buildings; they were consulted on curriculum and gave lectures; they contributed money to pay for books and teachers; and if families were considered wealthy, parents even paid tuition (Robinson, 1986, p.79).

The combination of decentralisation to local Party leadership and self-reliance in funding was designed to ensure that education was both politically correct and inexpensive for the state. *Minban* schools were the second leg of the policy of 'walking on two legs' in education. They were established to provide diversity and popularisation in an educational system characterised by standardisation and selectivity. But the two legs ended up running on two different tracks. So-called 'people's management' provided legitimacy for the move to decentralise as it did for the call for relevant—rather than expert—education. In the process, promotion of *minban xuexiao* exacerbated the inequalities between urban and rural areas and between experts and non-experts. These were exactly those inequalities that

Mao Zedong had thought structures like *minban* schools would improve (Zedong, 1956).

Conflicts were also engendered because other groups had different objectives for the schools. Peasants wanted to enhance the status of their children through the acquisition of diplomas, so they questioned the low status of a *minban* education. Central education officials and educational experts joined peasants in finding fault with the quality of education offered in mass-run schools. Although relatively quiet in 1957 and 1958 (during the height of the Great Leap Forward), as recentralisation progressed over the next few years, officials from the central education ministry used their new strength to attack *minban xuexiao* with full force.

3. Post-Leap Schools: The Return to Two Tracks

In 1959 the new minister of education, Yang Xiufeng, deplored *minban* schools as being far below acceptable levels and urged the development of 'key' schools to ensure quality education. Not coincidentally, this policy removed control over education from Party and local officials to the coterie of experts in the centre and provincial capitals. A general report issued by the central Ministry of Propaganda in 1962 alleged that the 'pace of growth [of *minban* schools] was too fast and too much power was delegated to the lower echelons; there was too much labour and too few classes; chaos prevailed and it greatly hurt the schools' (*Jiaoyu geming*, 6 May 1967; see also *NCNA*, 28 April 1959; *Current Background*, no. 577, 14 May 1959; and *Renmin ribao*, 14 April 1961). Local control of *minban* schools was seen as sacrificing long-term educational development to the petty desires of the masses (*Renmin ribao*, 31 October 1960). The critical point was not only the low quality of *minban* education but also the question of where authority should rest. From the perspective of officials in Beijing, control should belong to the experts. The equation of decentralisation with mass control but low quality became an institutionalised fixture of the educational expert mentality.

The central bureaucracies pre-empted decentralisation and any form of mass (or official Party) participation in education by averring that quality education could be ensured only with direct leadership and control by the experts in the ministry. Yet the two-leg, two-track system did not come to an end in 1962. *Minban* schools just became the even poorer stepchild of the educational family (Xiao and Yang, 1960). Control of the schools was no longer in the hands of local Party cadres, although funds for schooling still came from the villages. Yet centralised management of *minban* schools did not mean that the local schools would be improved. Rather, as emphasis was placed on professional teaching and the development of key schools and individual achievement through book learning, the *minban* schools were judged inadequate.

Between 1961 and 1963—a period of severe economic depression—the lack of local funds and the condemnation by experts that *minban* schools were 'irregular' led to the closure of many schools. Yet, as in the 1950s, some survived the experts' assault. Schools came under the 'centralised and unified' leadership at higher levels; school districts, under the authority of the central education ministry, supervised all policy affecting the schools (*Guangming ribao*, 6 February 1962; 6 December 1964).

Centralisation was clearly the leitmotiv of education policy. Quality was thought to be enhanced not by Party control but rather by control emanating from the ministry. Indeed, the role of the Party as an agency of decentralisation associated Party cadres with policies in opposition to quality control. By 1963 key schools were well entrenched, and proponents of *minban xuexiao* had no convincing arguments to counter the claim that people-run schools offered very little.

4. The Cultural Revolution: One Track, Committee Control

The Cultural Revolution saw the decentralisation of schools once again, the expansion of *minban xuexiao* run by poor and lower-middle peasants associations, the promotion of politico-ideological education, and the development of labour-oriented schooling. These characteristics reflected a decrease in the authority of the central bureaucracy and a return to Maoist and populist influences over education. Part of the loss of central power was due to direct attacks on the bureaucracy from radical contingents within the leadership and the population. It was also, however, connected with the relegitimation of people-managed education. *Minban* schools symbolised the radical critique of standardised education and represented a massive attack on the way in which 'walking on two legs' had been structured for Chinese education. A two-track system might be necessary, given China's stage of development, but that did not mean, according to the Maoist radicals, that the two legs should diverge along totally different paths.

In 1962 Mao's criticism of inflexibility in the administration of education meant that between 1963 and 1965, *minban* schools grew again, stimulated by the Socialist Education Movement. However, as usual, the schools were subject to easy destruction when bureaucratic interests reasserted themselves in the tumultuous period before the Cultural Revolution. In fact, it was not until the later period of the Cultural Revolution that *minban xuexiao* gained some (short-term) measure of security.

The propaganda of the Cultural Revolution of 1967 and 1968 launched an assault on key schools as 'little treasure pagodas' (*xiao baota*) that created a two-track system, imputed inferiority to students and teachers in people-managed schools, encouraged self-interest, and fostered antagonism to hard work among the people (*Remin ribao*, 17 December 1967). The new *minban* schools, in contrast, embodied many of the same principles as the schools of the Great Leap and Yan'an. Peasants with political consciousness and practical experience in production became teachers; the policies of enrolling students in any season and utilising flexible timetables allowed children to help parents and communes in production or political work; and local units were responsible for site selection, teaching staff, and administration (*Hongqi*, November 1968, pp.46–52; *Renmin ribao*, 24 October 1968; *Renmin ribao*, 28 October 1968; *Renmin ribao*, 14 January 1969; and *Guangming ribao*, 1 January 1969). The schools generally followed the principle of creating three-in-one committees for the management of (what was now termed) revolutionary education. Party secretaries of production brigades or counties, appointed by local revolutionary committees as principals, were joined by poor and lower-middle peasants and revolutionary students and teachers on the management committees. Later, People's Liberation Army (PLA) representatives also served on some school committees. Rather than expert authorities, it was the committees that had the 'last say in all matters, such as choosing the teachers, the arrangement of the curriculum, the building of the school premises, and the allocation of graduates' (*Remin ribao*, 4 November 1968; see also 24 October 1968 and 15 November 1968). This reincarnated decentralisation operated on the theoretical principle that quality could be ensured by popular participation. The participation did not include the setting of policy (by other than revolutionary committee members), but it did involve peasants in the adjustment of policy to local conditions.

Decentralisation increased the authority of the masses *vis-à-vis* professional teachers, principals, and education experts (Shirk, 1979). *Minban xuexiao* in particular presented new opportunities for the non-professional. Combined with the responsibilities for funding and equipping the schools, working with committees enhanced the peasants' role in educational decision making and gave them a greater stake in the policy process. The comparatively greater authority that the peasants had over teachers and educational professionals during this period would lead them in the 1980s to conflict with the central authorities over the role of teachers in local policy-making.

5. The Post-Mao Era: Two Tracks, Uneven Legs, Central Control

By the time Mao Zedong died, recentralisation of education had become the order of the day. Quality control, selectivity, and professional management of the school system have been accompanied by frequent attacks on people-run schools. As in the early 1960s, the key words in the criticisms are low quality. The grudging acceptance of the schools is based on lack of financial resources to provide better alternatives. Whereas the argument for *minban xuexiao* during the periods of the Great Leap Forward and the

Cultural Revolution had been that they were vehicles for popular participation, relevant education, and nonbureaucratised administration, their *raison d'être* by 1980 was their cheapness.

The attack on the Cultural Revolution that helped to establish the legitimacy of the post-Mao leadership pointed (among other things) to the destruction caused by decentralisation and popular participation in rural primary schools. It was accepted that slogans such as 'poor and lower middle peasants, not intellectuals, must run the schools' failed to ensure the development of pupils (Foreign Broadcast Information Service, 16 December 1980). Furthermore, *minban* schools were disorganised, staffed by untrained teachers, and prone to too much independence from central objectives. Yet even these harsh criticisms allowed a place for *minban xuexiao* in the new educational order. The development of education was seen as crucial for the country's socialist modernisation, and investment in capital construction was to be diverted to education. Noting that even with this radical step the state would not have enough money to universalise primary education, the state proposed that 'Communes, production brigades, factories, mines, enterprises, all industries and all professions [should] run schools. Private individuals should also be allowed and encouraged to run schools as a supplement to schools run by the state and collectives' (*Renmin ribao*, December 1980). Educational policy called for continuing to walk on two legs. While the central ministry and provincial bureaus were developing texts, curricula, teacher training institutes, and well-equipped key schools, the masses were told to raise their own funds to run schools in their local villages. 'Decentralisation' was invoked. Provincial education bureaus sent the word down that operation of schools by production brigades was not an 'unreasonable responsibility' (*Yunnan ribao*, 16 June 1981).

To the present, the reliance on localities for funding continues unabated. In most of the provinces, local units—from villages to prefectures, from households to brigades—have contributed the money to keep the schools alive (Robinson, 1986, p.83). In Shandong, where almost Y500 million was invested in school buildings between 1979 and 1983, 75 per cent of the financing came from brigades and peasant households (*Renmin ribao*, 27 August 1983). Party leaders in Hunan have approved an additional levy of 25 per cent on agricultural taxes for use by education departments for rural schools (Hunnan Provincial Service, 25 September 1983). In all cases, the Party and the state have lauded the 'voluntary' contributions of the masses while noting that neither the authorities nor the peasants 'should regard taking money from the peasants to run education as an increase of the burden on them' (Henan Provincial Service, 8 August 1983, in Joint Publications Research Service [*JPRS*], no.84332, 15 September 1983).

These proposals have created some conflict at the local level. In an era when responsibility has meant a greater measure of autonomy in economic practices, peasants may have assumed that the same held true in education.

However, as in earlier periods, paying for schools does not necessarily mean managing or controlling them. The struggle between the peasants' view of local control and the central education authorities' is most clearly seen in disagreements over the role and treatment of teachers and in the attendance and behaviour of students.

The teacher issue is complex. Traditionally, Chinese culture has revered teachers and intellectuals. But intermittently throughout the history of the PRC, teachers have suffered dreadfully for their élite status and educational attainments. Official attitudes toward well-trained professional teachers have varied, and so, of course, have official attitudes toward *minban xuexiao* teachers. When 'redness' and 'decentralisation' were paramount, teachers in people-run schools were valued in the same way as barefoot doctors; they represented the community integration of red and expert and 'serving the people'. However, since the push toward the Four Modernisations barefoot doctors and *minban* teachers have suffered a loss in prestige. Peasants are of two minds: they look down on teachers in people-run schools as uneducated, unqualified, and drain on village or brigade resources. At the same time, there is an awareness that these teachers are the only game in town.

The conflicts between *minban* teachers and villages are used to rationalise both increasing governmental involvement at the local level and greater control by experts. For instance, *minban* teachers have been physically beaten by villagers for failing to produce students who pass the exams for entrance into higher schools. School property, originally contributed by peasants, has been looted by local villagers (*Guangming ribao*, 24 July 1982; Hebei Provincial Services, 23 November 1982 in *JPRS* no.82615, 11 January 1983; *Renmin jiaoyu*, July 1981; *Sichuan ribao*, 5 January 1983). Most widespread, however, is the attitude that if peasants have to pay the salaries of the teachers, the teachers must work. And work means labour in the fields. Brigades and villages have been withholding wages from teachers until they perform assigned field work. In some localities, teachers are forced to accept contracts for responsibility plots; in other areas, teachers want the contracts, for then they too can earn more money. In a smaller number of cases, teachers have been forced to adopt the contract system for their work in schools and to guarantee that pupils will pass exams or be accepted into state-run middle schools (Liaoning Provincial Service, 27 November 1982 in *JPRS*, no.85248, 27 December 1982).

Related to this is the negative attitude expressed by peasants toward these village 'intellectuals'. In a time when the CCP is striving to upgrade the status of teachers and intellectuals by raising their salaries, by inducting them into the Party, and by giving them special concessions, peasants' abuse and humiliation of teachers is unacceptable. Yet, when the central administration asks villages to pay local teachers higher salaries, peasants refuse by saying, 'Old barefoots, why should they be superior to us?' (*Renmin jiaoyu*, July 1981, p.52).

In the face of all this, central and provincial education officials have re-established their authority over people-run schools. Focusing on quality, cost, and control, the administrative experts have approached the new round of *minban xuexiao* in ways that exhibit only the narrowest level of decentralisation. Selection and evaluation of teachers is now a function of the provincial bureaus. The new standards of teaching quality give exceptional power to provincial officials; it is they who decide who will teach the peasant children and what they will be taught.

The standardisation extends beyond staffing to such issues as salaries and benefits. In the effort to protect and secure the interests of teachers, central authorities have opposed village leaders and established national compensation levels for *minban* teachers. In some provinces, distribution of salaries has also been centralised. Furthermore, throughout the country, the state issues subsidy payments for teachers in people-run schools. This change in monetary control has two important repercussions. First, it changes the relationship between *minban* school teachers and local residents. Although teachers in people-run schools may now be better qualified, they no longer have the connection to local authorities that they had when villagers decided on wage scales and staffing. In this situation, teachers have less stake in the school or the community. Second, the new system removes all authority from the local level. Villages and brigades dispense funds and equipment, but they no longer have any way to control their schools. Their reaction is seen in the increase in violence and antipathy directed toward *minban* school teachers. In essence, peasants have traded some local control for a minimum increase in quality.

Student attendance and behaviour in the people-run schools have also been a source of conflict. Structured to enable pupils to learn as well as to help with their family's agricultural work, earlier versions of *minban* schools fit in well with the labour needs of Chinese agriculture. As people-run schools have been centralised, flexible schedules have been lost; new guidelines call for 'making sure students study, avoiding drifting and not letting anyone suspend classes or make disorder out of school plans' (*Renmin jaioyu*, July 1981, p.52). Less leeway is given to individual schools in order to have more disciplined educational administration. Yet in spite of these new rules, some families keep their children home occasionally to help fulfil household agricultural contracts (*China Daily*, 4 August 1983). And villages take out their frustrations about local education on the school teachers. Indeed, it is the teachers who are the most obvious losers here. They face dismissal from the authorities because of poor training or lack of skills, and they face beatings and no salaries from their village neighbours.

The thrust of the new policies is to use educational expertise to universalise primary education. Indeed, in May 1985 the Central Committee of the CCP introduced new reforms, including a nine-year compulsory system. Junior middle school is to be universal in the countryside within ten years.

The history of people-run schools has convinced education experts that the only way to ensure continuous quality education in the village is to centralise the administration of the schools as much as possible, to standardise its operations, and to professionalise its ranks. This is how success has been achieved in the 'normal' schools. This is also how control can be wrested from local authorities—on the basis of greater efficiency and success. In the villages, this approach has come into conflict with the peasants' own sense of what local education should offer.

Conclusion

The protagonists in the drama of *minban xuexiao* have changed over time. In the 1950s and 1960s the conflict was fought among Party and state leaders, with the CCP promoting greater levels of decentralisation. Since the beginning of the 1980s the most significant conflict has been local interests versus central authorities. This reflects the varying interests and objectives that bear on local education. Central authorities from both the Party and the state are concerned with broad issues of modernisation and see specialisation and standardisation as the ultimate objective for public education. In the short run, educational administrators attempt to ensure basic and inexpensive education in the countryside. Local officials, in contrast, are concerned with maintaining their authority at the basic level; the short-run aims of central administrators have put local administrators in a position of having to promote sometimes unpopular policies because parents in the countryside question the value and the expense of a *minban* school education. Bearing the cost of a substandard education makes no sense to these peasants, especially in a period when to 'get rich' is the dominant political slogan.

The conflicts are finally over the question of control. Peasants in rural China have found that decentralised education does not necessarily mean better, more participatory, or even cheaper education. Education officials have learned that decentralisation may encourage conflict rather than providing a means for integrating different interests in society (Grindle, 1980). The end result in this case is a great vulnerability in local education and a growing dissatisfaction with decentralisation as a panacea for educational development problems.

This trend in China is matched by recent analyses of education, decentralisation, and development by Western scholars. Often decentralisation and local participation have served as pretexts for the extraction of additional resources from the population without providing any significant increase in local control over education (see Weiler, 1982), nor necessarily more effective education (Bock, 1982; Rothenberg, 1980). Policies with regard to *minban xuexiao* do suggest several additional, if still tentative, conclusions about the relation between education and decentralisation.

First, as the competence and expertise of administrators in developing societies increase, greater centralisation will be the trend. We saw that criticism of people-managed schools grew as the Ministry of Education and provincial bureau incumbents gained experience and skill. Over its history, more and more of the decisions relating to *minban xuexiao* have been transferred from the local level to education offices at provincial and higher levels. It is not only the increasing competence of experts that is crucial but also the growing gap in knowledge between experts and the general population. Especially in terms of education, peasants who at best have only basic literacy skills cannot compete with highly trained officials. Whereas decisions about hiring teachers, choosing texts, and writing examinations were once made at the local level, these functions are now performed at provincial or central levels. This is because experts are concentrated at more central levels *and* because expertise is valued in its own right.

By mid-1985, the PRC had proceeded in this centralisation effort. A new State Education Commission was established to eliminate the chaos in China's educational system (*Renmin ribao*, 9 June 1985). Indications are that investment in education will also increase, but the emphasis will be on key schools, especially at the university level (*Renmin ribao*, 4 July 1985). There have been critiques of the differentiation between key schools and mass-based schools, and in June 1986 Shanghai abolished its key junior schools (*China Daily*, 18 June 1986). However the status of rural *minban xuexiao* does not seem to have been altered; reports indicate that no significant changes in investment or control are forthcoming (*Beijing Review*, 30 December 1985, p.23).

Second, the more narrow the functional decentralisation, the more likely it is that the local authorities will be allowed control. For instance, in the contemporary period, local communities raise funds for school buildings and major portions of teachers' salaries. They are constrained from setting salaries as well as deciding what goes on inside the school building. When more extensive decentralisation is allowed, such as on curriculum issues and staffing, the appearance of local authority obscures strong links to central and expert élites. In these instances, Party cadres are placed in leadership positions, as during the Great Leap Forward and the Cultural Revolution.

Third, the case study suggests that local self-governing institutions will not be encouraged unless there is strong central control over local interests. Even during the periods when people-managed schools were promoted as participatory organisations, they were guided by Party cadres, and Party cadres remained subject to the democratic centralism of the organisation. In other words, there has never been, not even in the halcyon days of Yan'an, a time when *minban* meant autonomous people's control.

Finally, the history of *minban xuexiao* should remind us to distinguish between decentralisation and local autonomy. In single-party states, where fear of loss of authority is an ever-present characteristic, decentralisation qua local autonomy can represent a major challenge to the élite. In fact, this probably was the intention of Maoist support for *minban xuexiao* in the fifties and sixties. Decentralisation during both the Great Leap Forward and the Cultural Revolution was intended to unleash revolutionary fervour and initiative from below in order to attack the privileges and bureaucratism of the élites in society. Mao's expectation was that the division of policy-making and policy implementation between central and local authorities would enhance mass involvement at the local level and make policy more relevant to local conditions. Yet to decentralise control from the Ministry of Education to villages, communes, or revolutionary committees was to transfer control to the élite of that local authority but, at the same time, to exacerbate tensions between the populace, local authorities, and central policy-makers. Thus, despite even the most radical intentions, decentralisation remains subject to élite control and is far removed from local autonomy. What we see here is the continuation of a world in which authority is seen as finite, a world in which peasants, local authorities, and experts remain in conflict.

CHAPTER 16

Community Participation in the Financing of Education in Guyana

UNA M. PAUL, EVELYN M. HAMILTON AND
RANDOLPH A. WILLIAMS

In 1976 the Government of Guyana assumed full responsibility for and control of education, which became free from the nursery to university levels. Community financing has remained important, however, and is encouraged by the Ministry of Education.

This chapter begins by outlining the main community bodies involved in school financing. It then discusses in turn the main types of community contribution, and mechanisms for central support and control.

1. Nature of the Community

Seven main types of community have been or still are involved in educational financing in Guyana. They are:

1. *Religious Bodies.* These were at one time the most vibrant group. In 1966, the year that Guyana became independent, 51 per cent of primary schools were denominational ones. Originally, the main aim of religious groups was to win converts. The work of the churches gradually expanded and improved until some of the best educational institutions were run by them. However, since the 1976 nationalisation of schools, inputs from religious bodies have declined.

2. *Local Government Bodies.* District and village councils have power to establish, equip and manage schools, and to make financial grants to individuals and institutions. District and village councils are elected by their communities, and are directly responsible to them. Local government bodies are generally willing to support initiatives taken by members of the community in the education sector.

3. *Parent–Teacher Associations.* These consist of the parents or guardians of students, plus the teaching staffs of particular schools. Some PTAs include other interested persons in the community. For example, honorary membership can be granted to people who are neither parents nor guardians but who have given valuable service.

4. *Parent Action Committees*. These chiefly exist at the nursery school level, and result from a recent Ministry of Education initiative. The intention is to stimulate parental involvement by providing an avenue whereby parents can contribute to construction and running of nursery schools.

5. *Old Students' Associations*. These are most active among the secondary schools. Although all former students are free to join these associations, not all are actively involved.

6. *Adoption Agencies*. These are government agencies and public corporations which have agreed to sponsor a school. For example, if a school is sponsoring a dance, advertising may be arranged or paid for by the adoption agency. In areas where the community is dominated by one large company, aid may be provided on a large scale. For instance, in the major bauxite-producing area (Region 10), schools have benefited from grants by the two major companies which prior to 1970 were owned by multinational corporations and which have since been nationalised. The corporations even top up teachers' salaries in order to attract staff to the mining community.

7. *Friends of Schools*. These organisations consist of interested members of the community who have a philanthropic desire to aid educational development. They are usually informal bodies from which interested people come forward when the need arises. For example, a school may make a direct appeal for help to obtain some piece of equipment.

2. Types of Community Contribution

Financial contributions are the most obvious form of community contribution. They may be solicited from members of the community, business associations or even the nation as a whole. Alternatively they are raised through fairs, bring-and-buy sales, craft sales or bingos. When interest in building a school is spread over a wide area, the extent of fund-raising may be considerable. For example, financial contributions to the President College, built for students throughout the country, have so far totalled more than G$4 million.

Supply of materials is another aspect of community financing. Members of the community, such as businessmen who sell construction materials, may donate wood, nails, paint, electrical fittings, etc. These donations are often in lieu of a direct financial contribution. President College has benefited from donations of materials worth over G$600,000.

In rural communities, contributions of labour are more prominent, for few people have incomes high enough to permit direct financial contributions. For example, in Bush Lot and Winifred Gaskin secondary schools, contributions of labour defrayed around one third of the total building cost. Self-help labour has also helped construct rural schools under a project financed by the Netherlands Government. The aid donors have looked more favourably on requests for assistance from communities which have demonstrated willingness to make some contribution. Some of the schools built between 1979 and 1985 with the help of labour from the community are: Kato, Waipa, Morawhanna, Kamarang, Mahdia, Moco-Moco and Aishalton nursery schools; and Great Troolie Islands, Hotaquai, Surama, Great Falls, Silver Hill, Ketley, Lima Sands, Kabacaburi, Wallaba and Chinaweing primary schools.

In addition, many communities provide help with maintenance and general running of schools. During 1982–3, the Ministry of Education surveyed the scope of this type of activity. Replies from 37 per cent of the schools suggested that the most common activities were fencing compounds, repairing toilets, constructing and repairing furniture, maintaining buildings, providing custodial and security services, and constructing playing fields.

Finally, some communities make important donations of land. For instance, since 1970 eight schools have been built on donated land totalling over 20 acres.

3. Central Support and Control

Through head teachers, community organisations can draw on resources and skills at the Ministry of Education. Most often, assistance is given in the technical sphere. The Ministry of Education does everything in its power to encourage community organisations in order to deepen the links between schools and communities. Sometimes, the plan to build or upgrade facilities emerges from surveys undertaken by the Ministry.

Where formal structures exist, community organisations are governed by a constitution which must be approved by the Ministry of Education. Often this approval is given in an *ad hoc* manner because of the involvement of education officers, school welfare officers and head teachers in the formation of these organisations.

Although committees may identify the need for education facilities in the development of their areas, projects must have the approval of the Ministry of Education. The authorities ensure that building plans conform to the regulations governing space norms, general organisation of schools, zoning, etc. Once the Ministry approves a request, community groups make their contributions within the guidelines laid down for accountability in school finance. Projects are supervised by the Ministry and by approved technical consultants.

Sometimes, parents raise part of the required funds and are then given permission to negotiate with local and international charitable organisations. For example, USAID has contributed funds to Parika Salem Community High School and to Seeburg Secondary School.

Schools are not obliged to obtain approval from the Ministry for purchase of equipment. However, regulations require donations to be reflected in the schools' inventories and checked by the Ministry's audit section. Many schools are reluctant to submit annual returns because they fear that their funds will have to be placed in the national treasury. The Ministry is making strenuous efforts to assure schools and communities that this will not happen, and that the requirement of reports is simply to assist monitoring and to ensure that schools have proper accounting procedures.

Conclusions

In 1976 the government made itself responsible for fee-free provision of education at all levels. Since that time, community financing has been less prominent than it used to be. However, various types of community have continued to provide funds for their schools, and in recent years the government has strongly welcomed this type of contribution.

Because statistics are not collected centrally, it is hard to assess the overall contribution of community financing. In several schools, however, community sources have provided about one-third of construction costs. Recently, the Ministry of Education has devised mechanisms to help school administrators assess self-financing activities that involve non-monetary contributions, and in conjunction with the Ministry of Finance has run short courses in accounting. These activities reflect the desire of the government for community financing mechanisms to be strengthened.

PART III

Policy Implications

CHAPTER 17

Policy Implications and Conclusions

MARK BRAY

The policy implications of this study should be assessed from the separate viewpoints of governments and non-government organisations. This chapter devotes more space to the former than to the latter, because governments set the framework within which other bodies operate, and the types of readers likely to be most interested in this book will also be most keen to discern the policy implications at this level. Nevertheless, the views of non-government bodies should not be neglected.

1. Implications for Governments

The many examples given in this book show that in some countries communities can and do provide a lot of resources. However, the extent and forms of community financing vary widely, and some aspects of community financing may have negative consequences. In turn, this means that government policies must vary widely. What may be possible and appropriate in one context may be impossible and inappropriate in another.

Accordingly, this part begins by summarising some of the reasons why some governments strongly favour community financing but others oppose it. It then discusses ways in which governments which do favour community financing can encourage it. The third section turns to controls, indicating both those that may be needed and obstacles to their implementation. One obstacle noted is the nature of many bureaucracies, and this leads to discussion in the fourth section on centralisation versus decentralisation. The final section comments on specific features of the Kenyan experience, to throw further light on the extent to which other governments may either be able or want to emulate it.

(a) Should Community Financing be Encouraged?

In most countries, the strongest argument in favour of community financing is a financial one. Governments find themselves hard pressed, and welcome community support as a way to spread financial burdens. In some cases, this book has pointed out, support is extensive. Lillis and Ayot's chapter reports that unaided secondary schools in Kenya comprised 56.0 per cent of the total in 1983. Robinson indicates that in parts of China communities have provided well over half the primary schools and teachers (see also Wu, 1984). In Nepal 60 per cent of the labour for school construction is said to be provided free of charge by communities (Yannakopulos, 1980, p.125), and data from Burma indicate that communities have been responsible for 73.7 per cent of schools' non-salary costs (Kyi, 1977, p.48).

An added attraction to many governments is that community initiatives are often able to mobilise resources which are far beyond the reach of the government tax collector. In the Kenyan context, for example, Mbithi and Rasmusson (1977, p.16) comment:

> It is a common feature in Harambee meetings to see women and men contributing their personal property such as beads and ear-rings, eggs, foods and artifacts. . . . It is usual for people to work, dance and work day in and day out, hungry, cold, thirsty and un-complaining on a project they are strongly committed to. When this is compared with participation in pre-independence forced labour or to development efforts initiated by local governments before 1965, . . . the performance of Harambee is outstanding.

In addition, the authors point out (p.164), self-help contributions may divert resources from consumption to investment. Harambee attracts resources from the prosperous as well as the lower tiers of society, and helps channel wealth from conspicuous consumption, often of imported goods, to rural development. Although Kenya's official taxation system has recently become more progressive, its capacity to tap the incomes of the rich is much lower than, for example, that of Tanzania, Sweden or the United Kingdom. Harambee therefore acts as an unofficial taxation system which helps achieve some of the same objectives as the official one.

Some educationists also feel that local support helps make communities more interested in education, and that participation and self-reliance are themselves aspects of development. They point to the widespread failures of centralised planning, and consider that bottom-up approaches are more likely to be successful (e.g. Unesco, 1984a, pp.5–6).

However, during the present century the balance of school sponsorship in most systems has changed, and governments have come to view provision of education as their responsibility. Whereas in the last century the majority of Third World schools were run by religious bodies, this is no longer the case. When community financing constitutes a large proportion of education budgets, therefore, governments may feel embarrassed that they are failing to meet their own responsibilities.

Problems may also arise over the quality of provision in self-help schools. For example, Kenya's harambee secondary schools have been described as abysmal in quality (Wellings, 1983, p.24), and the unaided sectors in other countries often have equally poor reputations. Moreover, even good quality can cause problems, for the government may feel embarrassed at the poor performance of its own schools.

In addition, whether they perform poorly or well, unaided schools are likely to be instruments for social stratification. If unaided schools are qualitatively superior to government ones, they may foster the development of an élite; but if they are inferior they perpetuate inequalities and make the government schools appear élitist. Chapter 7 highlighted the ways in which self-help schemes can also enlarge geographic inequalities.

In addition, many self-help schemes are badly planned and wasteful. Table 17.1 shows that in Kenya the number of abandoned projects has sometimes been higher than the number of completed ones. Olembo (1985, p.18) points out that one reason for this has been that:

> a majority of head teachers and primary school committees embark on fund-raising and in fact the construction of school facilities without even estimating the total cost of the facility.

Particularly serious in many cases is the failure to assess the recurrent implications of capital investment. This causes a large number of projects to remain uncompleted; and even when projects *are* completed it leads to strife because villagers complain that organisers have swindled them. Chapter 5 pointed out that projects may also waste resources if communities have inadequate expertise in construction and the choice of appropriate designs.

Olembo also points out that community financing can distort educational priorities. Thus, he suggests (1985, p.24), head teachers have to work closely with school committees; but in their efforts to raise funds and supervise the construction of facilities, head teachers may have to neglect pedagogic matters. Chapter 3 added that schools' attempts to run businesses may similarly distort the curriculum.

Governments also have to decide how far they are prepared to tolerate education systems run by religious bodies. Just because Ahmadiyya, Hindus, Ismailis, Roman Catholics, Mormons, Jehovah's Witnesses and other groups are prepared to finance schools does not necessarily mean that

TABLE 17.1 *Flow of Self-Help Projects, Kenya, 1971–3*

	Continued from previous year (cumulative)	Newly started	Abandoned	Completed	Continued into next year (ongoing)
1971	5,074	6,597	3,325	1,841	6,505
1972	6,010	2,841	1,057	1,800	5,994
1973	7,190	3,064	740	1,704	7,810

Source: Government of Kenya, reproduced in Mbithi and Rasmusson (1977, p.40).

they should be encouraged to do so. Quite apart from the political and cultural questions that are raised when schools are run by such bodies, there is often a danger that institutions will make it uneconomic to provide other schools in the same areas for people who are not members of the religions. When this happens, outsiders are forced either to attend the schools run by the religious bodies or to forego schooling altogether.

Moreover, when self-help movements generate their own momentum, they may distort carefully-laid official priorities, leading for example to a greater supply of people with particular educational qualifications than the economy can absorb. It is worth recalling comments on the political framework in Kenya. Keller (1980, p.52) quotes the Minister for Labour:

> *they are a political thing* and even though I am not very happy with what they are doing, I myself am building these schools. . . . This is political and cannot be helped. (emphasis original)

Under such circumstances, governments may consider it less risky to prohibit self-help projects altogether. Trinidad is one country in which the government has made this decision.

(b) If Governments do Favour Self-Help, How can they Encourage it?

Few governments go so far as the Trinidadian one however. Most are prepared at least to tolerate community support, and some actively encourage it. Moreover, because of increasing financial stringency, the number of governments in the latter group is growing. The question then changes from 'whether' to 'how'. This section outlines ten ways in which governments can encourage community financing.

(i) Neglect of education

This strategy is in effect widely used, though it is hardly to be recommended. Many self-help ventures have arisen simply because communities have perceived needs which governments are not meeting, and have decided to bridge the gap themselves. This has happened even in developed countries, where it is has become increasingly common for PTAs to supplement school resources by buying books and other materials that governments are no longer able to supply.

In some cases, the gap between supply and demand for schooling exists despite high government expenditures. Thus Lillis and Ayot report the Kenyan government to be allocating 30 per cent of its recurrent budget to education, and it could hardly be criticised for not allocating more.

In other cases, however, government expenditures are low. For instance, the Pakistan government only allocates about 7 per cent of its budget to education, which is well below the 17 per cent developing country mean (World Bank, 1985, p.74). In 1972 the Pakistan government decided for ideological reasons to nationalise all schools. However, the measure had a disastrous effect on the system. It was reversed in 1979, and within a short period the private sector again mushroomed (Jimenez and Tan, 1985, pp.52–7). China has also allocated low amounts to education (World Bank 1985, p.45), which partly explains the prominence of *minban* schools. Similar factors apply to the secondary school sector in Tanzania (Carr-Hill, 1984; Cooksey, 1986).

(ii) Publicity

This is a more positive approach. Governments often publicise the virtues of self-help through official channels and through announcements at public meetings which are likely to be reported in the newspapers and on the radio.

One common problem with such measures is that they have very broad target audiences, and they rarely indicate what initiatives will *not* be welcomed—schools run by particular minorities, with specific curricula, etc. To solve these difficulties, governments have to supplement overall publicity with detailed information on relevant regulations. In Kenya, a special harambee unit has been established at the Ministry of Education headquarters, part of the function of which has been to distribute information. Because of organisational problems, the unit has not always worked effectively; but that has been the fault of implementation strategies rather than of the initial concept.

Many governments have also recognised the importance of district-level community development staff, education officers and chiefs. Through formal and informal contact with communities, these officers can play a particularly important role. They should be able to advise on government regulations and assist with overall design and implementation of projects.

(iii) Offering grants

Many governments encourage self-help by giving grants. Matching grants can be particularly effective, for they give communities an incentive to maximise their contributions. Many are 'dollar-for-dollar' allocations, but the proportions can be varied according to the availability of government resources, the extent to which communities are thought to need a 'carrot', and the extent to which regional inequalities seem to be developing. However, one Indian experience has been cited to stress the need for governments to make careful initial calculations of the strength of demand. Offers of matching grants can sometimes lead to stronger responses than the authorities are able to cope with.

(iv) Permitting fees and levies

Some governments have ideological objections to fees and levies, which, they point out, can be discriminatory. These governments recognise that schooling is a critical determinant of individual and group social mobility, and feel that it is unfair that some children should be excluded from school simply because their families cannot afford fees. Exclusion may also hinder the recognition and development of talented children, and may thus deprive the nation of valuable resources.

However, few self-help schools can operate without fees, and Chapter 4 points out that fees are not necessarily inegalitarian. If imposed and collected by the central government they tend to be inflexible, but when imposed locally it is easier to make allowance for needy cases. Local fees may also encounter smaller collection costs than central fees.

As implied by Figure 3 in the Introduction, tuition fees have a narrower base than that of the full community, for they are usually paid only by the parents or guardians of children who actually attend schools. However, they may be especially important for institutions with large catchment areas, because it is hard to foster voluntary contributions when people live far away from projects.

(v) Defining and reducing school catchment areas

Following on the previous point, because primary schools usually have smaller catchment areas, it is often easier to foster community support for them than for secondary schools. In addition, communities whose children go to several schools are unlikely to support the institutions as strongly as communities whose children all go to the same school. Governments can improve community identification by clearly demarcating school catchment areas and making them as small as possible. Economies of scale often make it desirable to have large institutions, but it may be easier to develop community support for smaller, more local schools (Bray, 1987, pp.27–8).

(v) Promise of take-over

Where communities are running schools merely in order to bridge gaps, promise of government take-over encourages them to establish institutions and to meet laid-down requirements for facilities. Mbithi and Rasmusson (1977) point out that this has been a major force in Kenya, for example.

At the same time, governments which want to encourage religious or other groups could promise *not* to take over schools unless invited. Such promises, of course, have to be demonstrated by actions as well as words.

Policy swings of the types found in Pakistan and Zaire make communities very cautious about large commitments of money and energy.

(vii) Technical Assistance

Many communities need help with construction. In some countries, staff have been recruited to advise communities on the designs of buildings and to help them secure materials. The governments of Peru, Nepal and Burma have produced simple, well illustrated manuals. Separate booklets have been written for administrators, project overseers and community leaders, approaching objectives from different angles.

(viii) Management advice

In many countries, government officers are already represented on secondary school Boards of Governors. They can be encouraged to take an active role, and to assist with the overall management of schools. Accounting procedures are particularly important, for many self-help projects collapse following embezzlement of funds. Accounts do not need to be complicated—indeed they should be clear and comprehensible to ordinary people. Inspectors could do a great deal just by asking to see the accounts every time they visit a school. Even if they do not check accounts in detail, the mere action of asking to see the accounts can have a beneficial impact.

(ix) Organising workshops

Experience in India, Papua New Guinea, Nepal and other countries has shown that a lot can be achieved through district level workshops at which community leaders, government officers and others share ideas. These need not be expensive, for communities are often willing to provide free accommodation, and individuals may pay their own travel expenses. Young and Aarons (1986) point out that school committees in Nepal have been very hazy about the extent of their responsibilities and their powers, and that in one district workshops have greatly improved the situation.

(x) Relaxing regulations on income from abroad

Some governments insist that all money received from abroad has to be channelled through the National Planning Office or a similar body. These regulations have been devised as monitoring and control mechanisms. However, sometimes they inhibit projects. It may be useful to allow communities to negotiate directly with foreign organisations for money and teachers.

(c) Controls and their Implementation

If governments really want to encourage communities to provide resources, they may also have to relinquish some control over their school systems. Many governments are unwilling to do this however, and thorny questions arise on the most appropriate controls in particular circumstances.

Among the most critical policy decisions is whether to permit parallel unaided systems. Okoye (1986) comments that Anambra State of Nigeria has avoided many of Kenya's problems by insisting that all secondary schools must be part of a state system. Communities are responsible for facilities, but teachers are employed by the government. This structure allows the government to control the curriculum and to avoid many qualitative problems by posting good teachers to disadvantaged areas. Chapter 12 indicates that the government of Botswana is moving in a similar direction.

This system may be inflexible and costly, however. Some schools run by religious bodies prefer to remain independent because they wish to have their own curricula. A unified system also requires the government to recruit and pay teachers and on occasions to deny communities the opportunity to have their own schools. In many countries political and financial forces preclude the operation of unitary systems.

Chapter 8 pointed out that most governments insist that even unaided schools should be registered before they are permitted to operate. And before schools are allowed to register, governments often require owners to agree that the institutions will be open to children of all races and religions, that they should include certain subjects on the curriculum, and that class-sizes should not exceed a specific number. They may also check the demographic circumstances of the area in which the school will be sited, to assess its impact on geographic and social inequalities.

In many systems, schools are also subject to periodic inspection. If their toilets do not meet health standards, for example, the schools may be closed; and the laboratories and teaching staffs can be required to meet specific standards before pupils are allowed to sit public examinations.

Imposition of strong controls encounters various problems, however. First, there is a danger that they will stifle community initiatives and reduce the extent of provision. In Zambia, for example, the government has faced a dilemma on overall provision. In order to widen access to poorer groups, the Zambian government would like to impose a ceiling on the fees charged in non-government schools. So far, however, it has resisted doing so because it fears that the schools might withdraw their services altogether (Kaluba, 1986, p.167).

In some countries, policies also face thorny regional implications. For example, the governments of Kenya and Anambra State of Nigeria, have had to relax controls in less developed areas in order to prevent initiatives being stifled altogether (Mbithi and Rasmusson, 1977; Okoye, 1986).

In addition, although Igwe's chapter in this book suggests that in Imo State of Nigeria self-help seems to flourish even when controls are very stringent, one suspects that supervision problems arise. Controls that are not implemented lose respect; but controls that *are* implemented may incur considerable manpower costs.

Further, this book has pointed out in several places that most governments are regrettably short of information. It is relatively rare for Ministries of Education to have detailed data even on the number of pupils in unaided schools, let alone on their academic achievements and the nature and extent of community contributions. Without such information the operation of effective controls is very much a hit or miss affair. But one reason why they lack information may be that regulations are fierce and communities are reluctant to expose themselves to government scrutiny.

(d) Centralisation versus Decentralisation

These issues of control are partly linked to questions of decentralisation. Psacharopoulos, Tan and Jimenez (1986, p.17) are among the strong advocates of decentralisation as a way to increase community financing. By this, they chiefly mean decentralisation to the school level rather than to provincial or local governments. Rarely are policies and processes straightforward, however.

In this connection, it is worth drawing out the lessons from Robinson's chapter on China. The overall lesson from her paper is that the history of decentralisation as it relates to *minban* schools has not been positive, and her evidence accords with experience elsewhere.

During the 1940s, Robinson relates, *minban* schools in China were hailed as institutions that made education more relevant to local conditions, but were under the centralised direction of the Party. This system ran into problems. In 1952 the Ministry of Education stipulated that people-run schools could be accredited only after three years of operation, during which time they had to fulfil the same requirements as public schools. The regulation made it almost impossible for *minban* schools to operate, since they had neither the funding nor the staff to adhere to the same standards as state-supported schools.

Yet attempts over the next few decades to decentralise and solve these problems encountered new ones of quality, selectivity and institutional management. Thus the last decade has witnessed recentralisation. Education experts, Robinson indicates, have become convinced that 'the only way to ensure continuous quality of education in the village is to centralise the administration of the schools as much as possible'. But this still conflicts with peasant interpretations of what local schools should offer, and restricts their enthusiasm for contributing to schools.

These tensions have also been felt elsewhere. For example, Chapter 12 points out that in Botswana concerns about the quality of Community Junior Secondary Schools have led to government support. However, this is so extensive and is accompanied by so many controls that 'what was originally seen as government support for community initiative is fast becoming a government programme with community support'. The chapter suggests that it is now questionable whether the CJSSs are really community schools at all.

Central authorities may also be hampered in their work by inability to rely on staff at lower levels of the system. In this respect, the comments on Nepal by Young and Aarons (1986), quoted in Chapter 8, are instructive. The authors referred to a successful project run jointly by Unesco, Unicef and the UNDP, but comment negatively on the prospects for another one to be run by the government. Widespread corruption, they suggest, poses a serious obstacle to success.

Moreover, even in countries without serious problems of corruption, there often remain difficulties arising from the overall outlook of the bureaucracy. As a Unesco document points out (1984a, p.13), most bureaucracies were initially created more to control than to render services. Their origins lay in needs to collect taxes, raise armies, conscript labour and otherwise marshall the forces of production, and the concept of a modern government's responsibility to render services to *all* people and not just the powerful upper and middle classes is relatively recent. Because of this, most bureaucracies are oriented upwards—junior personnel are more concerned about their accountability to their seniors than to 'mere' villagers, and in project design and development will usually 'play safe'.

In the context of community financing, this means that although official government policy may assert the value and even the right of communities to participate in their own affairs, staff often place so many obstacles in the way that in effect they oppose participation. And the traditions of bureaucracies being what they are, it is doubtful whether many governments would encourage staff to do otherwise.

In other words, decentralisation and community participation are frequently just a model to which it is fashionable to pay lip service. Governments are pleased to accept the resources and the grass roots initiatives which coincide with their own concepts; but they are rarely willing to relinquish control and place themselves in a position where their policies can be undermined.

(e) Other Tensions

Some other serious tensions must also be considered, and are examined in this section with reference to the Kenyan experience. Although this book has shown that harambee schemes are among the most productive, the environment that promotes these activities is to some extent unique, and is arguably undesirable. It is important to consider the causes of the activity in Kenya as well as its outcomes, for other governments might be misguided if they hope to achieve the same outcomes in their own countries.

Beginning with the social background of harambee, Mbithi and Rasmusson (1977) point out that it has long indigenous roots in the areas in which it is most successful, such as Nyanza and Central Provinces. In North Eastern Province by contrast, traditions are much more shallow. Harambee there is more of a top-down process initiated by government officers, and is much less successful. Governments often find it hard to generate activities where the necessary social structures do not already exist.

Perhaps even more important, although in the post-independence era harambee was widely associated with the rallying cries of President Kenyatta, much of its momentum was generated by feelings of relative deprivation and inappropriate central planning. Strategies of favouring some areas so that other areas feel deprived, or of developing bad central planning strategies so that groups react against them, are hardly to be recommended.

Moreover, much of the cohesion of harambee groups has been based on opposition to the central government, and has been exploited by disaffected politicians (Godfrey and Mutiso, 1974; Mbithi and Rasmusson, 1977). During the early 1960s, the ruling Kenya African National Union (KANU) suppressed regionalism by absorbing leaders in the Kenya African Democratic Union and the Akamba People's Party. This was effective at the national level, but created conflict between KANU groups who had been long associated with the party and those who had not. It was administratively contained by centralising provincial administrations, but during the late 1960s enforcement of a rigid party line displaced several national leaders who moved into competition at the regional level.

In order to regain their positions, some of these politicians exploited the potential of harambee. This benefited the communities, because it often gave them access to more resources. However, inspiration for specific projects was frequently derived from strategies and goals which deliberately diverged from those advocated by the central planners, and which in non-political terms were hard to justify. Also, in order to promote solidarity, many harambee groups found it desirable to stress grievances against other clans, regions and ethnic groups. Sometimes, reasons for antagonism to other groups were invented if they did not already exist.

Although the political forces may have produced valuable outcomes in the form of self-help efforts, therefore, they also produced less desirable results. Governments in other countries might welcome the self-help outcomes of the conflicts, but it is doubtful whether they would welcome the conflicts, or consider the desirable outcomes sufficient to justify the costs.

2. Implications for Non-Government Organisations

It is clear that the range of non-government organisations which support education is very wide. On the one hand are large religious bodies such as Christian and Islamic missions, and on the other hand are village development associations which have much smaller bases.

Yet whatever, the size and coverage of the organisation, all must generally work within the framework of government policies in the countries concerned. Kenyan and other experiences have shown that political forces can be manipulated and that official regulations can sometimes be ignored, but only at considerable risk.

Several other broad policy implications may also be discerned:

(i) Selection of good leaders

Mbithi and Rasmusson's case studies (1977, pp.103ff.) showed that village projects which were most likely to be successful had a leadership that was selected or elected from a broad range of groups and had some continuity over time across different project phases. Projects in which the leaders appointed themselves, or in which there was either too little or too much overlap between project initiation, organisation and implementation phases had high failure rates.

(ii) Securing powerful sponsors

At the same time, the most successful schools established by village communities are often ones with powerful patrons. These may be politicians, government officers or others. They may be able to secure resources for their schools and to protect their interests.

Though rather different in nature and magnitude, similar remarks apply to larger non-government organisations. When there are pressures to nationalise schools, organisations are in much stronger positions when they have influential advocates in government circles.

(iii) Liaison with governments

Clearly it is desirable for non-government organisations to make their views known to governments—the reasons why they want to fund schools, the extent of the resources which they can command, and the nature of their requirements on curriculum and staffing. In many countries there is scope for considerable 'trading' on these issues.

At the village level, leaders need to acquaint themselves with official regulations. Communities are usually required to provide specific facilities, follow certain types of curriculum, and register their managers with the government. In turn, they may be eligible for grants and technical advice.

(iv) Assessment of commitments

Schools are expensive, and commit their owners to particularly high salary costs. It is essential for sponsoring agencies to assess the nature of commitments before they open schools, and to match these against resources. Many projects have collapsed because leaders have underestimated the demands that schools can make. Mbithi and Rasmusson's (1977) case studies showed that small projects which were not in competition with others and which had limited time scales were among the ones most likely to be successful.

(v) Examining strategies for quality control

When churches run systems that are entirely independent of governments, they need their own inspectors and supervisory personnel. Though voluntary agencies can usually recruit teachers trained in government institutions, they sometimes need separate systems for training staff. As in Papua New Guinea and Lesotho, for example, Church Education Secretaries or similar personnel can be employed to look after administrative arrangements. If churches require pupils and teachers to be members of their faiths, they must be aware that they may have to tolerate lower academic standards than if they aim for quality regardless of religious belief.

Though local communities cannot contemplate employment of inspectors, occasionally they sponsor individuals for training on the understanding that the individuals will return to teach in local schools. This is rare, however, and because communities are local in focus, they often recruit staff from a small pool with unsatisfactory selection procedures. Communities may decide that it is important to recruit local staff and students, but they should be aware that the small size of the catchment area can have a negative effect on quality.

(vi) Fostering international links

Many religious bodies in poor countries obtain aid from corresponding bodies in richer nations. International links can generate considerable resources.

Though village level communities are rarely in a position to develop the same types of links, many secondary schools have gained staffing assistance from foreign volunteer bodies. Sometimes, volunteer teachers also act as channels for donations of equipment and books.

(vii) Including the value of non-monetary inputs in applications for matching grants

Occasionally, this is prohibited in the terms of the grants. Where it is not, however, it helps communities to maximise their incomes. Allowance can be made for labour inputs as well as donations of land and materials.

(viii) Devising proper accounting procedures

The importance of proper accounts cannot be stressed too strongly. Good accounts should be an instrument for planning. Even more important, they should be an instrument to reduce temptations to embezzle funds and to protect those who have not embezzled funds but who find it hard to explain how money has been used. Accusations of misuse of money are among the most common causes of collapse of self-help projects.

In most cases, it is unrealistic to expect government officers to examine the accounts of every school. Self-help groups should therefore devise their own procedures, and Boards of Governors can insist on presentation of accounts at every meeting. Schools which are part of a church or other network may have an advantage not shared by those run by village development associations. But even in the latter case it ought to be possible to devise ways to have accounts convincingly audited. Usually this can be done by the village priest or a similar respected figure. Alternatively, communities might be able to arrange for neighbouring schools to check accounts in the way that neighbouring schools often invigilate each others' examinations.

While few schools appear to have good systems for auditing monetary accounts, even fewer have good systems for accounting for labour and goods. These aspects of community support are less likely to cause major strife, but they can still be important.

One final point concerns accounting for 'unofficial' receipts—i.e. for fees or other payments which have been collected in contravention of government policies. Clearly these require sensitive handling, and communities would be unwise to advertise them too openly. However, accounts are needed for these receipts as much as for others; and if communities feel that official policies are inappropriate, they should inform the authorities of their views.

(ix) Collecting information

The comments made above about government information systems often apply as much to non-government organisations. The latter frequently lack detailed information on the demand for their facilities, on the resources that local congregations and other bodies can command, and on the academic achievement of their pupils. It is unrealistic to expect village-level communities to embark on major research projects, but there are occasions when clearer understanding of labour market trends and comparative performance of pupils in different systems would be very desirable.

Conclusions

There is a danger of idealising the role that communities can play in the education system. For example, it was noted in the Introduction that Phan and Cao (1973, p.109) assert that increased use of community resources has the advantage that:

> The government will receive no more requests from parents asking for building more schools because they have already felt that they are responsible for their own community. In this respect, the government has gained a notable spiritual advantage. Parents and people in the community have really made their contribution to the common national plan with the spirit of a 'responsible man' because they are directly concerned with the education of their children. They will, therefore, play a more important role after having acquired a better knowledge of education and of their own community problems.

They advanced no data to back up their assertions, and it is doubtful whether they could have done so. In many cases, self-help efforts are only stop-gap measures because communities consider government provision deficient either in quantity or type, and it is naive to expect promotion of self-help to lead to a reduction in demands for government inputs. Indeed, the Kenyan and other experiences show that the reverse is more likely to occur.

Likewise, most efforts to involve the community in curriculum matters have had very limited success. The Cameroonian experience has been highlighted here as a project with ambitious objectives but disappointing results because of coordination and pedagogic difficulties (see Chapter 3). While governments may extol the virtues of community financing as a way to encourage citizens to take a stronger interest in education, rarely are they keen on people extending their interest too far into curriculum matters. Indeed, even when community resources are urgently required, it is uncommon for governments voluntarily to relinquish control over the structure and major components of schooling.

In addition, while this book has recognised that community resources can provide a valuable supplement to government ones, it has also shown that community endeavours are often badly organised, lead to poor quality schools, and sometimes defeat official attempts to reduce geographic and social inequalities. It is very dangerous to regard community initiatives as a panacea for the ills of education systems.

Nevertheless, community support will remain important, if only for the negative reason that most Third World governments will remain too hard-pressed to meet all the demands on them. Indeed, in many countries populations are growing rapidly, expectations about the education levels to which individuals may legitimately aspire are escalating, and economies are stagnating. This suggests that community support will become even more important during the next few years.

In this light, more detailed analysis of specific contexts is urgently required. This book has drawn on literature which is wide but mostly superficial. Writting this book has therefore been like assembling a jigsaw with half the pieces missing. Only in Kenya has extensive research been conducted on the topic, and even there many questions remain unanswered.

Moreover, one result of the availability of studies from Kenya and the paucity of literature from countries has been an imbalance in the basis for this book. While the Kenyan literature highlights concerns to which governments, voluntary organisations and communities in other countries should pay attention, it is no substitute for detailed local information. Even within Kenya societies vary widely, and in the Third World as a whole variations are much more extreme.

Finally, far too many governments quote their own expenditure data as if that is all that is spent on education in their countries, and are disquietingly ignorant of the nature and impact of self-help projects. Ironically, one reason for this is that self-help does not cost governments anything. Most items which do appear in official budgets are scrutinised much more carefully. It is one contention of this book that it is precisely because self-help efforts do *not* cost governments money that they deserve more careful investigation.

Bibliography

ABERNETHY, David B. (1969) *The Political Dilemma of Popular Education: An African Case*, Stanford University Press, Stanford.

AGA KHAN FOUNDATION (1985) *Programme Interests*, Geneva.

ALABI, Anthony (1985) 'The Politics of Education: Some Issues from the Scheme for Free Secondary Education in Oyo State of Nigeria', M.A. dissertation, University of London Institute of Education.

ABREU, Elsa (1982) *The Role of Self-Help in the Development of Education in Kenya 1900–1973*, Kenya Literature Bureau, Nairobi.

AINSWORTH, M. (1984) 'User Charges for Social Sector Finance: Policy and Practice in Developing Countries', Country Policy Department, The World Bank, Washington.

ANDERSON, John (1969) 'The Harambee Schools: The Impact of Self-Help', in JOLLY, Richard (ed.), *Education in Africa: Research and Action*, East African Publishing House, Nairobi.

ANDERSON, John (1970) *The Struggle for the School*, Longman, Nairobi.

ANDERSON, John (1973) *Organization and Financing of Self-Help Education in Kenya*, IIEP, Paris.

ANDERSON, John (1975) 'The Organisation of Support and the Management of Self-help Schools: A Case Study from Kenya', in BROWN, Godfrey N. and HISKETT, Mervyn (eds.), *Conflict and Harmony in Education in Tropical Africa*, George, Allen & Unwin, London.

ASHUNTANTANG, G. T., BERGMANN, H., BUDE, U. and DIVINE, V. J. (1977) 'Environmental Studies (Agricultural and Social Aspects) Report', in IPAR-BUEA, *Report on the Reform of Primary Education*, Institute for the Reform of Primary Education, Buea, Cameroon.

AWANOHARA, Susumu (1985) 'A Rich Ideology, or the Poor Teaching the Poor to be Poor', *Far Eastern Economic Review*, 10 January.

BARBADOS, Government of (1981) *Education Act 1981*, Supplement to Official Gazette 14 May 1981, Bridgetown.

BERGMANN, Herbert and BUDE, Udo K. (1976) 'An Analysis of Existing School-Community Participation in a Central African Country', in KING, Kenneth (ed.), *Education and the Community in Africa*, Centre of African Studies, University of Edinburgh.

BERTHE, Adama (1985) 'Participation des Communautés Locales au Financement de l'Education au Mali', Ministère de l'Education National, Bamako/Division of Educational Policy and Planning, Unesco, Paris.

BIAK CIN, Robert and SCANDLEN, Guy B. (1985) 'Loving Kindness and the Five Gratitudes: Burmese Cultural Values Underlying Community Participation in the Primary School Improvement Programme', paper presented to the Unicef-Unesco Regional Education Meeting, Pattaya, Thailand.

BIRDSALL, Nancy (1983) 'Strategies for Analysing User Charges in the Social Sectors', Country Policy Department, The World Bank, Washington.

BIRDSALL, Nancy *et al.* (1983) 'Demand for Primary Schooling in Rural Mali: Should User Fees be Increased?', Country Policy Department, The World Bank, Washington.

BOCK, John C. (1982) 'Education and Development: A Conflict of Meaning', in ALTBACH, Philip, ARNOVE, Robert F. and KELLY, Gail P. (eds.), *Comparative Education*, Macmillan, New York.

BOLNICK, B. R. (1974) *Comparative Harambee: History and Theory of Voluntary Collective*

Behaviour, Working Paper No.34, Institute of Development Studies, University of Nairobi.

BOTSWANA, Republic of (1977a) *Education for Kagisano: Report of the National Commission on Education*, Ministry of Education, Gaborone.

BOTSWANA, Republic of (1977b) *National Policy on Education*, Government Paper No. 1, Government Printer, Gaborone.

BOTSWANA, Republic of (1978) *Education (Private Secondary Schools) Regulations 1978*, Ministry of Education, Gaborone.

BOTSWANA, Republic of (1979) *Supplementary Report of the National Commission on Education*, Ministry of Education, Gaborone.

BOTSWANA, Republic of (1980) *National Development Plan 1979–85*, Ministry of Finance and Development Planning, Gaborone.

BOTSWANA, Republic of (1985) *National Development Plan 1985–91*, Ministry of Finance and Development Planning, Gaborone.

BRAY, Mark (1981) *Universal Primary Education in Nigeria: A Study of Kano State*, Routledge and Kegan Paul, London.

BRAY, Mark (1983a) 'The Politics of Free Education in Papua New Guinea', *International Journal of Educational Development*, Vol.2, No.3.

BRAY, Mark (1983b) 'Community Schools or Primary Schools? A Reform of the 1970s Reconsidered', *Yagl-Ambu: Papua New Guinea Journal of the Social Sciences and Humanities*, Vol.10, No.1.

BRAY, Mark (1984), *Educational Planning in a Decentralised System: The Papua New Guinean Experience*, University of Papua New Guinea Press, Port Moresby/Sydney University Press, Sydney.

BRAY, Mark (1986) *New Resources for Education: Community Management and Financing of Schools in Less Developed Countries*, The Commonwealth Secretariat, London.

BRAY, Mark (1987) *Are Small Schools the Answer? Cost-Effective Strategies for Rural School Provision*, The Commonwealth Secretariat, London.

BRAY, Mark and BOZE, Kangu (1982) 'Community School Wastage and Non-Enrolment in the Western Province', *Papua New Guinea Journal of Education*, Vol.18, No.2.

BRAY, Mark, CLARKE, Peter B. and STEPHENS, David (1986) *Education and Society in Africa*, Edward Arnold, London.

BRAY, M., DONDO., J. M. C. and MOEMEKA, A. A. (1976) 'Two Case Studies from Nigeria and Kenya', in KING, Kenneth (ed.), *Education and the Community in Africa*, Centre of African Studies, University of Edinburgh.

BRODERSOHN, Mario (1978) 'Public and Private Financing of Education in Latin America: A Review of its Principal Sources', in *The Financing of Education in Latin America*, Inter-American Bank, Washington.

BROKENSHA, D. W. (1966) *Social Change at Larteh, Ghana*, Clarendon Press, Oxford.

BURMA, Government of (1952) *The Pyidawtha Plan: Education for a Welfare State*, Ministry of Information, Rangoon.

CARR-HILL, Roy (1984) *Primary Education in Tanzania: A Review of the Research*, Swedish International Development Authority, Stockholm.

CAYAGO, Salome (1979) *Community School Survey*, Research Report No.28, Educational Research Unit, University of Papua New Guinea.

CAYMAN ISLANDS, Government of (1984) *The Education Law 1983 (Law 35 of 1983)*, Supplement No.1 printed with Gazette No.2 of 1984, Georgetown.

COLCLOUGH, Christopher, LEWIN, Keith and OXENHAM, John (1985) 'Donor Agency Support for Primary Education: Strategies Reconsidered', *International Journal of Educational Development*, Vol.5, No.4.

COLLINS, J. (1981) *Strategies for Success: A Study of Three Harambee Schools*, Bureau of Educational Research, Kenyatta University College, Nairobi.

COOKSEY, Brian (1986) 'Policy and Practice in Tanzanian Secondary Education since 1967', *International Journal of Educational Development*, Vol.6, No.3.

COOMBE, Trevor and LAUVAS, Per (1984) *Facilitating Self-Renewal in Zambian Education*, Norwegian Agency for International Development, Oslo.

COOMBS, Philip H. (1985) *The World Crisis in Education: The View from the Eighties*, Oxford University Press, New York.

COURT, David and KINYANJUI, Kabiru (1980) 'Development Policy and Educational Opportunity: The Experience of Kenya and Tanzania', in CARRON, Gabriel and TA NGOC Chau (eds.), *Regional Disparities in Educational Development*, IIEP, Paris.

CRUZ, Leopoldo and CALADO, Rene R. (1975) *Financing Secondary Education in the Philippines*, Financing Education Systems Case Study 11, IIEP, Paris.

DORE, Ronald (1976) *The Diploma Disease: Education, Qualifications and Development*, George, Allen & Unwin, London.

EASTERN NIGERIA, Ministry of Education (1967) *Annual Report 1964*, Official Document No.4 of 1967, Government Printer, Enugu.

EDUCATION REFORM IMPLEMENTATION PROJECT (1985) 'Survey of Primary Schools', University of Zambia, Lusaka.

EICHER, J. C. (1984) *Educational Costing and Financing in Developing Countries: Focus on Sub-Saharan Africa*, Staff Working Paper No.655, The World Bank, Washington.

EL HAGGAZ, H. M. and GARVEY-WILLIAMS, F. T. (1978) 'Community Participation in the Provision of School Facilities in Sudan', paper presented at the Unesco seminar on The Mobilization of Domestic Resources for Formal and Non-Formal Education, ED-78/CONF.734/REF.4.4, Unesco, Paris.

EZE, A. (1983) *Economics of Education: The Nigerian Experience*, New Africa Publishing Company, Owerri.

FAFUNWA, A. Babs (1974) *History of Education in Nigeria*, George, Allen & Unwin, London.

FÄGERLIND, I. and VALDELIN, J. (1983) *Education in Zambia: Past Achievements and Future Trends*, Education Report No.12, Swedish International Development Authority, Stockholm.

FIAH, Solomon (1979) 'Ghana's Universal Primary Education Scheme: A Review', M.Sc. dissertation, University of Edinburgh.

FISHER, Humphrey J. (1975), 'The Modernisation of Islamic Education in Sierra Leone, Gambia and Liberia: Religion and Language', in BROWN, Godfrey N. and HISKETT, Mervyn (eds.), *Conflict and Harmony in Education in Tropical Africa*, George, Allen & Unwin, London.

GALABAWA, J. C. J. (1985) 'Community Financing of Schools in Tanzania', paper presented at the Commonwealth Secretariat workshop on Community Financing of Schools, Gaborone, Botswana.

GHANA, Government of (1981) *Ghana Education Bill (1981)*, Ghana Publishing Corporation, Accra-Tema.

GODFREY, M. and MUTISO, G. C. M. (1974) 'The Political Economy of Self-Help: Kenya's Harambee Institutes of Technology', in COURT, D. and GHAI, D. (eds.), *Education, Society and Development*, Oxford University Press, Nairobi.

GRANT, Sandy (1976) 'A Very Remarkable School', *Botswana Notes and Records*, Vol.8.

GRINDLE, Merilee S. (ed.) (1980) *Politics and Policy Implementation in the Third World*, Princeton University Press, Princeton.

GURUGE, Ananda W. P. (1977) *Planning the Location of Schools: Sri Lanka*, IIEP, Paris.

HADDEN, Susan (1980) 'Controlled Decentralization and Policy Implemention: The Case of Rural Electrification in Rajasthan', in GRINDLE, Merilee S. (ed.), *Politics and Policy Implementation in the Third World*, Princeton University Press, Princeton.

HANSON, E. Mark (1983) 'Administration Development in the Columbian Ministry of Education: A Case Analysis of the 1970s', *Comparative Education Review*, Vol.27, No.1.

HANSON, E. Mark (1984) 'Administrative Reform in the Venezuelan Ministry of Education: A Case Analysis of the 1970s', *International Review of Education*, Vol.XXX, No.2.

HENEVELD, Ward and KARIM, Abdul (1984) 'Outline of a Pilot Programme for Self-Help School Construction in the Northern Areas of Pakistan', Aga Khan Foundation, Geneva.

HEYMAN, R. D., LAWSON, R. F. and STAMP, R. M. (1972) *Studies in Educational Change*, Holt, Rinehart & Winston, Toronto.

HILL, M. (1974) 'Self-help in Education and Development: A Social Anthropological Study in Kitui, Kenya', Bureau of Educational Research, University of Nairobi.

HILL, M. (1975) *The Roots of Harambee*, Occasional Paper No.3014, Bureau of Educational Research, Kenyatta University College, Nairobi.

HINDSON, Colin E. (1985) 'Kiribati—The Search for Educational Alternatives in a Pacific Micro-State', *International Journal of Educational Development*, Vol.5, No.4.

222 *Bibliography*

HOLMQUIST, F. (1979) 'Class Structure, Peasant Participation and Rural Self-Help', in BEKAN, J. D. and OKUMU, J. J. (eds.), *Politics and Public Policy in Kenya and Tanzania*, Heinemann, Nairobi.

HOUGHTON, Harold and TREGEAR, Peter (1969) *Community Schools in Development Countries*, Unesco Institute for Education, Hamburg.

IMO STATE OF NIGERIA, Government of (1978) *Ministry of Education Annual Report 1977/78*, Government Printer, Owerri.

IMO STATE OF NIGERIA, Government of (1980) *Education Law 1980*, Gazette No.33, Vol.5 of 16th October, Government Printer, Owerri.

IMO STATE OF NIGERIA (1984a) 'Regulations and Guidelines for Communities Building New Secondary Schools', Ministry of Education & Information, Owerri.

IMO STATE OF NIGERIA (1984b) 'Request for Permission to Collect P.T.A. Levy', State Schools Management Board, IM/SSMB/ADS/250/137, Owerri.

INTERNATIONAL LABOUR OFFICE (1981) *Zambia: Basic Needs in an Economy under Pressure*, Jobs and Skills Programme for Africa, Addis Ababa.

IPAR-BUEA (1977) *Report on the Reform of Primary Education*, Institute for the Reform of Primary Education, Buea, Cameroon.

JAYASURIYA, J. E. (1984) *The Organization and Management of Community Support for Education: A Synthesis Study*, Occasional Papers in Educational Planning, Management and Facilities No.8, Unesco, Bangkok.

JIMENEZ, Emmanuel and TAN, Jee-Peng (1985) *Educational Development in Pakistan: The Role of User Charges and Private Education*, Report No.EDT16, Education and Training Department, The World Bank, Washington.

JIMENEZ, Emmanuel (1986) 'The Public Subsidization of Education and Health in Developing Countries: A Review of Equity and Efficiency', *The World Bank Research Observer*, Vol.1, No.1.

KALUBA, L. H. (1986) 'Education in Zambia: The Problem of Access to Schooling and the Paradox of Private Education', *Comparative Education*, Vol.22, No.2.

KAUNDA, A. H. (1985) 'Deliberate Steps towards the Achievement of Basic Education on the Copperbelt', unpublished, Ndola.

KEINO, E. (1980) 'The Contribution of Harambee in the Development of Secondary School Education in Kenya: A Case Study in Kericho', Ph.D. thesis, Harvard University.

KELLER, Edmond (1975) *The Role of Self-Help Schools in Education for Development: The Harambee Movement in Kenya*, Bureau of Educational Research, Kenyatta University College, Paper P–11.30.

KELLER, Edmond (1980) *Education, Manpower and Development: The Impact of Educational Policy in Kenya*, Kenya Literature Bureau, Nairobi.

KELLER, Edmond (1983) 'Development Policy and the Evaluation of Community Self-Help: The Harambee School Movement in Education', *Studies in Comparative International Development*, Vol.18, No.4.

KENYA, Government of (1969) *Kenya Development Plan 1970–1974*, Government Printer, Nairobi.

KENYA, Government of (1974) *Kenya Development Plan 1974–1978*, Government Printer, Nairobi.

KENYA, Government of (1979) *Kenya Development Plan 1979–1983*, Government Printer, Nairobi.

KENYA, Government of (1984a) *Economic Survey 1984*, Central Bureau of Statistics, Nairobi.

KENYA, Government of (1984b) '8–4–4 System of Education,' Government Printer, Nairobi.

KENYA, Government of (1984c) *Kenya Development Plan 1984–1989*, Government Printer, Nairobi.

KEMELFIELD, Graeme (1972) *A Community-Based Education System: A Proposal*, Educational Research Unit Report No.3, University of Papua New Guinea.

KENNEDY, Margrit I. (1979) *Building Community Schools: An Analysis of Experiences*, Unesco, Paris.

KINAHAN, Timothy (1976) 'Education and the Community in Ethiopia: The Example of the Asra Hawariat School, Addis Ababa', in KING, Kenneth (ed.), *Education and the Community in Africa*, Centre of African Studies, University of Edinburgh.

KLEES, Stephen (1984) 'The Need for a Political Economy of Education: A Response to Thobani', *Comparative Education Review*, Vol.28, No.3.

KRYSTALL, A. (1980) 'Women's Access to Education in Kenya', in *Proceedings of a Conference on Research in Education in Kenya*, Bureau of Educational Research, Kenyatta University College, Nairobi.

KULAKOW, A. M., BRACE, J. and MORRILL, J. (1978) 'Mobilizing Rural Community Resources for Support and Development of Local Learning Systems in Developing Countries', Academy for Educational Development, Washington.

KWONG, Julia (1979) 'The Educational Experience of the Great Leap Forward 1958–59: Its Contradictions', *Comparative Education Review*, Vol.23, No.3.

KYI, Hnin Mya (1977) *A National Case Study on the Management of Local Support to Education in the Socialist Republic of the Union of Burma*, Burma Educational Research Bureau, Rangoon.

LESOTHO, Government of (1985) 'The Lesotho Government View', paper presented at the Commonwealth Secretariat Workshop on Community Financing of Schools, Gaborone.

LINDSAY, Michael (ed.) (1950a) 'Directive on Development of Winter School Movement' [1944], in *Notes on Educational Problems in Community China*, Institute for Pacific Relations, New York.

LINDSAY, Michael (ed.) (1950b) 'Directive on Reorganisation of Primary Schools and the Strengthening of Education in Production among Pupils' [1943], in *Notes on Educational Problems in Communist China*, Institute for Pacific Relations, New York.

MAKAU, B. (1985) *The Concept of Quality in Education and its Evaluation in Kenya*, Institute of Development Studies, University of Nairobi.

MAKUNGA, George (1985) 'Notes on Community Junior Secondary Schools' (typescript), Ministry of Education, Gaborone.

MALAWI, Ministry of Education and Culture (1984) *The Impact of the Increase in School Fees on Primary School Enrolments in 1983*, Lilongwe.

MANALANG, Priscilla (1977) *A Philippine Rural School: Its Cultural Dimension*, University of the Philippines Press, Manila.

MBITHI, Philip M. (1977) ' "Harambee" Self-Help: The Kenyan Approach' *The African Review*, Vol.II, No.1.

MBITHI, Philip M. and RASMUSSON, Rasmus (1977) *Self-Reliance in Kenya: The Case of Harambee*, Scandinavian Institute of African Studies, Uppsala.

McKINNON, K. R. (1972) *A Handbook for Boards of Management in Primary Schools*, Department of Education, Port Moresby.

McVEY, Ruth (1983) 'Faith as the Outsider: Islam in Indonesian Politics', in PISCATORI, James P. (ed.) *Islam in the Political Process*, Cambridge University Press, Cambridge.

MEHRA, A. N. (1985) 'Distribution of Secondary School Enrolments in Zambia', paper presented at the National Seminar on Dissemination and Utilization of the 1980 Population and Housing Census Data, Lusaka.

MILONGO, J. C. and ROUAG, D. (1978) 'La Participation des Collectives Locales dans le Financement de l'Education en Republique Populaire du Congo', paper presented at the Unesco seminar on The Mobilization of Domestic Resources for Formal and Non-Formal Education, ED-78/CONF.734/REF.4.1, Unesco, Paris.

MINGAT, Alain and TAN Jee Peng (1985) 'Subsidization of Higher Education versus Expansion of Primary Enrolment: What can a Shift of Resources Achieve in Sub-Saharan Africa?', *International Journal of Educational Development*, Vol.5, No.4.

MKANDAWIRE, Donton J. (1985) 'Academic Standards in Malawi Schools', paper presented at the Commonwealth Secretariat workshop on Community Financing of Schools, Gaborone.

MORRIS, H. S. (1968) *The Indians in Uganda*, Weidenfeld and Nicolson, London.

MOTANYANE, A. (1985) 'A Non-Government View from Lesotho', paper presented at the Commonwealth Secretariat workshop on Community Financing of Schools, Gaborone.

MWIRIA, K. (1985) 'The Kenya Harambee School Movement: A Historical Perspective', Ph.D. dissertation, Stanford University.

MWIRIA, K. (1986) 'Education through Self-Help: The Experience of the Kenya Harambee Secondary Schools', unpublished paper, Bureau of Educational Research, Kenyatta University, Nairobi.

NACHISON, J. (1971) 'A Case Study in Kenya: Community Development Builds a Nursery School', *Community Development Journal*, Vol.6, No.1.

NAYAR, D. P. and VIRMANI, K. G. (1978) *Management of Local Support to Education in India: A Case Study*, National Staff College for Educational Planners and Administrators, New Delhi.

NG'ETHE, N. (1978) 'Harambee and Popular Participation: Notes on an Elusive Ideology', paper presented at the Workshop on Popular Participation and Rural Development, Nairobi.

NHAN, Nhoeng (1973) 'Use of Community Resources in Providing Low-Cost Education', in INNOTECH, *Use of Community Resources in Providing Low-Cost Primary Education: Report of a Regional Seminar*, Saigon.

NIGERIA, Federal Republic of (1975) *Third National Development Plan 1975–80*, Federal Ministry of Economic Development, Lagos, Vol.I.

NIMPUNO, Krisno (1976) 'Design for Community Education: General Proposition and Case Study Material on Community Education Centres in Tanzania', in KING, Kenneth (ed.), *Education and the Community in Africa*, Centre of African Studies, University of Edinburgh.

NWAFOR, J. C. (1978) 'The role of Communities in the Provision of Educational Spaces in Nigeria: The Example of Anambra State', in UIA WORKING GROUP ON EDUCATIONAL SPACES/UNESCO, *Self-Reliance in Educational Facilities*, Athens.

OKOYE, Mary (1986) 'Community Secondary Schools: A Case-Study of a Nigerian Innovation in Self-Help', *International Journal of Educational Development*, Vol.16, No.4.

OLEMBO, J. O. et al. (1984) *Financing Kenya's Primary School Education: One of the Corner Stones to Quality in Education*, Bureau of Educational Research, Kenyatta University College, Nairobi.

OLEMBO, J. O. (1985) *Financing Primary School Buildings in Kenya*, Transafrica Press, Nairobi.

OMARI, I. M. et al. (1983) *Universal Primary Education in Tanzania*, International Development Research Centre, Ottawa.

ORATA, Pedro T. (1977) 'Barrio High Schools and Community Colleges in the Philippines', *Prospects*, Vol.VII, No.3.

OTA, C. C. (1985) 'A Non-Government View from Zimbabwe', paper presented at the Commonwealth Secretariat workshop on Community Financing of Schools, Gaborone.

OTA, C. C. (1986) 'Community Financing of Schools in Zimbabwe', *Prospects*, Vol.XVI, No.3.

OXENHAM, John (ed.) (1984) *Education versus Qualifications?*, George Allen & Unwin, London.

PADHYE, Nilakantha Rao (1976) *Financing First-Level and Second-Level Education in Nepal*, Financing Educational Systems Specific Case Study 8, IIEP, Paris.

PAPUA AND NEW GUINEA, Territory of (1970) *Education Ordinance*, Government Printer, Port Moresby.

PAPUA NEW GUINEA, Department of Education (1974) *Proposed Five Year Education Plan*, Department of Education, Port Moresby.

PAPUA NEW GUINEA, Independent State of (1983) *Education Act*, Government Printer, Port Moresby.

PAPUA NEW GUINEA, Department of Education (1985) *Growth of Education since Independence, 1975–85*, Department of Education, Waigani.

PARSONS, Q. N. (1972) *The World of Khama*, Nec-Zam, Lusaka.

PARSONS, Q. N. (1984) 'Education and Development in Pre-Colonial and Colonial Botswana to 1965', in CROWDER, Michael (ed.), *Education for Development*, Macmillan, Gaborone.

PAYNE, Monica and HINDS, Jennifer (1986) 'Parent–Teacher Relationships: Perspectives from a Developing Country, *Educational Research*, Vol.28, No.3.

PHAN Cong Ming and CAO Minh Khai (1973) 'Some Opinions Concerning the Use of Community Resources in Providing Low-Cost Primary Education', in INNOTECH, *Use of Community Resources in Providing Low-Cost Primary Education: Report of a Regional Seminar*, Saigon.

PHILLIPSON, S. (1948) *Grants in Aid of Education in Nigeria*, Government Printer, Lagos.

PRESTON, Rosemary (1985) 'Community and the School Economy in Papua New Guinea', Division of Educational Policy and Planning, Unesco, Paris.

PRESTON, Rosemary and KHAMBU, John (1986) 'Between the Community and its School: Boards of Management in Papua New Guinea—Stage I: The Bereina Case Study Report', Educational Research Unit, University of Papua New Guinea.

PSACHAROPOULOS, George, TAN Jee-peng and JIMENEZ, Emmanuel (1986) *Financing Education in Developing Countries: An Exploration of Policy Options*, The World Bank, Washington.

PUTSOA, Bongile (1985) 'A Non-Government View from Swaziland', paper presented at the Commonwealth Secretariat workshop on Community Financing of Schools, Gaborone.

RAHARDJO, M. Dawan (1975) 'The Kyai, the Pesantren, and the Village: A Preliminary Sketch', *Prisma* (English-language edition), Vol.1, No.1.

RANGER, Terence (1965) 'African Attempts to Control Education in East and Central Africa, 1900–1939', *Past and Present*, No.32.

RASHID bin Muhammed Nor and HARITH bin Muhammed Liki (1973) 'Malaysia's Experience and Some Suggestions in the Use of Community Resources in Providing Low-Cost Primary Education', in INNOTECH, *Use of Community Resources in Providing Low-Cost Primary Education: Report of a Regional Seminar*, Saigon.

ROAKEINA, S. G. (Chairman) (1984) *A Statistical Review of the Education Sector*, Education Sector Committee, Ministry of Education, Port Moresby.

ROBERTS, Martin (1985) 'The Marigot Foundation High School in Dominica', paper presented at the Commonwealth Secretariat workshop on Community Financing of Schools, Gaborone.

ROBINSON, Jean C. (1986) 'Decentralization, Money, and Power: The Case of People-run Schools in China', *Comparative Education Review*, Vol.30, No.1.

ROTHENBERG, Irene Fraser (1980) 'Administrative Decentralization and the Implementation of Housing Policy in Colombia', in GRINDLE, Merilee S. (ed.) *Politics and Policy Implementation in the Third World*, Princeton University Press, Princeton.

SAITOTI, George (1985) 'Major Issues in Implementing District Focus' (excerpts), *Daily Nation*, Nairobi, 8 March.

SALIH, Leila Taha (1986) 'Costs of Primary, Intermediate and Secondary Schools in Sudan', Prg.CT/86.264, IIEP, Paris.

SAMARANAYAKE, M. R. (1985) *Introduction of School Clusters in Sri Lanka*, Occasional Paper No. 67, IIEP, Paris.

SELDEN, Mark (1971) The *Yenan Way in Revolutionary China*, Harvard University Press, Cambridge.

SELIM, M. and BOLTON-MAGGS, J. (1978) 'Community Participation in the Provision of Educational Facilities: The Bangladesh Experience' paper presented at the Unesco seminar on The Mobilization of Domestic Resources for Formal and Non-Formal Education, ED-78/CONF.734/REF.4.3, Unesco, Paris.

SEYBOLT, Peter (1971) 'The Yenan Revolution in Mass Education', *China Quarterly*, Vol.48, No.4.

SEYBOLT, Peter (1973) *Revolutionary Education in China*, M. E. Sharpe, New York.

SHAO Delin (1973) 'The Introduction of Work-Study Programme and the Realization of Free Primary Education', in Unesco, *Universal Primary Education and its Significance for Rural Development in China*, ED–84/WS.68, Paris.

SHELINE, Y. E., PAPAGIANNIS, G. and GRANT, S. R. (1984) 'The Effect of School Sponsorship on Academic Achievement: A Comparison of Catholic, Protestant and Government Secondary Schools in Zaire', *Comparative Education*, Vol.20, No.2.

SHENGANNING BIANCHU ZHENGFU BANGONGTING (1944a) *ShenGanNing Bianchu Jiaoyu Fangzhen* [The Educational Policy of the ShenGangNing Border Region], Yan'an.

SHENGANNING BIANCHU ZHENGFU BANGONGTING (1944b) *Sige Minban Ziaoxua* [Four People-Managed Schools], Yan'an.

SHIRK, Susan (1979) 'Educational Reform and Political Backlash: Recent Changes in Chinese Educational Policy', *Comparative Education Review*, Vol.23, No.2.

SHUE, Vivienne (1980) *Peasant China in Transition*, University of California Press, Berkeley.

SIMON, M. (1984) 'Equity in Secondary Education in Botswana', in CROWDER, Michael (ed.), *Education for Development in Botswana*, Macmillan, Gaborone.

SMITH, Brian (1980) 'Measuring Decentralization', in JONES, G. (ed.), *New Approaches to the Study of Central-Local Government Relationships*, Gower, Brookfield, USA.

SMITH, J. Stephen (1973) *The History of Alliance High School*, Heinemann, Nairobi.

SOLARIN, Tai (1970) *Mayflower: The Story of a School*, John Westgate Publications, Lagos.

SOMERSET, H. C. A. (1984) 'Factors Influencing School Quality in Kenya', typescript, University of London Institute of Education.

SRI LANKA, Government of (1959) 'Parent–Teacher Associations', Circular No.59, VGC 39, Education Department, Colombo.

SRI LANKA, Government of (1974) 'Parent–Teacher Associations', Circular No.345, SO 238/18, Ministry of Education, Colombo.

SRI LANKA, Government of (1977) 'Parent–Teacher Associations', Ministry of Education, Colombo.

SRI LANKA, Government of (1979) 'School Development Societies', Circular No.28, SO/7/125, Ministry of Education, Colombo [in Sinhala].

TAN Jee-Peng et al. (1984) *User Charges for Education: The Ability and Willingness to Pay in Malawi*, Staff Working Paper No.661, The World Bank, Washington.

TAN Jee-Peng (1985) 'The Private Direct Cost of Secondary Schooling in Tanzania', *International Journal of Educational Development*, Vol.5, No.1.

TANZANIA, Jamhuri ya Muungano wa (1982) *Mwongozo wa Usajili wa Shule Zisizo za Serikali, Kimetolewa na Wizara ya Elimu ya Taifa*, Dar es Salaam.

TANZANIA, Government of (1985) 'The Tanzania Government View', paper presented at the Commonwealth Secretariat workshop on Community Financing of Schools, Gaborone.

THAILAND, Ministry of Education (1984) *National Case Study on the Management of Local Support to Education*, Educational Planning Division, Bangkok.

THEMA, B. C. (1970) 'Moeng College: A Product of Self-Help', *Botswana Notes and Records*, Vol.2.

THOBANI, Mateen (1983) *Charging User Fees for Social Services: The Case of Education in Malawi*, Staff Working Paper No.572, The World Bank, Washington.

THOBANI, Mateen (1984a) 'Charging User Fees for Social Services: Education in Malawi', *Comparative Education Review*, Vol.28, No.3.

THOBANI, Mateen (1984b) 'A Reply to Klees', *Comparative Education Review*, Vol.28, No.3.

THOMAS, B. (1980) *Development through Harambee—Who Wins and Who Loses: Observations on Kenya's Experience with Self-Help Projects on Selected Rural Communities*, Clark University, USA.

TLOU, Thomas and CAMPBELL, Alec (1984) *History of Botswana*, Macmillan, Gaborone.

TONI, Malawa and BRAY, Mark (1984) 'Church Education Secretaries in the National Education System: An Equal or Unbalanced Partnership?', *Papua New Guinea Journal of Education*, Vol.20, No.2.

TOWNSEND-COLES, Edwin L. (1985) *The Story of Education in Botswana*, Macmillan, Gaborone.

UNESCO (1949) *Human Rights: Comments and Interpretations*, Allan Wingate, London.

UNESCO (1960) *The Needs of Asia in Primary Education: A Plan for the Provision of Compulsory Education in the Region*, Paris.

UNESCO (1961) *Conference of African States on the Development of Education in Africa: Final Report*, Paris.

UNESCO (1962) *Conference on Education and Economic and Social Development in Latin America*, Paris.

UNESCO (1966) *Conference of Ministers of Education and Ministers Responsible for Economic Planning in the Arab States*, Paris.

UNESCO (1982) *Improving the Primary School Environment through Community Efforts*, Educational Buildings Occasional Paper No.1, Bangkok.

UNESCO (1984a) *Community Participation for UPE at Local (Operational) Level*, Training Module on Planning and Management of Universal Primary Education (UPE), Bangkok.

UNESCO (1984b) *The Role of Non-Governmental Organizations (NGOs) in UPE Programmes*, Training Module on Planning and Management of Universal Primary Education (UPE), Bangkok.

UNGER, Jonathan (1980) 'Bending the School Ladder: The Failure of Chinese Educational Reform in the 1960s', *Comparative Education Review*, Vol.24, No.2.

UNICEF (1982) 'Plan of Action for Primary School Improvement Programme', Rangoon.

UNICEF (1984) *Situation Analysis of Women and Children in Kenya*, Unicef Eastern Africa Regional Office, Nairobi.

UNITED NATIONS (1973) *Human Rights: A Compilation of International Instruments of the United Nations*, New York.

VAN RENSBURG, Patrick (1974) *Report from Swaneng Hill*, Dag Hammarskjöld Foundation, Uppsala.

VICKERY, D. J. (1985) 'Communities and School Buildings: Developments and Issues', paper presented at the Commonwealth Secretariat workshop on Community Financing of Schools, Gaborone.

VISAYSACKD, Bounthong (1973) 'Use of Community Resources in Providing Low-Cost Primary Education', in INNOTECH, *Use of Community Resources in Providing Low-Cost Primary Education: Report of a Regional Seminar*, Saigon.

WAHLSTROM, Per-Ake (1985) 'The Village School Project in Tamilnadu: A Short History', in HOLGERSSON, T. and BLOMSTRAND, G. (eds.), *Formal and Non-Formal: A Report on Education in India*, Church of Sweden International Study Department, Stockholm.

WATSON, Keith (1980) *Educational Development in Thailand*, Heinemann Asia, Hong Kong.

WEEDEN, W. J. *et al.* (1969) *Report of the Advisory Committee on Education in Papua and New Guinea*, Canberra.

WEEKS, Sheldon G. (1975) *Community School in Africa: Is there a Lesson for Papua New Guinea?*, Educational Research Unit Report No.15, University of Papua New Guinea.

WEILER, Hans N. (1982) 'Educational Planning and Social Change: A Critical Review of Concepts and Practices', in ALTBACH, Philip, ARNOVE, Robert F. and KELLY, Gail P. (eds.), *Comparative Education*, Macmillan, New York.

WELLINGS, Paul Anthony (1982) 'Occupational and Educational Aspirations of Kenyan Secondary School Students: Realism and Structural Inequalities', *Educational Review*, Vol.34, No.3.

WELLINGS, Paul Anthony (1983) 'Unaided Education in Kenya: Blessing of Blight?', *Research in Education*, Vol.29.

WILLIAMS, Peter (1986) 'Non-Government Resources for Education with Special Reference to Community Financing', *Prospects*, Vol.XVI, No.2.

WILLIAMSON, P. D. (1983) *Evaluation of the Primary School Self-Help Construction Programme undertaken in Malawi under the Third IDA Education Project*, Ministry of Education and Culture, Lilongwe.

WORLD BANK, The (1980) *Education Sector Policy Paper*, Washington.

WORLD BANK, The (1984) *Controlling the Costs of Education in Eastern Africa: A Review of Data, Issues and Policies*, Report No.4907, Washington.

WORLD BANK, The (1985) *China: Issues and Prospects in Education*, Washington.

WU CHUN (1984) 'A Study Report on Universal Primary Education in Yongning Township, Jiangpu County, Jiangsu Province', Unesco, Bangkok.

XIAO Shu and YANG Fu (1960) 'The Party's Policy is the Guarantee of Revolutionary Strength', *Hongqi* [Red Flag], Vol.22, November.

YANNAKOPULOS, Polymnia (1980) 'Eleven Experiences in Innovations in Decentralization of Educational Administration and Management of Local Resources', Report C91, Division of Educational Policy and Planning, Unesco, Paris.

YOUNG, Beverley and AARONS, Audrey (1986) 'Implementation of NES Plan in Relation to Community Support', typescript, Unicef, Kathmandu.

ZAMBIA, Republic of (1966) *Education: Chapter 234 of the Laws of Zambia*, Government Printer, Lusaka.

ZAMBIA, Republic of (1973) *The Education (Primary and Secondary Schools) Regulations 1973*, Instrument No.254 of 1973, Lusaka.

ZEDONG, Mao (1969) 'On the Ten Great Relationships' [1956], in SCHRAMM, Stuart (ed.), *The Political Thought of Mao Tse-tung*, Praeger, New York.

ZHAI Yisi (1957) 'My Opinions concerning China's Middle and Primary Schools', *Renmin Jiaoyu*, March.

ZIMBABWE, Government of (1980) *Education (Registered Schools) (Amendment) Regulations, 1980*, Government Printer, Salisbury.

ZIMBABWE, Government of (1985) 'The Zimbabwe Government View', paper presented at the Commonwealth Secretariat workshop on Community Financing of Schools, Gaborone, Botswana.

Index

229

Notes on the Authors

Henry Ayot is Professor of Educational Communications and Technology at Kenyatta University, Kenya. He has written widely on educational issues and on the history of the Luhya and Luo peoples of Western Kenya.

Mark Bray lectures in educational planning at the University of Hong Kong. He has taught in secondary schools in Kenya and Nigeria and at the Universities of Edinburgh, Papua New Guinea and London. He has travelled extensively in Africa, Asia, the Caribbean and the Pacific. His other books focus on educational planning, sociology of education, and educational financing, and include *New Resources for Education: Community Management and Financing of Schools in Less Developed Countries* (Commonwealth Secretariat, 1986).

Robert Biak Cin is Burmese, and works for Unicef in Rangoon. He holds M.A. degrees from the Universities of Rangoon and Lancaster (UK), and previously lectured in the Department of English at Rangoon University.

Evelyn M. Hamilton works in the Planning and Research Unit of the Ministry of Education, Social Development and Culture, Guyana.

S. O. Igwe is Reader in Educational Management and Planning and former Dean of the School of Education at Alvan Ikoku College of Education, Owerri, Nigeria. He wrote his doctorate for the University of London Institute of Education on church-state relations in Eastern Nigeria.

L. H. Kaluba lectures in the Department of Education at the University of Zambia. He was recently a member of the Educational Reform Implementation Project (ERIP), commissioned by the Ministry of General Education and Culture and funded by the World Bank. He is currently Zambia's coordinator in the Educational Research Network for Eastern and Southern Africa.

Kevin Lillis teaches in the Department of International and Comparative Education at the University of London Institute of Education. He has

233

worked for many years in Kenya, as a school teacher, inspector and researcher, and has travelled extensively in other parts of the Third World. He is co-author of *School and Community in the Third World* (Croom Helm 1980), and editor of *School and Community in Less Developed Areas* (Croom Helm 1985).

Una M. Paul is Permanent Secretary of the Ministry of Education, Social Development and Culture, Guyana. She previously worked in the Planning and Research Unit of the Ministry.

Jean C. Robinson is assistant professor of political science at Indiana University, Bloomington, USA. She has conducted field research in China and in Eastern Europe, and has published articles on charismatic leadership, family policies and education.

Guy B. Scandlen works for Unicef in Rangoon. He holds an M.A. degree in international communications from the University of California, and previously lectured at Chulalongkorn University, Thailand. He has also worked for the National Family Planning Board in Malaysia, and for Unicef in Thailand.

J. R. Swartland is the Deputy Permanent Secretary of the Ministry of Education in Botswana. He trained as a teacher in South Africa, came to Botswana in 1965, and is now a citizen of Botswana. He holds degrees from the Universities of Leeds and Newcastle upon Tyne (UK), and has also worked as Senior Education Officer (Mathematics) and Chief Education Officer in charge of Curriculum Development.

D. C. Taylor is a planning officer in the Ministry of Education, Botswana. He is a British citizen, and has taught in secondary schools in Ghana, Botswana and England. For five years he lectured in Education at the university in Lesotho, and since 1979 he has held a lectureship at the University of Manchester, from which he is seconded to his current post.

Randolph A. Williams works in the Planning and Research Unit of the Ministry of Education, Social Development and Culture, Guyana.